One Year

Devotional
Prayer Book II
Living the Life

Thomas Nelson
Since 1798

NASHVILLE   DALLAS   MEXICO CITY   RIO DE JANEIRO   BEIJING

© 2010 by Thomas Nelson, Inc.

All rights reserved. No portion of this book may be reproduced, stored in a retrieval system, or transmitted in any form or by any means—electronic, mechanical, photocopy, recording, scanning, or other—except for brief quotations in critical reviews or articles, without the prior written permission of the publisher.

Published in Nashville, Tennessee, by Thomas Nelson. Thomas Nelson is a registered trademark of Thomas Nelson, Inc.

Thomas Nelson, Inc. titles may be purchased in bulk for educational, business, fundraising, or sales promotional use. For information, please email NelsonMinistryServices@ThomasNelson.com.

All Scripture references are from THE NEW KING JAMES VERSION® (NKJV) © 1982 Thomas Nelson, Inc. Used by permission. All rights reserved.

ISBN-13: 978-1-4041-7495-5

Printed in China

Introduction

~~~

I am excited to share with you that we have again joined hands with Jack Country-man and Thomas Nelson Publishers to bring you a second *One Year Devotional Prayer Book*. This edition compliments last year's devotional that was so well received by individuals and churches around the nation.

This new, beautiful book will take you on a journey of living the life God has intended for every Christian. Learning to be life giving is an essential role of all believers as we learn to fulfill the calling God has given each of us.

I have again chosen 51 devoted men of God to join me each week as we encourage you in your prayer and devotional life. Each contributor has written on meaningful topics that will enrich you spiritually.

May you be blessed daily as you draw closer to the Lord in prayer, Scripture reading, and devotional thought, leading you to live each moment in His presence.

Johnny M. Hunt

Dr. Johnny M. Hunt
Pastor, First Baptist Church of Woodstock
Woodstock, Georgia

Contents

One Year

Devotional
Prayer Book II
Living the Life

Week 1, Monday

Heavenly Father, Your grace is sufficient and abundant. Thank You for caring so deeply and dearly for Your family. Help me to honor You by representing You well today. I ask for opportunities to sow seeds in the lives of those around me that will bring a great spiritual harvest for Your glory. I pray this in Jesus' name. Amen.

But this I say: He who sows sparingly will also reap sparingly, and he who sows bountifully will also reap bountifully. So let each one give as he purposes in his heart, not grudgingly or of necessity; for God loves a cheerful giver.
2 CORINTHIANS 9:6, 7

Every farmer or hobby gardener knows that a seed in a basket will not produce a harvest. Yes, everyone knows that in order to reap, one must be faithful and diligent to sow the seeds. The principle is true not only in the field, but also in the life of every believer. To sow bountifully is to invest in God's kingdom. When we do this, our heavenly Father returns the investment with His rich blessing. Conversely, sowing sparingly will bring a small harvest and a small reward.

Since this is true, believers should give not out of cold-hearted calculation, but from warm-hearted jubilation. We should give not with a sense of obligation, but with a sincere heart of generosity. Remember that our Lord loves and delights in the kind of giving that comes from a cheerful attitude, and we are never more like Jesus than when we are giving. Take joy today in the privilege of blessing others through generous giving.

EVENING
Lord Jesus, this day is a gift from You. May Your graciousness toward me inspire a heart of gratitude and a hand of generosity toward You and others. You are indeed good, and Your teachings are true. Amen.

MORNING

Heavenly Father, help me realize today that You are more than enough to meet every need that I will be confronted with today. Help me feel with Your heart and touch with Your hand. I surrender afresh right now and bow in Your presence to confess, "You are Lord." In Christ's name, Amen.

Then Peter said, "Silver and gold I do not have, but what I do have I give you: In the name of Jesus Christ of Nazareth, rise up and walk." And he took him by the right hand and lifted him up, and immediately his feet and ankle bones received strength.
ACTS 3:6, 7

What is the greatest gift you have ever received? I think back to January 7, 1973, when I received the greatest gift of my life. I repented of my sins that day and placed my faith in the Lord Jesus Christ. That very instant, He gave me the gift of salvation and sealed my eternal destiny. As a result, my past is forgiven, my present is blessed, and my future is secure.

In today's passage, Peter and John did not apologize for not providing what the crippled man expected. The truth is, what the man requested was not his greatest need. This man didn't need silver or gold—he needed God's touch on his life. Only when we walk in spiritual discernment will we view people's greatest need—their need for the Lord. As in the first century, there will be needs we feel we cannot meet. However, there is no need that Jesus cannot meet! Live today in light of His name, touching others with His goodness and power.

EVENING

Jesus, what a wonder You are. You can heal and deliver the captives. As I walk in Your victory, may I join You in Your ministry. Amen.

Week 1, Wednesday

Lord, here I am beginning another new day, which is nothing short of a gift from You. May I treat this day in a way that acknowledges Your goodness in giving it. Bless You, Father. I give You thanks in Jesus' name. Amen.

> *Do not neglect the gift that is in you, which was given to you by prophecy*
> *with the laying on of the hands of the eldership. Meditate on these things;*
> *give yourself entirely to them, that your progress may be evident to all.*
> 1 TIMOTHY 4:14, 15

Undoubtedly, the gifts the Lord has placed within us are intended to serve as an encouragement to others. First Peter 4:10 says, "As each one has received a gift, minister it to one another, as good stewards of the manifold grace of God." Clearly, God intended spiritual gifts to benefit the whole body of Christ. When we neglect His investment in us, we rob the body of His ministry to them through us. Just think how wonderful it is that the Lord has given you a supernatural ability to use for His glory and the good of others. The Lord desires for you to use the gift He's put in you to advance His work—what a privilege!

As you live this day, "meditate on these things" and consider ways you can use your God-given abilities to benefit those around you. Be totally consumed with His will and His work. As you follow the Captain of our salvation to Christlikeness, others should be able to mark your progress. Live today in a way that counts for Christ.

EVENING

Lord, I pray that You would continually make me more like Christ and that Your work in me would be clear for others to see and follow. As I retire from another blessed day, I thank You for Your enabling power in my life. Amen.

Lord, help me not to face this new day without committing myself to all You have planned for me. May I not look for an easy road, but for the road You are on. In Jesus' name, Amen.

> *If anyone wants to sue you and take away your tunic, let him have your cloak also. And whoever compels you to go one mile, go with him two. Give to him who asks you, and from him who wants to borrow from you do not turn away.*
> MATTHEW 5:40–42

Jesus often challenges us to live and give in a way that even the law does not demand. I like to call it being "a second-miler" for Christ. It symbolizes a greater commitment to the way of love than the way of demanding our rights. We surrender our rights in order to follow His example. Odus Scruggs taught me during my college days that "you will never miss anything you give away." When a task is laid on you, even under unreasonable circumstances, don't do it as a grim duty to be resented; do it as a service to be rendered gladly. We dislike giving up our rights or possessions and often forget that nothing truly belongs to us. We are only stewards of what belongs to God.

What Jesus has demanded calls for one main thing: death to self. Turn away from possessiveness and offer all you have to God for His use. He may call on you today to meet a genuine need, so walk through this day with open-handed generosity and stay alert to His leading.

EVENING

Lord, everything I possess is a gift from You. I thank You for Your abundant provision and ask You to help me to be ready always to give freely, even as I have received. Amen.

Week 1, Friday

Lord, I know that my actions clearly reflect what is in my heart. Help me to be a reflection of You today as I seek to radiate Your precious presence. I pray this in Jesus' name. Amen.

Jesus said to him, "If you want to be perfect, go, sell what you have and give to the poor, and you will have treasure in heaven; and come, follow Me."
MATTHEW 19:21

I once heard this great quote by Amy Carmichael: "You can give without loving, but you cannot love without giving." You see, giving has a way of exposing the true nature of one's heart. Just as He was during His days on earth, Jesus today is looking for a person of faith who is willing to surrender to Him regardless of the cost. His call to selfless generosity often reveals that we love our possessions and ourselves more than we love our neighbors. Money has a unique way of showing whether we truly recognize Jesus is Lord of all, and generosity is one of the many indicators of spiritual maturity.

It should be our constant prayer that we would not be tight-fisted with our resources. Jesus said, "Where your treasure is, there your heart will be also" (Matthew 6:21). When we learn that the real treasure is the kingdom of God, our hearts will not hesitate to put all our resources into it. Deepen your relationship with Christ by living with open hands in loving surrender to Him.

EVENING
Lord, I am certainly a greedy person apart from You working in my heart. Purify my heart, Father, and grant me opportunities to display my great love for You in the way I live and give. May my hands be open in order to receive from You and give freely to others. Amen.

Heavenly Father, I realize that it is one thing to acknowledge that all I have comes from You, but it is another thing altogether to realize You are a giver and that I should seek to emulate You. May I learn to give rather than accumulate, so that my life pictures You. In Christ's name, Amen.

> *"Be angry, and do not sin": do not let the sun go down on your wrath, nor give place to the devil. Let him who stole steal no longer, but rather let him labor, working with his hands what is good, that he may have something to give him who has need. Let no corrupt word proceed out of your mouth, but what is good for necessary edification, that it may impart grace to the hearers.*
> EPHESIANS 4:26–29

Jesus is concerned about believers' words and actions. When believers allow the Enemy to have his way in their lives, it changes the way they talk and walk. Jesus often spoke of having "good eyes," referring to eyes that not only see needs, but actively look for needs to meet. Can you picture yourself praying each morning for "good eyes" so you can identify needs the Lord has blessed you with the means to meet?

Jesus was providentially in places in order to meet particular needs (for example, the woman at the well in John 4). Likewise, He places us in particular situations where we can become aware of a need and then feel His gentle prompting to meet it. It may be a word of encouragement, or it may be a gift of time or money. God knows the need, and He knows how to meet it. No matter the specifics, trust Him today to lead you to those in need and to enable you to help them.

EVENING

Almighty God, You are the One who has met my every need and my deepest need. May I be a conduit through which You meet needs in the lives of those around me. Amen.

Lord, remind me today that You are all I need. Amen.

*Now godliness with contentment is great gain. For we brought
nothing into this world, and it is certain we can carry nothing out.
And having food and clothing, with these we shall be content.*
I TIMOTHY 6:6–8

———————————— ❧ ————————————

What would it take for you to feel content? For most of us, our days are filled with ordinary moments like getting the kids ready for school and waiting in traffic to and from work. The little personal time we steal for rest can be quickly forgotten in the nervous pace of our daily lives. Are we content? Or is there a restlessness for something more just below the surface?

As I write this devotion I am in New York City, the financial capital of the world. I am reminded everywhere I turn that the dreams of this world can be summed up in one phrase: "Give me more."

John Wesley once said, "Earn all you can. Save all you can. Give all you can." The twenty-first century's philosophy seems to be the opposite: "Get all you can, can all you get, sit on the can, and poison the rest." The desire for "more" never brings contentment. Our Scripture for today says that "godliness with contentment is great gain." The New Testament word *godliness* is one word made up of two words in the Greek language. The first word is *eu* and it means "good." It survives in English in the word *eulogy*, literally meaning a "good word" about a person at their funeral. The second part of the word is the Greek word *sebias*. We get the English name *Sebastian* from this word, and it means "worship." So the word translated as "godliness" carries the idea of "good worship." Contentment is found in "godliness," which from a practical standpoint means being a "good worshiper"! God promises the "good worshiper" a contentment we can actually call "gain." In other words, godly contentment is the way forward—it's a profit. So when you feel restless, content yourself in worship and you will share in God's rich reward.

———————————— ❧ ————————————

EVENING
Father, let me content myself in You. Amen.

Lord, today I want to live out my faith and share the Good News. Amen.

> *Sanctify the Lord God in your hearts, and always be ready to give*
> *a defense to everyone who asks you a reason for the hope that is in you,*
> *with meekness and fear; having a good conscience, that when they defame*
> *you as evildoers, those who revile your good conduct in Christ may be ashamed.*
> 1 PETER 3:15, 16

D oes it ever seem to you that the good you do goes unnoticed by the unchurched world? It sometimes seems like the cynic who said, "No good deed goes unpunished," was right. Nowhere is this more evident than when we witness for Christ. Who hasn't felt the sting of criticism for sharing his or her faith?

Yet when it comes to sharing the Good News, we have a mandate from the Lord to "live out loud" and share Christ with others. In today's passage, the Bible calls our salvation "the hope that is in [us]" and says we should "always be ready to give a defense" of that hope. In other words, we have to be prepared not only to "step up" and live the Christian life, but also to "speak up" for Jesus. Unbelievers should be able to see the Good News in both our conduct and our conversation.

In December 2008, a journalist named Matthew Parris wrote an article for *The Times of London* entitled, "As an atheist, I truly believe Africa needs God." Having grown up in Malawi, Parris understood the people there. Going back years later, he saw the positive impact of Christian evangelism. He said, "It . . . embarrassed my growing belief that there is no God,"[1] and added, "I've become convinced of the enormous contribution that Christian evangelism makes in Africa."

Our ready defense of the hope within us can literally leave our critics ashamed of their slander when they see the good our God does through us!

EVENING
Father, bless those who could see and hear Jesus in me today. Amen.

Lord, today let me love the people I meet as a ministry to You. Amen.

Above all things have fervent love for one another, for "love will cover a multitude of sins." Be hospitable to one another without grumbling. As each one has received a gift, minister it to one another, as good stewards of the manifold grace of God.

1 PETER 4:8–10

D o your priorities change when you have a deadline? A pastor friend of mine frequently reminds his staff that people don't do what's expected; they do what's inspected. Most of us know the feeling of cramming for a final exam or rushing to tidy a room before company comes. But what about even bigger issues, like our main purpose for living? If we recognized a "deadline" for that, would we be more focused and intentional?

Scripture teaches that history itself has an ending point. First Peter 4:7 says, "The end of all things is at hand." The apostle Peter clarified what we are to do in light of the end of all things. Of course, realizing history has a deadline makes seriousness and prayer essential, but we are also commanded to "have fervent love for one another."

The word fervent literally means "to stretch out." We might say that we are to love beyond our comfort zone as the end nears. According to Scripture, that kind of stretched-out love includes being hospitable, which is a combination of two Greek words—one meaning "love of friends" and the other "strangers." So hospitality involves willingness to love those we do not know as if they are our brothers and sisters.

The Christian message is revolutionary in every way, and we require God's help if we hope to live it! No wonder Scripture reminds us in today's passage that we will demonstrate this "end-time love" when we exercise our spiritual gifts (v. 10). When we love like that, we literally dispense the blessings of God toward others as a gift!

EVENING
Father, let me "stretch out" in love and hospitality as I live in Your grace. Amen.

Father, thank You for opening doors of service and ministry today. Thank You for the spiritual gifts You have blessed me with. Use me, I pray! Amen.

If anyone speaks, let him speak as the oracles of God. If anyone ministers, let him do it as with the ability which God supplies, that in all things God may be glorified through Jesus Christ, to whom belong the glory and the dominion forever and ever. Amen.

I PETER 4:11

I believe in spiritual gifts! Three passages of Scripture—Romans 12:6–8, 1 Corinthians 12:7–10, and Ephesians 4:11—contain lists of spiritual gifts. Some of them are mentioned in more than one list, while others are unique to only one list.

The apostle Peter did not make a list, but he did point out that every believer has at least one spiritual gift, and he suggested a simple way to categorize the various spiritual gifts. He said in today's passage, "If anyone speaks, let him speak as the oracles of God. If anyone ministers, let him do it with the ability which God supplies." In this brief encouragement, Peter gave two broad categories that nearly every gift fits into: "speaking gifts" and "serving (ministry) gifts." A speaking gift would include prophecy and teaching, as well as other gifts requiring spoken communication. A serving gift would be administration, mercy, or service, along with the more action-oriented gifts.

Which category do you most "super-naturally" fit into? The discovery of your spiritual gifts can mark the beginning of one of the most rewarding journeys of the spiritual life. After discovery comes the development and deployment of your gifts. Ultimately your gifts are spiritual and given by the Holy Spirit to help you live the Christian life and glorify God "through Jesus Christ." God has gifted you and He wants to work through your gifts today!

EVENING

God, thank You for Your gifts in my life. May I always use them to build up Your church and to glorify You. Amen.

Lord, I have one simple request this morning: Oh God, make me a person of prayer. In Jesus' name I pray. Amen.

> *Ask, and it will be given to you; seek, and you will find; knock, and*
> *it will be opened to you. For everyone who asks receives, and he*
> *who seeks finds, and to him who knocks it will be opened.*
> MATTHEW 7:7, 8

J. C. Ryle observed in his booklet entitled, "A Call to Prayer" that in the history of Christianity, God has used people of nearly every denomination and theological persuasion for His purposes. A common denominator among them is not immediately apparent. However, Ryle noticed one similarity: "They have differed in all kinds of ways, but one thing they all have had in common: they have all been people of prayer."[2]

In one of the first lessons on prayer in the New Testament, Jesus taught some of the basic principles of an effective prayer life. He said, "Ask, seek, and knock."

Like many others, I hate to ask directions if I'm traveling. When I can't find something in a store, my wife usually says, "Ask someone," which I find hard to do. Yet as much as we resist asking for directions or assistance, Jesus said prayer includes asking!

Jesus said, "Seek," which implies a diligent search for the answer. He also said, "Knock." When we knock on the door of a friend's house, we are requesting to be accepted—we are asking for the door to be opened. Prayer is like that. Prayer is an expression of a desire to find what we do not have, and it is the hope that doors will be opened to us.

Just this week I saw a strange message in graffiti painted on a wall that said, "Do not pray for me." We can only imagine what motivated that kind of request. But the truth is, nothing can stop the power of prayer. Those we pray for can resist our love, our words, and our actions, but nothing can stop our prayers. We ask, we seek, and we knock, and God promises answers, discovery, and open doors!

EVENING
Thank You, Lord, for hearing my prayer. I will keep asking, seeking, and knocking until I joyously meet You face-to-face someday in heaven. Amen.

Father, today, give me the gift of peace and contentment. Amen.

> *He said to His disciples, "Therefore I say to you, do not worry about*
> *your life, what you will eat; nor about the body, what you will put on.*
> *Life is more than food, and the body is more than clothing. Consider the*
> *ravens, for they neither sow nor reap, which have neither storehouse nor*
> *barn; and God feeds them. Of how much more value are you than the birds?"*
>
> LUKE 12:22–24

America is a worried nation. According to the *L.A. Times*, one man in Santa Fe was so nervous about the use of electronics, he sued his neighbor for half a million dollars because she used a cell phone, Wi-Fi, and dimmer switches in her house down the block. The man was nervous that the use of electronics would make him sick. It appears that there is something new to worry about every day!

Jesus wants us to live without anxiety and worry, so He encourages us to consider how God feeds the birds of the air by providing food for them. His point is clear: if God provides for birds, will He not be even more willing to care for those created in His image and saved by His Son?

One day as I was preparing a sermon on this subject, I heard a knocking sound against the window of my study. I ignored it until I noticed it was a bird outside my window seeing his reflection and trying to get in. As I looked closer, I noticed that the tree outside my window was covered with red berries and the tree was full of birds busily eating the thousands of berries growing there.

I couldn't believe it. It was as if God reminded me at the instant I was considering His promise that I can trust Jesus when He tells me not to worry. The One who cares for wild birds cares even more for His children. Worry, you might say, is "for the birds."

EVENING
Lord, let me be an instrument of Your peace. Amen.

Father God, I confess with Job that "naked I came from my mother's womb, and naked shall I return" (Job 1:21). May I use this life You have given me for eternal matters. I recognize that all I possess comes from You, and I pray that You would guide me in wisdom and generosity so I may give life to others. I thank You that even though the Lord Jesus was rich, He became poor that we might become rich in His salvation. In Jesus' name, Amen.

Command those who are rich in this present age not to be haughty, nor to trust in uncertain riches but in the living God, who gives us richly all things to enjoy. Let them do good, that they be rich in good works, ready to give, willing to share.
1 TIMOTHY 6:17, 18

⟿

God has so blessed us as Christ-followers with every spiritual blessing in heavenly places in Christ (Ephesians 1:3), and He has also blessed us with every material blessing to supply the basic necessities of life, such as food, clothing, and shelter. The blessings of God are not just for our *enjoyment*, but also for our *employment*. We should *employ* the benefits He gives to us to bless others.

The Lord Jesus taught us to lay up treasures for ourselves in heaven (Matthew 6:20), that is, to be rich toward God. Invest your life not in the fleeting "pretty bubbles" of this passing world, but in that which is eternal by supporting the things that advance God's kingdom. Monetary wealth is here today and gone tomorrow, but money invested in lives for Christ's sake will last forever. As Martin Luther said, "I have held many things in my hands, and I have lost them all; but whatever I have placed in God's hands, that I still possess."

⟿

EVENING
Abba Father, teach me to give life through daily generosity. Just as You gave Your one-of-a-kind Son so I could live eternally, may I live with a heart of gratitude and give to others. Bring to my mind someone who is in need that I may refresh and bless them with an act of sharing and caring. Amen.

MORNING

Holy, Holy, Holy are You, Lord God Almighty! All of creation declares Your glory, and I pray that my life created in Christ Jesus for good works will declare Your glory today. May this day be used to impact the lives of those with whom You allow me to interact in the course of my life. I pray in Jesus' wonderful name. Amen.

Who is wise and understanding among you? Let him show by good conduct that his works are done in the meekness of wisdom.

JAMES 3:13

———

Being a life-giving influence comes from living with wisdom. Wisdom is gaining the knowledge of God's character and desires and applying it to daily life. Wisdom is seeing the world through the eyes of Christ.

In Mark 8:22–25, our Lord Jesus healed the blind man at Bethsaida and caused him to be restored and see everyone clearly. Wisdom comes to us by the touch of our Lord, enabling us to see everyone clearly—not as things in our lives to avoid, but as people for whom Christ died. We are to view people as objects of God's love; He desires for us to show His love and goodness to them. The spiritual life of Christ is imparted to others through our lives when we walk in humble wisdom, seeing others through Jesus' eyes.

I recently saw this principle in action when a mission team from our church in the United States went to Guatemala to construct two houses for impoverished families. As a result of the "good conduct" that displayed Christ's love, many people were introduced to the saving power of the Lord Jesus Christ.

As we humbly follow the Savior, He will eternally change lives around us. Be a life-giving influence in your world today by allowing Christ to display His goodness through your conduct and to declare His good salvation with your lips.

———

EVENING

Father God, I pray that any good thing that has come from my life today would praise You. May my life display the radiant splendor of who Jesus is and His mission to seek and save the lost. May my life point others to You and impact lives for eternity. Open my eyes to see people not as moving objects to avoid, but as living persons whom You love. In Jesus' name I pray. Amen.

Week 3, Wednesday

Heavenly Father, as I begin this new day I ask that You would order my steps according to Your Word. May I follow Your heart in leading some soul to You. Place me in the path of an individual who needs You. Manifest Your compassion and love through me this day. I pray in Jesus' mighty name. Amen.

Brethren, if anyone among you wanders from the truth, and someone turns him back, let him know that he who turns a sinner from the error of his way will save a soul from death and cover a multitude of sins.

JAMES 5:19, 20

The writer James confronts us with the reality that any one of us at any given time can wander from the truth. There is never a day that we can coast in our spiritual walk with the Lord. We must actively pursue the Lord with a holy passion to please Him and guard our hearts from the deceptive allurements of the Evil One.

To give life to others through our daily walk with the Lord Jesus means that we are to be soul winners. We are to be actively and intentionally seeking to turn back sinners from their ways and restore them to a right relationship with the Lord. Soul winning is not just directed toward spiritually lost sinners but also toward passively misguided saints. We are to speak the truth in love and seek to turn sinners from their ways.

The gospel is only good news if people hear it in time. Be sensitive to the Spirit's leading in your life today to turn some soul to the Lord.

EVENING

Father God, You are mighty to save and change lives by the power of Your risen Son. As I lay down to sleep this night, I pray that You will increase my burden for those who are wandering from the truth. Give me a passion to follow You and influence others to follow You. May my life gather many to You and never scatter any from You. I humbly pray in Jesus' name. Amen.

MORNING

Father God, this morning I am mindful that You are thinking of me. You know when I rise and when I lie down. You are aware of my thoughts as they wander far off and of my words before one of them is spoken. May the words of my mouth and the meditations of my heart be pleasing to You this day. I pray this in the name of my living Redeemer, Jesus Christ. Amen.

> *My son, if your heart is wise, my heart will rejoice—indeed, I myself;*
> *yes, my inmost being will rejoice when your lips speak right things.*
> PROVERBS 23:15, 16

These are the words of a king written to his son on the proper conduct of royalty. He is encouraging his son to walk in the path of wisdom and to avoid the fallacies of folly. The king takes great joy in hearing his son speak right things and knows that what is in the abundance of his son's heart his mouth will speak (see Matthew 12:34). The right communication of the son's lips reveals the right character of his son's life, which gives a cause of great rejoicing to the father-king.

As children of God by faith in Jesus Christ, we must never forget that we are royal princes and princesses of the everlasting King of kings. Our heavenly Father desires that we live lives of honor, worthy of His calling to our adopted position (Ephesians 4:1). He takes great delight in hearing us speak words of honor, dignity, and grace that reflect His eternal calling on our lives. As our heavenly Father and King hears us speaking words that give life to others, He rejoices in His inmost being. The words that give Him the greatest joy are those that share the life-giving message of the gospel of His Son. May the Father's heart rejoice as our "lips speak right things"!

EVENING

Lord God Almighty, thank You for calling me by Your amazing grace to be Your child and serve You in Your eternal kingdom. I pray that the words of my mouth and the meditations of my heart have been acceptable to You this day. Please forgive me for speaking words that were not reflective of my position in Christ. I desire to cause Your heart to rejoice by sharing words that impart life to others. In Jesus' name, Amen.

Abba Father, I confess that all I have and all that I am comes from You. You, the Almighty Creator, spoke the entire universe into existence. You are the Giver and Sustainer of all life. I bow in surrender to You with my hands open before heaven. My greatest joy is to worship You. Amen.

Nor is He worshiped with men's hands, as though He needed anything,
since He gives to all life, breath, and all things. And He has made from one
blood every nation of men to dwell on all the face of the earth, and has determined
their preappointed times and the boundaries of their dwellings, so that they should
seek the Lord, in the hope that they might grope for Him and find Him, though
He is not far from each one of us; for in Him we live and move and have our
being, as also some of your own poets have said, "For we are also His offspring."
ACTS 17:25–28

In this passage, the apostle Paul was on his second missionary journey, preaching the resurrected Christ in Athens. He was invited by the city's philosophers to the Areopagus where he preached about the "Unknown God" who had "made Himself known" in the person of Jesus Christ. He declared that this "Unknown God" was the One who created the heavens and the earth by His power and might. Further, he declared that this Creator God did not need anything from humans but had given life to all that they might know Him. He proclaimed that the Creator had sent His Son to be their Savior.

God desires that we would seek Him and know Him as the Creator, Redeemer, and Lord of our lives. He has given us life that we may give our lives in worship to Him! May our worship glorify Him as the one true, living God who sent His Son to save the world.

EVENING

Almighty Father, thank You for giving me life this day. I realize that it is because of You that I live and move and have my being. I bless You for giving me physical life on the day I was born and for giving me spiritual life on the day of my second birth. May my life be a song of praise that brings glory to Your name! Amen.

MORNING

Father God, I rejoice that the Holy Spirit who raised Christ from the dead dwells in me. I pray that by the Spirit's power You would enable me to give the life of Christ to others. I rejoice in the law of the Spirit that is life in Christ Jesus. May Your Spirit lift me above my natural fleshly tendencies and help me live supernaturally in spiritual victory over my flesh, the world, and the devil. In Jesus' name, Amen.

I remind you to stir up the gift of God which is in you through the laying on of my hands. For God has not given us a spirit of fear, but of power and of love and of a sound mind.
2 TIMOTHY 1:6, 7

The apostle Paul wrote his beloved spiritual son in the ministry, Timothy, to encourage him. Timothy was a young pastor of a local church and his spiritual fervor had diminished from when he first began the ministry. Paul exhorted him to fan the flame of the Spirit's work in his life. Spiritual fires that once burned hot can cool down to a flicker in seasons of discouragement, whether it is in one's ministry or one's spiritual life.

Paul reminded Timothy of the day of his spiritual commissioning, when Paul laid hands on him. He also reminded Timothy of the One who dwelt within him. The Spirit of God who indwells the Christ-follower does not cause one to live with timidity and anxiety when facing perplexing problems. God's Spirit gives power to face the pressures, Christlike love to love our enemies, and a sound mind to think clearly in confusing situations. We, like Timothy, must learn to live lives fully dependent on the Spirit and not on ourselves.

EVENING

Abba Father, as I come to the close of this day, I ask for Your Spirit to fall fresh on me. Melt me, mold me, make me, use me! Fan Your flame once again in my heart and give me fresh courage to face the crises of life and ministry. Give me clarity of thought to know the mind of Christ. Bring to my remembrance the promises of Your Word, for You will keep me in perfect peace when my mind is stayed on You. Amen.

DR. MICHAEL LEWIS, PLANT CITY, FL

Week 4, Monday

Dear heavenly Father, give me a heart that seeks after You, a mind that thinks like Christ, and a spirit that desires to know and follow Your Word. Empty me of myself, fill me with Your Spirit, and drive the truths of Your Word deep into my heart. I pray in Jesus' name. Amen.

Let nothing be done through selfish ambition or conceit, but in lowliness of mind let each esteem others better than himself. Let each of you look out not only for his own interests, but also for the interests of others. Let this mind be in you which was also in Christ Jesus.
PHILIPPIANS 2:3–5

Many great things seemed to be going on in the Philippian church, but one issue threatened their strength: division in the body. Where there is division, there can be no unity. And when the body of Christ is not in unity, the ministry for Christ is hurt.

Divisiveness is a very real danger to every healthy church. Why? Because self gets in the way. The answer in a word is ego. However, God gives an answer to sinful, human thinking in Philippians, and we can break it down into five brief, clear points.

First, don't be selfish. Unity in the church starts with slaying the giant of selfishness, which is egotism. A personal desire to advance one's self is always destructive and disruptive. Second, don't be conceited. This refers to seeking after personal glory. Third, regard others as more important. Unity is born out of humility. Fourth, don't look out for only your own interests. We are to be passionately involved in the causes of others. Fifth, be genuinely concerned for others.

If the church lives by the standard of conduct God has set for us, we will eliminate competition and divisiveness. God's standard is very high. The only One who ever lived it to perfection was Jesus Christ. He is our model. Therefore, let us follow Him!

EVENING

Lord Jesus, help me to be a team player, someone who brings unity and not division. My heart's desire is for people to see You in me, to be salt and light. Fill me with Your compassion for the world's spiritual brokenness. I pray in Jesus' name. Amen.

MORNING

Father, give me eyes that see You and ears that hear You today. In Jesus' name, Amen.

Let us hold fast the confession of our hope without wavering, for He who promised is faithful. And let us consider one another in order to stir up love and good works, not forsaking the assembling of ourselves together, as is the manner of some, but exhorting one another, and so much the more as you see the Day approaching.

HEBREWS 10:23–25

I hear people say, "I don't really need to attend church consistently. I can live a good Christian life by myself." Really? There is a story about a lion who roamed the hill country looking for food. He saw a herd of buffalo and was afraid to attack them while they were all together. He thought, "If I could just find one of them straying from the herd, then I could kill it and have a good feast." So he stalked the herd, day after day, for months, but he could never find one alone. Then one day, a buffalo got up earlier than the others and went out to eat. His family criticized him for getting up earlier to eat the best grass and called him selfish. He criticized them for being lazy. As a result of the argument, they separated, which was exactly what the lion had been patiently waiting for. The lion stalked a buffalo, killed him, and had a royal feast. In a few days, he killed another, and he eventually killed the whole herd.

First Peter 5:8 says, "Be sober, be vigilant; because your adversary the devil walks about like a roaring lion, seeking whom he may devour." We are weak and vulnerable to the devil's schemes. By ourselves we are no match for him. We need the strength that comes from the unity and fellowship with other Christians. Continually build up other believers and join them in worship, Bible study, and Christian service, and together you will stay guarded from attacks.

EVENING

Lord, give me the wisdom to know that being together is better than being alone. Thank You for forming the church and the community of believers. Help me encourage others and minister in the name and love of Jesus. Amen.

Father, today is the day You have made, and I will rejoice and be glad in it. Thank You for knowing everything I will face. Grow me today for the cause of Christ. Amen.

gird up the loins of your mind, be sober, and rest your hope fully upon
the grace that is to be brought to you at the revelation of Jesus Christ; as
obedient children, not conforming yourselves to the former lusts, as in your
ignorance; but as He who called you is holy, you also be holy in all your conduct.
1 PETER 1:13–15

Is it possible for a group of Christians who are facing escalating persecution to live victoriously and joyously? The apostle Peter asserted that it is not only possible, it is necessary! He urged believers to have a lifestyle void of bitterness, rooted in hope, and focused on the Second Coming of the Lord.

Peter encouraged the saints with four main ideas. First he told them, "Gird up the loins of your mind," which simply means, "Pull your thoughts together! Have a disciplined mind!" The image is that of a robed man tucking his skirts under the belt so he can be free to run. Our equivalent might be, "Roll up your sleeves and get to the task." When you center your thoughts on Christ's return and live accordingly, you escape the worldly things that would encumber your mind and hinder your spiritual progress.

Second, Peter said, "Be sober." Believers are to be steadfast, self-controlled, clear-headed, and morally decisive. Know what you believe. Outlook determines outcome and attitude determines action. Don't let things distract your spiritual focus. Third, he instructed them to rest their hope in Jesus' Second Coming. You will be amazed what you can endure in the light of His coming. Fourth, they were to be holy, set apart from those around them, because the Lord is holy. As children we should reflect our Father. American clergyman, James H. Aughey said, "Holiness is not the way to Christ, but Christ is the way to holiness."

It is the certainty of our future inheritance that forms the basis for a victorious Christian experience. Fix your mind on Christ, put your hope in Him, and become more like Him every day.

EVENING
Lord, I pray that people saw Jesus in me today. In Christ's name, Amen.

MORNING

Dear heavenly Father, today I pray what Moses prayed: "Show me now Your way" (Exodus 33:13). I want to know Your ways, Your Word, Your love, and Your power. Speak to my heart and give me the grace to see this life is not about me, but You, dear Lord. I pray in Jesus' name. Amen.

> *if there is any consolation in Christ, if any comfort of love, if any*
> *fellowship of the Spirit, if any affection and mercy, fulfill my joy by being*
> *like-minded, having the same love, being of one accord, of one mind.*
> PHILIPPIANS 2:1, 2

Paul made a plea to the Philippian church for unity. There is probably nothing that can cripple a church faster than disunity. When people start fussing, the church quits evangelizing. When Christians bicker, the sinners snicker. We see churches in our generation split over music, ministry, or a lack of doctrinal teaching. We watch churches divide over too many changes taking place, or because folks refuse to change at all.

However, the message of the church must reach the culture in which it lives. The church has no message if the members have no unity. In Philippians 2, we see the motives for unity in verse 1 and the marks of unity in verse 2. The bottom line is, if we are in Christ—walking in the Spirit and aiming to glorify God—we will think alike, love one another, and be united in one spirit, intent on one purpose. Our society has been producing selfish, self-indulgent, egotistical, introverted, consumptive, materialistic people, and it's had a devastating impact on the church. The question is, are you part of the problem or part of the solution? Look around you and identify where your church and greater community need revival, and make it start with you!

EVENING

Dear Father, search my heart, reveal to me anything that needs to be weeded out. Help me to be a healer and not a divider. May I be one who sees the best in people, one who weeps for the lost and wants to reach them, and one who unites with others for the cause of Christ. Amen.

ROB ZINN, HIGHLAND, CA

Dear heavenly Father, thank You for life! Thank You for the blessings that come from being Your child. Today let me be reminded of all that I have and all that You have provided for me because of Your great love. May I have an attitude of gratitude and may the light of Jesus shine through me today. I pray in Jesus' name. Amen.

Know that the LORD, He is God; it is He who has made us, and not we ourselves; we are His people and the sheep of His pasture. Enter into His gates with thanksgiving, and into His courts with praise. Be thankful to Him, and bless His name. For the Lord is good; His mercy is everlasting, and His truth endures to all generations.

PSALM 100:3–5

One could say that the Bible is a "Him" book, and Psalm 100 is a "Him" psalm. This psalm is all about Him. We are to know that the Lord, Yahweh, our covenant God, is also Elohim, our Creator. We are His people, the sheep of His pasture. We are to enter His gates and thank Him and bless His name. And how are we to enter His courts? With praise! The Hebrew word for praise, *tehillah*, means "to celebrate, to exalt, to laud someone who is praiseworthy." Who is more praiseworthy than God?

We are His creation, His sheep, and His children. It is because of whose we are that we have purpose and meaning in life. It is He who made us—with feelings, emotions, intellect, and the ability to reason, to live, to enjoy, and to have a personal relationship with Him. And if that's not enough, verse 5 gives us three more reasons to be thankful and praise Him. First, the Lord is good. He is the source and perfect example of goodness. Second, His mercy and unfailing love are everlasting. Third, His truth, His promises, and His faithfulness endure to all generations.

Remember the great blessings of belonging to God and live today with a grateful heart in worship to Him!

EVENING

Oh Father, I am so grateful to be in Your family. Thank You for Your unconditional love, grace, and peace. Tonight, cause me to reflect upon Your greatness and to be reminded of all that I have in You. In Jesus' name. Amen.

Dear Father, open my eyes today to see Your truth and understand Your will. Help me to have a heart that desires to please You. In Jesus' name. Amen.

> *Now, Israel, what does the LORD your God require of you, but to fear the LORD your God, to walk in all His ways and to love Him, to serve the LORD your God with all your heart and with all your soul, and to keep the commandments of the LORD and His statutes which I command you today for your good?*
> DEUTERONOMY 10:12, 13

God defines five basic requirements for His people in this verse. First, His people are to fear Him. They are to hold Him in awe and live in His presence with holy reverence. Second, they are to walk in all His ways—not their ways, but His. They are not free to do their own thing; they are to follow the road He sets for them. Third, they are to love Him, to set their affection on Him and Him alone. They are commanded to love God with all their heart, soul, mind, and strength (Mark 12:30). Fourth, His people are called to serve Him. They are to do His will, His bidding, with all their being and be grateful for the privilege. Fifth, they are to keep His commandments.

You might say, "But we are under grace, not the law," and I say, "Amen." It is not about what I *have* to do, but rather, what I *want* to do, *choose* to do, and *desire* with my whole heart to do.

For so many, Christianity has become a mere intellectual assent to certain beliefs. They have embraced the doctrines without the doctrines embracing them. Faith that neither changes a life nor causes one to burn some energy for God is not true, saving faith. Christ makes no apologies for requiring faithful service from His children. Jesus' question is, "Why do you call Me 'Lord, Lord,' and not do the things which I say?" (Luke 6:46). Today, demonstrate that you are one of God's children, eager to love and obey Him at every turn.

EVENING
Lord, prepare my heart tonight to hear Your Word tomorrow and to worship You in spirit and in truth. Thank You for loving me unconditionally. Amen.

ROB ZINN, HIGHLAND, CA

Week 5, Monday

Father, as I face this new day, I come before You in total surrender to Your will. I ask You to fill me with Your Holy Spirit. Please bring someone across my path whom I can encourage today. Help me understand that the Christian life is not about me, but about You. In Christ's name, Amen.

If anything is revealed to another who sits by, let the first keep silent. For you can all prophesy one by one, that all may learn and all may be encouraged.

1 CORINTHIANS 14:30, 31

This is a day when Christians need to be encouraged. Too many have forgotten that we are on the winning side. In 1 Corinthians 14, the apostle Paul dealt with disorderly worship services brought about by misunderstanding and abusing spiritual gifts. Paul reminded believers that genuine worship of God should produce two specific results in their lives. First is enlightenment ("all may learn") and second is encouragement ("all may be encouraged"). When the Holy Spirit is in charge of the worship service, these two results will become reality.

Many Christians are discouraged today because of division within their local churches. There is too much fussing, feuding, and fighting going on, and it seldom has anything to do with spiritual gifts. Often it has to do with people not getting their own way. One of the most enlightening and encouraging events that a Christian can experience is Spirit-inspired worship in their church. As you go to church this Lord's Day, ask the Holy Spirit to bring unity in your community of believers and to enable you to learn from Him and be encouraged by Him.

EVENING

Father, thank You for every act of encouragement in my life today. I pray that I may have encouraged someone else. Tonight, I praise You for Your presence throughout this day. In Jesus' name I pray. Amen.

MORNING

Good morning, Father! With all my heart I love You and long to serve You today. Make me a blessing to others as I manifest Jesus Christ and His love. Amen.

> *I want you to know what a great conflict I have for you and those in*
> *Laodicea, and for as many as have not seen my face in the flesh,*
> *that their hearts may be encouraged, being knit together in love,*
> *and attaining to all riches of the full assurance of understanding,*
> *to the knowledge of the mystery of God, both of the Father and of Christ.*
> COLOSSIANS 2:1, 2

———

Verses like these often send the child of God into hiding. Somehow the word mystery leads us to think this is a text beyond our comprehension. Not so! Paul shared his heart with his friends at Colosse. He wanted them to know that it was the driving passion of his life ("great conflict") to see all believers encouraged, including believers who knew him and those who had never seen his face. He wanted his life to be an encouragement to others, and we should want our lives to be the same.

You probably know people who are a constant source of discouragement. They are always down and their philosophy is "misery loves company." But don't you also know people who encourage you every time you are around them? Do you know why they are like that? First, they understand what it means to be "knit together in love." Second, they understand the great "mystery of God," which is Jesus Christ Himself. Those people have attained the spiritual riches that come from Christian maturity. Yes, there are barriers that attempt to divide the people of God, but Christ unites us. Seek to live in unity with others believers, and be an encourager today!

———

EVENING

Father, thank You for letting me understand that real riches do not come from the worldly possessions I may attain, but from growing in my understanding of Your Son and His love. May others have seen Him through me today. Amen.

Week 5, Wednesday

Father, today I will face conflict because I live for You. Thank You that Jesus is my Lord and that He is strong in battle. There is no conflict too hard for Him. I submit myself to His Lordship today. Amen.

> *Who is this King of glory? The LORD strong and mighty,*
> *the LORD mighty in battle. Lift up your heads, O you gates!*
> *Lift up, you everlasting doors! And the King of glory shall come in.*
> PSALM 24:8, 9

Psalm 24 was sung by the people of God as they went to the temple for a time of worship. How wonderful worship today would be if all God's people sang their way to church! This psalm is about the true King of Glory. That title could never have belonged to David, Solomon, or any other king of history. Only Jesus is the real King of Glory.

How encouraging it is for believers to remember the Person of Jesus. He is our King and our Lord. His kingdom, of which all believers are a part, has no geographical boundaries. It is strong and mighty and has no equal. Some oppose it and some denounce it, but forever it will stand because our King is eternal.

In a day of great political uncertainty in this present world, it is encouraging to know that we are pilgrims and strangers here. We are citizens of another world. We are simply passing through on our way to the Father's house. Do not be dismayed, child of God, in the valley of despair. Lift up your heads! Behold your King! We see Him now by faith, but soon we shall see Him face-to-face!

EVENING
Father, thank You for loving me throughout this day and standing with me in spiritual warfare. Thank You that I am not a victim, but a victor; not overcome, but an overcomer. Amen.

Father, thank You for giving me another day to live. The desire of my heart today is to walk in praise to You. I will praise You with my soul, my hands, and my mouth. Amen.

Because Your lovingkindness is better than life,
my lips shall praise You. Thus I will bless You while I live;
I will lift up my hands in Your name.
My soul shall be satisfied as with marrow and fatness,
and my mouth shall praise You with joyful lips.
PSALM 63:3–5

It is obvious that David was encouraged when he wrote these words. He was on a spiritual mountaintop. It is difficult to offer praise to God out of despair, but when your life has been encouraged by the Lord, praise becomes natural.

Notice three encouraging truths about the Lord from these verses. First, He is a God of lovingkindness. His love is steadfast. Love is not a fickle emotion; it is an act of the will. God doesn't love you because you are cute, warm, and fuzzy. He loves you because He wills to love you. He loves you with an everlasting love that can never be cancelled. It is a love that is better than life!

Second, He is a God who satisfies. "Marrow and fatness" speak of the richest of foods available to a person. Food can be satisfying, but it is a satisfaction that soon passes. Jesus told the woman at the well that if she would take just one drink of the water of life, she would never thirst again (John 4:14). That's satisfaction!

Third, He is a God of joy. Joyful lips come from a joyful heart, and a joyful heart comes from experiencing the joy of Jesus. Don't just sit there . . . PRAISE HIM!

EVENING

Heavenly Father, today You have loved me, satisfied the longing of my soul, and given me joy unspeakable. I praise You for who You are and what You have done! Amen.

Father, thank You for Your eternal love. Thank You that Your love is not passive, but active. Today Your love will watch over me, protect me, and strengthen me. Your banner over me is love. Thank You! Amen.

> *The LORD is your keeper; the LORD is your shade at your right hand.*
> *The sun shall not strike you by day, nor the moon by night . . .*
> *The LORD shall preserve your going out and your coming in*
> *from this time forth, and even forevermore.*
> PSALM 121:5, 6, 8

The encouragement we need as Christians does not come from circumstance or experience, but from the Lord Himself. Look how these verses present Him. He is our keeper, our shade, and our preserver. A keeper is a watchman, an overseer, one who stands guard. God's eyes are ever on us, and His arm ever protects us. The "shade at your right hand" reminds us that God is an ever present shelter who stands between His children and every threat that may come against them at any time, day or night. He is our blessed defender. Paul said, "If God is for us, who can be against us?" (Romans 8:31). The idea is that since God is for us, who cares who is against us? We are in the shade, under His shadow. He defends us from enemies.

Verse 8 says, "The LORD shall preserve." The phrase "shall preserve" is the verb form of the noun "keeper" in verse 6. The psalmist encourages us by telling us that the One who keeps us never leaves us or takes a vacation. He guards us in all of our going out and coming in, that is, in all of our life. When life on earth ends, He will still keep us, protect us, and defend us for eternity. Glory!

EVENING

Dear Father, it has been a day of many challenges, but through it all I have not spent one second out of Your love nor out of Your care. Thank You for being a loving Father to me. Amen.

MORNING

Gracious Father, today I will come in contact with many people, some of whom are my brothers and sisters in Christ. I yield myself to You so that Your encouragement may flow through me to others. Amen.

> *Humble yourselves in the sight of the Lord, and He will lift you up.*
> *Do not speak evil of one another, brethren. He who speaks evil of a*
> *brother and judges his brother, speaks evil of the law and judges the law.*
> *But if you judge the law, you are not a doer of the law but a judge.*
> JAMES 4:10, 11

God encourages you so that you may encourage others. As we humble ourselves before the Lord, He encourages us. As we humble ourselves before others, we encourage them. A Christian never encourages those he or she reviles or condemns. We know better than to blaspheme ("speak evil of") the Lord, but how often we forget that we are not to speak evil of our brothers and sisters in Christ.

The Bible tells us to love one another, comfort one another, pray for one another, prefer one another, greet one another, serve one another, be kind to one another, forgive one another, edify one another, receive one another, and even admonish one another, but it never tells us to speak evil of one another or judge one another. To do so is to contradict the Word of God, which we profess to believe. It is also an indication of a lack of humility in our hearts. Remember, it is the lowly one who will be lifted up. Jesus said, "He who humbles himself will be exalted" (Matthew 23:12). Be encouraged and be an encourager!

EVENING

Dear God, Abba Father, as I reflect on this day, I give You thanks for every opportunity You gave me to be a vessel through which Your love could flow. May I ever live by the words, "Not I, but Christ!" Amen.

Precious Lord, thank You for this new day that opens before me. I recognize it as a gift of love from Your gracious hand. Please help me to have the fragrance of Christ resting upon all that I do and think. May every step I take, every thought I have, and every word I speak be seasoned with grace and kindness. Grant that everyone whose path I cross be reminded of the sweetness and loveliness of Christ, whom I love and serve. In Jesus' name, Amen.

> *As the elect of God, holy and beloved, put on tender mercies,*
> *kindness, humility, meekness, longsuffering; bearing with one*
> *another, and forgiving one another, if anyone has a complaint*
> *against another; even as Christ forgave you, so you also must do.*
> COLOSSIANS 3:12, 13

As alluring and appealing as it may seem, we cannot live in a make-believe world or disconnect from the practical concerns of everyday life. The harsh truth is, real life is troublesome and messy. It is excessively cluttered with broken hearts, severed relationships, and shattered dreams.

Job stated it well when he sadly lamented, "Man who is born of woman is of few days and full of trouble" (Job 14:1). In light of that somber truth, Paul carefully instructed believers as to how we are to conduct ourselves in the midst of a fallen and depraved culture. We are to "put on" tender mercies, kindness, humility, meekness, and longsuffering. The words "put on" picture someone dressing in a garment and clearly describe a daily choice every one of us must make.

And once we have learned how to *dress ourselves*, then, and only then, will we be able to *address others* who have wounded or offended us. Since Jesus forgave us, why would we dare do less to those who have hurt us? Today, put on the garments of Christ in Colossians 3:12, 13 so you can represent Him well in our real-life, messy world!

EVENING

Lord, before I close my eyes in sleep tonight, please remind me if I have harmed or wounded any person today. If my words have been unkind arrows of hurt, if my thoughts have been too centered on self, or if my steps have rushed to judgment, I ask You to forgive me in simple faith. In Jesus' name, Amen.

MORNING

Lord Jesus, at the beginning of this day, please help me dress myself in the robes of love that my ways may be overshadowed by Your ways. Help me today to die to my desires and be alive to Yours. Guard my steps that I will not stumble—and if I should fall, please pick me up quickly that I may not hinder those who may be following behind me. Amen.

> *Above all these things put on love, which is the bond of*
> *perfection. And let the peace of God rule in your hearts,*
> *to which also you were called in one body; and be thankful.*
> COLOSSIANS 3:14, 15

Charles Dickens wisely said, "A loving heart is the truest wisdom." In today's verse Paul went even further than that when he majestically described love as "the bond of perfection." I find it very interesting to consider the different ways various translators have rendered that phrase. James Moffatt translated it this way: "For love is the link of the perfect life." W. J. Conybeare rendered it, "That which binds together and completes the whole." The Revised Standard Version® says love is "that which binds everything together in perfect harmony." And J. B. Phillips summarized it this way: "For love is the golden chain of all the virtues."

Because it is the culmination of all the virtues, William Blake said this of love: "Love seeketh not itself to please, nor for itself hath any care, but for another gives its ease, and builds a Heaven in Hell's despair."

Those who have discerned the incalculable value of love have astutely discovered something even more wonderful than that: *when love reigns in your spirit, God's peace will rule in your heart!* Now that's an unbeatable combination! Choose to put on God's love today, and you'll find His peace flooding your heart, too.

EVENING

Loving Master, Your grace has sustained me through yet another day. As I lie down to sleep, I thank You that Your love knows no boundaries. It embraces the unlovely, seeks the uninterested, forgives the unworthy, and cares for the unthankful. Left to my own selfish will and my own wicked way, I would never have desired You—much less loved You. As I close this day, I gladly pause to thank You that even when I did not love You, You were faithful to love me. In Jesus' name, Amen.

JUNIOR HILL, HARTSELLE, AL

Week 6, Wednesday

Loving Master, as I arise to face a new day, may I be keenly aware of Your direction in everything I do. Help me to never forget that anything that is big to You must be big to me. As the servant looks to the hand of his master for instruction, may my eyes be turned to Your ways and my ears open to Your soft and gentle guidance. Cause me to remember what You have taught me in the past and to be ever open to what You want to reveal to me today. I ask it all in Your dear name. Amen.

This is My commandment, that you love one another as I have loved you. Greater love has no one than this, than to lay down one's life for his friends.
JOHN 15:12, 13

Loving others is never a choice—it is always a command. It is grounded in the unshakable principle of divine repetition. We are to love others because Jesus loves us. While it may be possible to love others without loving Jesus, it is highly unlikely anyone will ever love Jesus without loving others.

That's why Jesus so emphatically declared, "By this all will know that you are My disciples, if you have love for one another" (John 13:35). Our attitude toward others always reveals our attitude toward the Lord. It is the indisputable mark of genuine conversion. It authenticates our salvation. That's why John could so solemnly warn, "If someone says, 'I love God,' and hates his brother, he is a liar; for he who does not love his brother whom he has seen, how can he love God whom he has not seen?" (1 John 4:20).

While most of us will never be asked to lay down our life for a friend, a willingness to do so puts us in the best of all company—the dear Lord Jesus, who laid down His life for us. May God graciously place in each of us that unshakable commitment to demonstrate His love at any cost.

EVENING

Dear Father, while today's sun may be swiftly setting, I give You praise that Your love and grace never grow dim. Your light always shines upon me, and Your presence never leaves nor forsakes me. I thank You that I can lay down in peace tonight and be comforted by that sweet truth. In Jesus' name, Amen.

MORNING

Dear Lord, as I open my eyes to this new day, I praise Your dear name that I am alive in You and that the hope of eternal salvation rests in my soul. May I never forget where I once was and where Your grace has now brought me. Keep my soul in peace, my mind uncluttered, my thoughts pure and undefiled, and my words tempered with grace and kindness. Make me a blessing to everyone I meet today. I beg this in Your wonderful name. Amen.

The love of Christ compels us, because we judge thus: that if One died for all, then all died; and He died for all, that those who live should live no longer for themselves, but for Him who died for them and rose again.
2 CORINTHIANS 5:14, 15

Every person has something that motivates him. While the reason for one's actions may not always be apparent, it is apparent that there is always a reason. Henry Ward Beecher rightly discerned that truth when he wrote, "God made man to go by motives, and he will not go without them, any more than a boat without steam or a balloon without gas."

What grips a person's heart generally directs his or her steps. That's why Paul could declare in today's passage that "the love of Christ compels us." The word *compels* is the Greek word *sunecho*, which means, "to hold together, to compress, to arrest, or compel." Richard Weymouth translates the word, "over masters us," while the New English Bible® renders it, "leaves us no choice." *Compels* is a word that defies timidity and infers an unbridled passion and an all-consuming commitment.

Paul was so moved that Christ had died for all and risen again that he could no longer fathom people living "for themselves." And neither should we. If Christ has indeed died for our sins, then how can we possibly be oblivious to that magnificent truth? May His love compel you to live passionately for Him today and always!

EVENING

Gracious Father, Your merciful hand has once again upheld me. You have fed my hungry body, comforted my discouraged spirit, and reassured by troubled heart. You have graciously reminded me that "this is the day the Lord has made" (Psalm 118:24). I gladly praise You and rejoice in it. Thank You, dear Jesus. Amen.

JUNIOR HILL, HARTSELLE, AL

Week 6, Friday

Loving Savior, I thank You for another day and the delightful privilege of loving and serving You. I rejoice that Your ways are not grievous and that Your commands are not harsh. I praise You that Your instructions to me are for my good and for Your glory. Help me today to yield quickly to them. Give me a listening ear, a discerning heart, and an obedient spirit. May Jesus be magnified in all that I do today. In Your dear name, Amen.

There should be no schism in the body, but that the members should
have the same care for one another. And if one member suffers,
all the members suffer with it; or if one member is honored, all the members
rejoice with it. Now you are the body of Christ, and members individually.
1 CORINTHIANS 12:25–27

Few things are as distressing to the Holy Spirit as churches with broken fellowships. When Paul exhorted the Corinthians that there should "be no schism in the body," he was obviously speaking about congregations split asunder by bitterness, and self-centeredness. The word *schism* means "clash, division, or discord." And the distressing shame is, few churches have been able to escape it. The religious body that has never been touched by open division among her members probably hasn't yet been organized!

Much, if not most, of that troublesome splintering of church harmony directly flows from a misunderstanding of the family of God. Paul specifically likened the fellowship of a local congregation to that of a human body with many different members. While the church is comprised of a great and varied number of individuals, *there is but one body.* That is always the emphasis of the New Testament church. And because it is, the sufferings, as well as the joys, of any one member must always be viewed as belonging to every member. If it hurts me, then it must hurt you, and if it blesses me, it must also bless you. May the Lord grant that every church member could embrace that precious truth!

EVENING

Wonderful Master, thank You for the precious body of Christ. If I have failed today to be sensitive to my hurting brothers and sisters, please forgive me. Cause me to remember that when they hurt, I should hurt—and when they rejoice, I should rejoice. In Jesus' name, Amen.

Dear Jesus, as I make my way through the ceaseless demands of yet another day, deliver me from senseless pride, arrogance, and smug feelings of self-importance. Help me today to walk humbly, speak kindly, and think purely. Give me a submissive heart so I can gladly and without complaint take my place in the body of Christ. In Your name, Amen.

> *I say, through the grace given to me, to everyone who is among you,*
> *not to think of himself more highly than he ought to think, but to think soberly,*
> *as God has dealt to each one a measure of faith. For as we have many members*
> *in one body, but all the members do not have the same function, so we,*
> *being many, are one body in Christ, and individually members of one another.*
>
> ROMANS 12:3–5

The most obnoxious characteristic of those who perceive themselves as being at the top is their condescending disdain for those they perceive to be at the bottom. The value people place on themselves is always determined by the value they place on others. That's why Paul's warning that people not think of themselves more highly than they should becomes especially important to those in the body of Christ.

Since each Christian is a member of one body and has been specifically assigned a place of service in that body, all are important—and none unimportant. As someone once wisely said, "In the family of God, nobody is anybody—but everybody is somebody."

Our value to Christ's body of believers is never determined by *where we are*, but by *what we do*. Some parts of the body are *unseen*, faithfully performing their invaluable function outside the admiring eyes of others. Some may even be viewed as *unnecessary*, a needless and unappreciated appendage. But when it comes to the members of the body of Christ, the words "unseen" or "unnecessary" never appear in God's dictionary! Thank God today for making you part of His body and for allowing you to serve Him gladly.

EVENING

Father, thank You that I am in Your body and that today I have been privileged to serve You. If I have in any way failed You and that transgression has hurt or offended some other member of the body, please forgive me and correct any damage I may have caused them. Amen.

JUNIOR HILL, HARTSELLE, AL

Lord, help me to see that by serving others, I serve You. Give me opportunities to serve in Your name today. Amen.

Be kindly affectionate to one another with brotherly love, in honor giving preference to one another; not lagging in diligence, fervent in spirit, serving the Lord.
ROMANS 12:10, 11

Have you ever met anyone who oozes kindness? You know—someone who is always full of God's love, even in the worst circumstances, and so full of God's Spirit that he or she leaks Jesus?

The truth is, we all leak. Whatever we fill our lives with is what leaks out of us when we get squeezed—and we all get squeezed. For me, mornings tend to squeeze me. That's right—I don't do mornings very well. I want to wake up every morning whistling a tune of gratitude and giving out smiles and waves like the Grand Marshall in some big parade. Unfortunately I never quite seem to remember that until my second cup of coffee . . . or 11:00 AM, whichever comes first. But because Christ Jesus lives in me, I do have hope! Although I don't always feel like smiling before lunch, I can choose to do what's right, even when I don't feel like it. I can be kind and affectionate because Jesus is and my life is hidden in Him.

When I need to, I can reach right down inside my heart and soul and pull out some Jesus and sprinkle it on a wound or a broken heart. When I am overwhelmed, I can breathe in Jesus like fresh oxygen. Since His love surrounds me, bright hope instantly rises like the sun on the freshest of spring mornings. The Bible tells us that "the Son of Man did not come to be served, but to serve, and to give His life a ransom for many" (Matthew 20:28). That being the case, when I serve with my whole heart, with eagerness and affection, I bring great joy to my heavenly Father and glory to His Son.

That's why I'm here! Not my preservation, but His proclamation! I want my life to reflect Him to everyone I come in contact with. May that be so for all of us today!

EVENING

Lord, fill my heart with the song of a grateful, glorifying servant. I pray in Your beautiful name, Jesus, for Your glory! Amen.

Jesus, help me find myself among the hurting and the broken, because that is where You are. When they gaze upon me, let them see You. In Your name and for Your glory. Amen.

Be of the same mind toward one another. Do not set your mind on
high things, but associate with the humble. Do not be wise in your own opinion.
Repay no one evil for evil. Have regard for good things in the sight of all men.
ROMANS 12:16, 17

Recently, on a visit to an orphanage inside a leper colony in Calcutta, India, a friend of mine met a beautiful young English woman. She was holding a diseased and severely disfigured crying baby to her chest. With all the warmth of heaven, she was singing a lullaby to the child. After observing this selfless act of maternal love, he asked the young lady, "Aren't you afraid you will catch that poor child's diseases?" With a gentle smile she replied, "Why would I be afraid? You see, sir, I've already died. I've been crucified with Christ, so my life now is His. He is the One who told me to care for these orphans. It is my joy and privilege to love these babies. This is what Christ would have me do."

The crucified life says, "My life is not my own. I've been bought with a great price. I now live to serve the One who rescued me from the misery of sin and death. I am His ambassador to the lowest of the low." The same Holy Spirit that provoked the King of the universe to get up from the table, gird Himself with a towel, and wash His disciples' feet will fuel us to be foot washers ourselves. Our blessing is that we can do these great acts of nothingness for the glory of God.

True Christianity cannot survive if it only lives on the highest rooftop. The greatest opportunities are in the deepest, darkest places where the hurting and broken people live. By bringing the healing hands of Jesus down into the valley, we discover His humility; we become so captivated with ministry that we no longer live for ourselves, but for Him. Ask God for a chance to be His healing hands today!

EVENING
Lord, help me always to pursue what is good and never ignore the hurting. In Your name. Amen.

Week 7, Wednesday

Jesus, let me think like You today and see the truth from Your perspective. May I have Your mind and look for ways to serve those around me. In Your precious name I pray. Amen.

> *Let this mind be in you which was also in Christ Jesus, who, being in the form of God, did not consider it robbery to be equal with God, but made Himself of no reputation, taking the form of a bondservant, and coming in the likeness of men.*
> PHILIPPIANS 2:5–7

Can you imagine the love that would provoke the great "Uncaused Cause" to step out of His heavenly domain, out of His perfect kingly adornment, and away from the greatest concert of all time (in His honor, mind you) to become one of us? Oh the depths of His great love! Oh the hope that is ours because of His great sacrifice! How can we comprehend it? Take just a moment and try. It's impossible, isn't it? No amount of generosity or sacrifice could ever match the gift He gave or the debt of love we owe Him.

Although we could never thank Him enough, we *can* do something. We can thank Him by loving selflessly like Jesus. We can heal like Jesus healed . . . with the hope and power of heaven. And we can serve like Jesus served . . . with joy unspeakable! Jesus laid His life down for us and for the glory of His Father. And because He lives in each of us who know Him, we have the same power . . . the power to empty ourselves.

Wait, think about it . . . empty ourselves? How liberating and empowering it would be to be completely free of myself—to love with selfless abandon, to serve the lowest and the broken in the humblest of circumstances with a soul full of holy laughter and joy, all the while realizing that I am a child of the King. There is great joy in making ourselves of no reputation, just as Christ did. Today, empty yourself of self and serve the King with selfless abandon!

EVENING

Father, use me today to give it all away! I want o give all of the love and all of the healing that comes when You use my hands and my heart to love and serve others. In Jesus' name and for His sake. Amen.

MORNING

Lord, thank You that each new day with You is truly a greater opportunity! Today, let me come along side someone and lift up their tired arms as they serve others in Your name. Amen.

As the body is one and has many members, but all the members of that one body, being many, are one body, so also is Christ. For by one Spirit we were all baptized into one body—whether Jews or Greeks, whether slaves or free—and have all been made to drink into one Spirit.

1 CORINTHIANS 12:12, 13

Truly no man is an island . . . Our "separateness" is lost to our "togetherness" as the body of Christ. When we believe and receive Christ at "salvation's moment" we receive His Holy Spirit and we are all made members of the body of Christ. The virtue of the indwelling of the Spirit makes us the church and makes us one. Our oneness accentuates the beauty and importance of our unique function as a part of the body of the Beautiful One, Christ Jesus! We are His body. He is our head and we are made one by the lifeblood of the Holy Spirit flowing through us. The church doesn't need to become united; it is united! The church doesn't need to strive to be as one. It is one! Just as the blood that flows through each of our bodies unites each part and brings it commonality and kinship, the blood of Christ that covers and cleanses us has brought us together and "grafted us into the vine" of the body of Christ. He is the head of the body. We are His parts. We are His hands to touch the world. We are His feet to carry the gospel. We are His eyes to see opportunity and need. We are His ears to hear the cries of the hurting. We are His heart that gives itself completely on the altar of ministry for the sake of the world and the pleasure of God. "Baptized," (vs. 13) means literally "to be placed into." Could it be that God has put you right where you need to be in order for you to function properly, doing your work as a part of His body, thus bringing Him glory?

EVENING

Lord, thank You for the good kind of tired, which comes from giving myself to the point of emptiness. It is here, when I am completely spent of myself for others in Your name, that I am truly filled! Amen.

RUSS LEE, MURFREESBORO, TN

Week 7, Friday

Lord, may Your Word truly be an illuminating window to my soul today. Give me ears to hear what You would say to me, Holy Spirit of God. Amen.

And we urge you, brethren, to recognize those who labor among you, and are over you in the Lord and admonish you, and to esteem them very highly in love for their work's sake. Be at peace among yourselves.
1 THESSALONIANS 5:12, 13

The young church at Thessalonica was full of zealous new converts, all eager to grow in their understanding of this new life they were experiencing. Just like young, energetic, curious children, the implication is that some of the young zealots had the tendency to question everything. Without a doubt, this was exhausting and time consuming for their leaders who were working hard to establish the church. When immaturity is ignored, it tends to breed rebellion, and that can be infectious and damaging among new believers with tender, shallow roots. I believe this is why Paul set out to establish the authority of the church leaders.

In his letter to the Thessalonians, Paul admonished his children in the Lord to respect and love those whom God had appointed to train them in their faith. Like all Christians, including you and me, they had a tendency to get ahead of themselves, to become impatient, and to be overcome with passion. Spiritual teaching and preparation are critical to effectiveness. We all must be taught to be used. It is better to learn our lessons from the wise who have gone before us than to allow our inexperience to lead us astray.

We know that our spiritual authorities have been placed in our lives by a loving heavenly Father who promises to complete the "good work" He began is us (Philippians 1:6). He uses our authorities, teachers, and His Holy Spirit to accomplish this. So trust today, listen with your heart, and obey. Remain teachable and you will find yourself always in the presence of the ultimate teacher!

EVENING
Lord Jesus, thank You for loving me enough to train me up in righteousness. Thank You for godly teachers and mentors. Thank You for the life lessons that shape me for Your glory. Help me to grow more like You every day as I listen, trust, and obey. In Your name and for Your glory, Amen.

MORNING

Lord, today help me to hear Your truth with Your mind and see this world through Your eyes. In Jesus' name, Amen.

Brethren, if a man is overtaken in any trespass, you who are spiritual restore such a one in a spirit of gentleness, considering yourself lest you also be tempted. Bear one another's burdens, and so fulfill the law of Christ.
GALATIANS 6:1, 2

When I read these verses, I am reminded of a soldier on the battlefield who puts his own life on the line for the sake of a fallen comrade. This is the scene that plays out in my mind as I consider the potential plight of a fallen soldier of the Lord. Too many times we see the wounded and hurting and we do nothing to rescue and restore them. Bearing another's burdens puts the strain and responsibility on the one who is stronger. He bears the weight gladly because he can. It is his privilege to help someone who is weaker than he is. He does it for the sake of the relationship, not as a favor or for bragging rights, but because it is a privilege.

Our responsibility as believers and followers of Christ is to lay down our lives, even for our weak brothers and sisters. They also are the body of Christ. We can never ignore His wounds and call ourselves "His body." If our bodies are broken and hurting, we tend to our physical needs. Our brothers and sisters who are wounded need the same care—they need us to be the hands and feet of Jesus and to run to their rescue. Not only are we to carry them from the battlefield of life to safety, but we are also to stay by their side and let God's Spirit use *us* as His medicine to heal them. One day soon, they will fight again.

EVENING

Lord Jesus, since I myself am also in constant need of mercy, help me to freely extend mercy to others the way You do. I pray this all in Your name, Jesus, for Your glory and their encouragement. Amen.

RUSS LEE, MURFREESBORO, TN

Week 8, Monday

Father, as I begin the day, I submit myself to You. I open my life to Your Word. I accept it as true and ask You to produce fruit in me. Do not allow me to harden my heart or be distracted by the cares of the world. I choose this day to focus my life on Jesus. In His name I pray. Amen.

These are the ones sown on good ground, those who hear the word,
accept it, and bear fruit: some thirtyfold, some sixty, and some a hundred."
MARK 4:20

This concluding verse of the parable of the soils contains three present participles that mark continuing action. Followers of Christ hear God's Word, accept God's Word, and bear fruit. Christians must not be people with hard hearts and shallow commitment, and they must not be distracted by the cares of this world. We are to be people of faith with hearts open to the Word of God, just as rich soil receives seed and produces abundance.

The production of spiritual fruit comes from the life-giving Spirit of God. However, there is action demanded from the believer. We are to hear the Word. I challenge you to have ears to hear what God's Word is saying to you. Read it and listen. Recently I read the testimony of J. Hudson Taylor, missionary to China in the late 1800s. Taylor read through the Bible every year for fifty consecutive years—a great habit we should all emulate. Make listening to the Word a continuous action in your life.

Next we must accept the Word of God. This involves study, understanding, and obedience. As one steps forward in volitional faith, God will open up the heart and mind to greater understanding of His revealed Word. Then comes fruitfulness. Every believer is not the same; each one is unique, and the Father produces thirty-, sixty-, or one hundredfold according to His will. God desires to be fruitful through you today, so prepare the soil of your heart—hear God's Word, accept God's Word, and you will bear much fruit for Him!

EVENING

Thank You, Father, for producing fruit in me today. I confess I cannot and did not produce spiritual fruit on my own, but I rejoice that You produced it through me. Let the fruit in my life be fruit of eternal significance—fruit that remains. In Jesus' name I pray. Amen.

Father, as I begin this day I submit to You as the Vinedresser. Prepare me for fruitfulness. Prune me if necessary. I welcome Your sovereign activity in my life. Thank You for providing the power of the Holy Spirit within me. Produce eternal fruit in me today, I ask. Amen.

> *I am the true vine, and My Father is the vinedresser. Every branch in Me that does not bear fruit He takes away; and every branch that bears fruit He prunes, that it may bear more fruit.*
> JOHN 15:1, 2

In the Gospel of John we find seven "I am" statements about Jesus. He is the Bread of Life (6:35); He is the Light of the World (8:12); He is the Door (10:7); He is the Good Shepherd (10:11); He is the Resurrection and the Life (11:25); He is the Way, the Truth, and the Life (14:6); and in today's text, He is the true Vine.

John 15:1, 2 describes a vine that has two kinds of branches—one that bears fruit and one that does not. Spiritually speaking, each believer is either a fruit stand or firewood— it all depends on fruitfulness. To ensure fruitfulness, the Vinedresser prunes the branch so it may progress into maximum wisdom. He removes all things in the believer's life that hinder fruit bearing.

Just as our earthly fathers correct us, so the heavenly Father chastens His children. Proverbs 3:11, 12 says, "My son, do not despise the chastening of the Lord, nor detest His correction; for whom the Lord loves He corrects, just as a father the son in whom he delights." This work is rarely joyful in the present, but it yields the gladness of righteousness in our lives. If you believe God wants to prune some attitude or behavior in your life, submit to His loving correction. He will produce much fruit in your life!

EVENING

Lord, thank You for the work You did in my life today. Remove everything in me that is not like Jesus. I submit to You for examination. Grant fruitfulness in my life. Cause love, joy, peace, long-suffering, kindness, goodness, faithfulness, gentleness, and self-control to be bountiful in me. In Jesus' name I pray. Amen.

Week 8, Wednesday

Father, as Your child I purpose to abide in You today. Open Your Word to me. Teach me to pray. Give me grace to keep my focus on You. May I walk with You in the fullness of the Holy Spirit. My desire is for You to bear fruit in my life this day. In Jesus' name, Amen.

Abide in Me, and I in you. As the branch cannot bear fruit of itself, unless it abides in the vine, neither can you, unless you abide in Me.
JOHN 15:4

W hen the *New York Times* bestselling author Andy Andrews autographs a book, he usually writes "Persist!" below his signature. In today's verse, Jesus did basically the same thing as a message to all believers. He said that the only legitimate believer is an abiding believer. To abide means to stay or remain. To *persist*. We are to persist in following Him. There will be no fruit in our lives if we are disconnected from the true Vine, the Lord Jesus. Persistently abiding in Christ is essential to being a fruit-bearing Christ-follower.

There are several keys to abiding in Christ. We must begin with an acknowledgement of our own inability to produce spiritual fruit. That leads us to a confidence in the sufficiency of Christ alone as our source of spiritual life. Abiding takes time. It is easy to get caught up in job-related, church-sponsored, or denomination-sanctioned efforts that keep us too busy to abide. Time alone in Bible study and prayer are required in order to abide in the Vine. As you live your life each day, walk in the presence of Jesus. Abide in Him and He will produce fruit in your life.

EVENING

Father, thank You for Your activity in my life today. I rest in Your sufficiency. Give me rest this night. Cause me to arise refreshed tomorrow as I meet You in the stillness of another morning. Amen.

Father, I confess that without You, I can do nothing. Thank You for the promise that I can do all things through Christ's strength. This morning I need that power so I can be a fruitful believer. My desire is to abide in You. Thank You for being the true Vine and for making me one of Your branches. Amen.

> *I am the vine, you are the branches. He who abides in Me, and I in him, bears much fruit; for without Me you can do nothing. If anyone does not abide in Me, he is cast out as a branch and is withered; and they gather them and throw them into the fire, and they are burned. If you abide in Me, and My words abide in you, you will ask what you desire, and it shall be done for you.*
>
> JOHN 15:5–7

Before we can pray, "Lord, Your kingdom come," we must pray, "Lord, my kingdom go." As a branch, we owe everything to the Vine, and we need to keep that perspective in mind. Jesus made a straight-shooting statement in today's text when He said, "Without Me you can do nothing." Some would protest at this declaration as they put forward their own accomplishments. Hard-working people will draw attention to what they have done, such as building a business or writing a book. While no one can accomplish anything unless the Lord gives him life, we do acknowledge that man has achieved some remarkable things. However, in one hundred years, what will be the reality of man-centered things? We may be able to accomplish some earthly things in our own strength, but apart from the Vine, we can do nothing of eternal value.

Our need today is to find our sufficiency and capability in the life of Jesus alone. Abide in Him! Without His touch, we wither and die. Without His sustenance, our branch can only be used as firewood and leave ashes behind. Abide in Him! Then prepare to see eternal work made manifest in your life today.

EVENING

Lord, forgive me for the times this day I have been driven by flesh instead of faith. Teach me to abide. Thank You for the power to bear eternal fruit through You. In Jesus' name. Amen.

DR. TED H. TRAYLOR, PENSACOLA, FL

Father, as I begin the day, I ask that You do in me what is required to make me holy. I confess that there is no good thing in me. However, I am confident that Jesus can produce in me the spirit and practice of holiness. I rest today in that assurance. In Jesus' name, Amen.

> *Now having been set free from sin, and having become slaves of God,*
> *you have your fruit to holiness, and the end, everlasting life.*
> ROMANS 6:22

I first heard these words quoted in a sermon preached by Dr. Stephen Olford, and my heart was moved: "Only one life, 'twill soon be past; only what's done for Christ will last." The poem was written many years ago by missionary C. T. Studd, but our lives are still to be lived from that point of view. We need to invest our lives here on earth in things that will matter for all eternity. And we cannot accomplish anything with eternal value apart from Christ. Our "fruit to holiness," the result of the Holy Spirit's continuing work of developing Christ's character in us, is not something that comes by striving, but by resting in Him. Jesus produces the fruit of holiness.

J. Hudson Taylor learned this from John McCarthy. McCarthy wrote to Hudson, telling of a great new sunrise that had dawned in his soul. He wrote, "The Lord Jesus received is holiness begun; the Lord Jesus cherished is holiness advancing; the Lord Jesus counted upon as never absent would be holiness complete." Mr. McCarthy then declared that it is defective faith that clogs the feet and causes many a fall.

Today I call you to the feet of Jesus. There you may rest. He is sufficient. Let Him make you holy.

EVENING

Lord Jesus, You are the sinless One. Without You I am at best striving in my flesh. I choose to die to my ability and live to Yours. Thank You for the anointing that enables me to have the fruit of holiness. In Your holy name I pray. Amen.

Father, thank You for entrusting me with the gospel. I am blessed to be Your child. As I live today, I ask that You shine the Good News through me. Place me in situations where I can reflect the light of Jesus. Grant me wisdom and boldness to be faithful with the witness. Make my life fruitful this day. In Jesus' name, Amen.

This man came for a witness, to bear witness of the Light, that all through him might believe. He was not that Light, but was sent to bear witness of that Light.
JOHN 1:7, 8

Spiritual fruit in the life of the believer comes in various forms. One of those fruits is influencing others to come to faith in Jesus Christ. We are to be soul winners. John the Baptist was a witness of the light of Jesus. We are to be like John. While we are not the light, we are to bear witness to the Light.

Pointing others to Jesus is a primary function of the believer. John exemplified this for us. He was a man of rock-solid character, not a reed shaken by the wind. John was also a man of self-denial. He was not a man in soft raiment. Rather, he was indifferent to material things. Living in the desert, John had one focus: pointing people to Jesus. He was God's messenger and luminary, aglow with the presence of Jesus.

The need of our day is for each of us to blaze with the light of the gospel. Then we will point others to our Master. No fruit produced in our lives is more critical to God's kingdom than the winning of one person to faith in Jesus Christ. May others see Jesus in you as you reflect His light today!

EVENING

Father, I confess to You that the world is lost and that I need a deeper concern for its lostness. Forgive for of being a hidden light. Give me courage and confidence to be a witness for Jesus. Thank You for the gospel. I realize You have entrusted it to me. I pledge to share the Good News. Amen.

Week 9, Monday

Father, thank You for another day to live and bring You glory. Help me this day to be like Your Son, who bore witness to the truth. In my life, in all I do and say, may others see Jesus in me and hear about Jesus from me. In His name I pray. Amen.

Pilate therefore said to Him, "Are You a king then?" Jesus answered, "You say rightly that I am a king. For this cause I was born, and for this cause I have come into the world, that I should bear witness to the truth. Everyone who is of the truth hears My voice."

JOHN 18:37

A s Jesus stood before Pilate, He announced to the earthly monarch, the governor of Judea, that He was indeed a king. And then Jesus told Pilate something revealing and profound. As a king, His main purpose was to bear witness to the truth. Jesus was a servant-king, a concept totally foreign to earthly kings or people of royalty like Pilate.

Our Lord's primary purpose was to honor the Father who sent Him on His mission. And that mission was to bear witness to the truth. The Greek word for witness is *martureo*, from which we get our English word *martyr*. God sent His Son on a mission of mercy, and it cost Jesus His life.

As His ambassadors today, we have also been commissioned to tell the truth, the whole truth, and nothing but the truth. And doing so may cost us our lives as well. Or it may cost us our teeth. Yes . . . teeth. Missionary Nathan Barlow served for sixty years in Ethiopia. He had to leave the country due to a painful toothache, so he had the dentist pull all his teeth and give him dentures so he could return to his work and not be hindered anymore by a toothache! Bearing witness to the truth of the gospel will cost us something, but the sacrifice does not compare to the honor of following in the steps of our King.

EVENING
In my life, Lord, be glorified today. Help me bear witness to the truth of who You are, both in what I say and how I live my life. I gladly hear Your voice and am willing to go to my neighbors and the nations. Here I am—send me!

Awesome, triune God—Father, Son, Holy Spirit—I come to You this new day, seeking You and asking You to use me for Your glory. Help me not to miss an opportunity to bear witness to You and Your power. Embolden me to speak the gospel and live the gospel. Assist me to proclaim and live in such a way that others are drawn to You. Amen.

There are three that bear witness in heaven: the Father, the Word,
and the Holy Spirit; and these three are one. And there are three that bear
witness on earth: the Spirit, the water, and the blood; and these three agree as one.
1 JOHN 5:7, 8

Our responsibility as followers of Jesus Christ is to proclaim the biblical Jesus to a lost world. Sadly, there are many groups today that proclaim a Jesus that is very different from the Jesus of the New Testament. John, the beloved pastor and apostle, also encountered heretics in his ministry. There was a group known as the Cerinthian Gnostics who taught that the Christ came upon Jesus at His baptism, but left Him before the Cross. The Gnostics did not believe that the Son of God could die. John corrected this faulty teaching in 1 John 5:8. The Holy Spirit bore witness to the true Christ, and so did the water (Christ's baptism) and the blood (Christ's death on the Cross).

Jesus Christ was fully God and fully man, and the Spirit bears witness that this Jesus Christ indeed died for the sins of the world, bodily arose from the dead, and is mighty to save all who call upon Him in faith. This is the Christ of the gospel; this is the Christ we proclaim. Hallelujah, what a wonderful Savior!

EVENING

Dear God, I thank You for who You are, and I am so grateful for Your Word that teaches me truth. Help me to forever ponder the great truths of Scripture, but not ponder only. Help me to live for and tell others about You. In Jesus' name I pray. Amen.

Week 9, Wednesday

Lord, thank You for another day to live. Help me to make an eternal investment in someone's life this very day. Help me introduce someone to You, and empower me to encourage a fellow believer in Christ. I am ready, Lord! Use me for Your glory. Amen.

I love those who love me, and those who seek me diligently will find me.
Riches and honor are with me, enduring riches and righteousness. My fruit
is better than gold, yes, than fine gold, and my revenue than choice silver.
PROVERBS 8:17–19

Every day I read the chapter in the Book of Proverbs that corresponds to what day it is. This habit is an integral part of my quiet time that I have been practicing for years. One of the things I love about Proverbs is that it teaches us about true riches. To know, fear, and love God is far greater than anything this world can offer.

In chapter 8, Solomon presents the characteristics and excellence of true wisdom. God, by His wisdom, created the world and all that is in it. And God gladly and freely offers this true wisdom to all who seek Him. Our passage for today is full of words of assurance and promise. If you love God and seek Him, He will lovingly bless you. And His blessings are far greater and more costly than the finest gold or choicest silver! Precious metals on earth cannot compare to the heavenly blessings that God showers upon His people.

This biblical text reminds me of the hymn written by Rhea F. Miller and sung by George Beverly Shea. It says, "I'd rather have Jesus than silver or gold; I'd rather be His than have riches untold; I'd rather have Jesus than houses or lands, I'd rather be led by His nail pierced hand. Than to be a king of a vast domain or be held in sin's dread sway, I'd rather have Jesus than anything this world affords today." Is this true for you? Would you rather have heavenly significance than worldly success? Would you rather have Jesus than anything this world can offer? May you choose wisely today!

EVENING
Father, thank You for using me today. Grant me rest and help me tomorrow to continue to focus on true riches and to share these eternal riches with others. Amen.

Week 9, Thursday

Some soul for Thee, oh God, some soul for Thee—this is indeed my earnest plea. I ask You to allow me the privilege and entrust to me the responsibility of leading some soul to You this very day. I can't wait to see how You use me today! Amen.

The fruit of the righteous is a tree of life, and he who wins souls is wise.
PROVERBS 11:30

God rewards the righteous with a blessed life. Psalm 1:3 says the righteous man "shall be like a tree planted by the rivers of water" that bears much fruit and that "whatever he does shall prosper." The church is God's instrument to reach the nations with the saving message of Jesus, and there is no other area where God wants to prosper us more than in our efforts to spread the Good News.

My daughter and I had the joy of leading a young man named Roman to Christ recently. Roman is from Russia and has lived in the United States for about ten years. He has many questions about Christianity, and we have been able to have an ongoing dialogue with him. Since he accepted Christ, he has been on fire! He witnesses at work and radiates the joy of Christ. Not long after he was saved, he ran through a stop sign and was pulled over by a police officer. After he received the ticket, Roman began sharing Christ with the officer. She told him, "This is a first; no one has ever witnessed to me after I pulled him or her over!" Though only a brand new Christian, Roman is pointing people to Jesus, and Proverbs says such a man is wise indeed.

The Hebrew word translated "win" in Proverbs 11:30 means "to take, receive, or acquire." To lead a soul to the saving grace of Jesus Christ is the greatest endeavor and the greatest thrill for the child of God. So how about you? Are you a tree of life offering spiritual shade and nourishment to those around you? Are you a wise man or woman of God who is winning souls to Christ?

EVENING

Father, my prayer is summed up in the following hymn—"Lord, lay some soul upon my heart, and love that soul through me; and may I bravely do my part to win that soul for Thee." In Jesus' name, Amen.

DANNY FORSHEE, AUSTIN, TX

Week 9, Friday

God, thank You for another day to live for You. I am Your servant; I am Your private, reporting to You, the general. Help me this day to be a healthy, responsible follower of Christ. Help me to bear good fruit worthy of Your name. Amen.

> *Every good tree bears good fruit, but a bad tree bears bad fruit.*
> *A good tree cannot bear bad fruit, nor can a bad tree bear good fruit.*
> *Every tree that does not bear good fruit is cut down and thrown*
> *into the fire. Therefore by their fruits you will know them.*
> MATTHEW 7:17–20

Jesus was the master teacher. He communicated deeply profound spiritual truths by using analogies from everyday life. In our text today, He told the disciples how citizens in God's kingdom are to live by comparing believers to trees. As followers of Christ, we will not be perfect here on earth, but we should consistently bear good fruit in service to God. Someone who habitually dishonors God in his or her life and speech is not a follower of Christ. First John 3:10 states, "In this the children of God and the children of the devil are manifest: Whoever does not practice righteousness is not of God, nor is he who does not love his brother."

The sixteenth-century reformer Martin Luther said some things that can inspire the child of God in any generation. He said, "My conscience is captive to the Word of God. I cannot and I will not recant, for it is neither safe nor honest to violate one's conscience." Luther also said, "There are two days on my calendar: this day and that day." We are to so live for Christ and bear good fruit (this day), for we will all appear before Christ and give an account of our lives (that day). If you repeatedly bear bad fruit, you need to become a new tree! Ask God to save you right now. If you know the Lord, keep bearing good fruit and get ready for that day!

EVENING

God, thank You for Your Word that speaks directly to my life. Jesus, as a good tree bears healthy fruit to eat, so I want my life to bear the fruit of the Spirit of God. Help me. Prune me. Enable me to bear fruit for You. Amen.

MORNING

God, I praise You and thank You for choosing me to know and serve You. Thank You for amazing grace that saved a wretch like me! Today, oh God, I ask that You do whatever You desire in my life that will bring You the most glory. Whatever You ask of me today, the answer is yes. In Jesus' name, Amen.

> *You did not choose Me, but I chose you and appointed you that*
> *you should go and bear fruit, and that your fruit should remain,*
> *that whatever you ask the Father in My name He may give you.*
> JOHN 15:16

If you know Jesus Christ as your personal Savior and Lord, then it is because of His amazing, sovereign grace. He chose you and appointed you to go on mission with Him and bear fruit that remains. As a child of God, note the promise Jesus makes to us: whatever we ask the Father in Jesus' name, He grants to us.

Today's text reminds me of Romans 8:30, which says, "Moreover whom He predestined, these He also called; whom He called, these He also justified; and whom He justified, these He also glorified." I was flying on an airplane not long ago, and the Lord sat me beside an agnostic who had many questions. He asked me how it could be that I cared so much about the things of God and he cared so little. I told him the reason God chose and saved me was for me to tell people like him how much God loves them!

God saved us not that we might sit, soak, and sour, but that we might have the privilege of bearing lasting fruit. Salvation from beginning to end is the work of God. And in His providence, He has selected you and me to broadcast freely His name and fame. Today, be about the work He handpicked you for!

EVENING

Father, this song captures the attitude of my heart: "Your grace still amazes me; Your love is still a mystery. Each day I fall on my knees; cause Your grace still amazes me."[3] Thank You for choosing me to tell others about You. Help me to bear fruit that remains for the glory of God. Amen.

DANNY FORSHEE, AUSTIN, TX

Lord, I rejoice in the living relationship I enjoy with You by faith in Jesus. Thank You so much for freedom from the law, for new life in Christ, and for the energy it brings to all that I do. I acknowledge that Jesus conquered sin, death, and the grave. So today, Lord Jesus, empower me to walk in Your resurrection power and to bear true, lasting fruit for You! Amen.

> *My brethren, you also have become dead to the law through*
> *the body of Christ, that you may be married to another—to Him*
> *who was raised from the dead, that we should bear fruit to God.*
>
> ROMANS 7:4

Leading up to Romans 7:4, the apostle Paul painted a grim picture of the fallen human race's relationship to God. We were dead to God and slaves to sin, enemies of God, and captive to our fallen nature. But Paul also dramatically introduced the wonder of God's grace that, in spite of the ravages of sin, we have been freed and redeemed by "the gift of God," which is "eternal life in Christ Jesus our Lord" (Romans 6:23).

Through the inspiration of the Holy Spirit, Paul made it plain in today's verse that our death to the law and our "marriage" to Christ are not just for eternal security or a home in heaven, but that we might "bear fruit to God."

How is that "fruit" to be characterized? Is it the fruit of winning souls to Christ? The manifestation of God's Spirit in us, resulting in the fruit of the Spirit growing in our character (Galatians 5:22, 23)? Is it the fruit of productive service and ministry for Jesus' sake? Probably not one in exclusion of the other, but rather, all together in concert and completeness.

Married to Christ for salvation—yes. That speaks to eternal life in heaven. But we are also presently joined to Christ—to bear fruit for His glory in the here and now!

EVENING

Lord, all glory and honor be to Your name for the joy of Your gospel and its great promises. Please bless whatever seed of Your grace I may have sown in my witness for Jesus, in my yieldedness to Your Spirit, or in my service for You. And thank You for the victory that is mine through the resurrection of Jesus. In His name I pray. Amen.

Thank You, Jesus, for the empowering ministry of the Holy Spirit. I want to honor You today by allowing Your Spirit to bear His fruit in me and direct me for the glory of Your name. Teach me afresh that it is not by my individual effort, power, or might that I can be more like You, but it is solely by the wonderful working of Your Spirit in me. Amen.

> *The fruit of the Spirit is love, joy, peace, longsuffering, kindness,*
> *goodness, faithfulness, gentleness, self-control. Against such there*
> *is no law. And those who are Christ's have crucified the flesh with its*
> *passions and desires. If we live in the Spirit, let us also walk in the Spirit.*
> GALATIANS 5:22–25

Having not been raised on a farm but being a self-confessed "city boy," there is a lot I don't know about trees. In fact, about the only way I can recognize any tree is if it is a fruit tree that has real, live, edible fruit. Then it's easy—an orange tree has oranges, an apple tree has apples, and so on.

The same dynamic is true of the fruit of the Spirit. How does one know that the Spirit of God is in charge of a person's life? Do they have the fruit of the Spirit of God? In other words, do His characteristics dominate that person's life?

Note that in these two verses we see *nine* characteristics of one fruit. It is only when all of these characteristics are evident simultaneously that we can be certain the Spirit is in control. There is one fruit but nine characteristics, just as an apple may be described as round, red, baseball-sized, etc. This miraculous, supernatural fruit is the evidence that God's Holy Spirit is present and in control—love, joy, peace, long-suffering, kindness, goodness, faithfulness, gentleness, and self-control.

How may a person evidence these characteristics? Only by walking in the Spirit (v. 25). May God grant that we be filled and go on being filled with His Spirit.

EVENING

Lord, as I end this day, I acknowledge afresh my complete dependence on You. Today I may have failed to be totally dependent on Your Spirit to bear Your fruit. Forgive me. Where and when I have manifested Your glorious character, I give credit to You. Thank You! Even as I sleep, may my thoughts and dreams be under Your control. Amen.

R. PHILIP ROBERTS, KANSAS CITY, MO

Father, how I rejoice today in the wonderful promises of Your Word. And there can be no greater one than the fact that Jesus is our High Priest and has offered for us the perfect sacrifice for our sin—His own shed blood. Please give me the spirit of gratitude and thanks as I delight in Your goodness. Let me share Your goodness and grace with those who might need it! Amen.

> *Therefore by Him let us continually offer the sacrifice of praise to God,*
> *that is, the fruit of our lips, giving thanks to His name. But do not forget*
> *to do good and to share, for with such sacrifices God is well pleased.*
> HEBREWS 13:15, 16

Today's passage begins in the New King James Version® with the word *therefore*. An important principle when that word appears is to remember that *therefore* is always "there" "for" a reason. The reason is that it serves as a reference to what has gone before. In this case it refers to the fabulous truths of all that the Book of Hebrews contains.

This great book recounts for all believers the completeness and supremacy of Christ's sacrifice for our sins. He is the great and perfect High Priest who offered the perfect, complete, and once-for-all sacrifice for sin. His sacrifice has, therefore, completed God's powerful plan of salvation so that it is based on faith in Jesus alone. Additionally, not only was Jesus a great priest, but a gracious one as well. Consequently, and due to His sacrifice, He receives all who come to Him in need and submission. In fact, it is our need that causes Him to respond out of His goodness to assist us in our hour of need.

While in many religious systems, pleadings for assistance to the deity may be limited to times of ceremonial sacrifice, Christ is ever ready to help. Therefore, we should also "continually offer the sacrifice of praise" and give thanks—the "fruit of our lips"—to His name.

EVENING

Oh Lord, I'm often so slow to give thanks to Your great name. The "fruit of my lips" is too often silent and unresponsive. Just as You sacrificed for me, so teach me day by day "to do good and to share" so that I may in some way sacrifice for You. I bless Your name! Amen.

Heavenly Father, please give me Your wisdom and grace throughout this day. Fill me with Your Holy Spirit so that I may be pleasing to You in all my ways. Thank You for using me as a reflection of Your glory! In Jesus' name, Amen.

The wisdom that is from above is first pure, then peaceable, gentle,
willing to yield, full of mercy and good fruits, without partiality and without
hypocrisy. Now the fruit of righteousness is sown in peace by those who make peace.
JAMES 3:17, 18

This great text had as its author "James, a bondservant of God and of the Lord Jesus Christ." While James was a common name in the first century (and there are several opinions as to who the author exactly was), the general consensus by most biblical scholars is that the author was James the half brother of Jesus. He had been a skeptic about Jesus and His claims prior to the Resurrection, but in a dramatic reversal, as a result of the risen Lord's appearance to him, James put his faith in Christ and assumed leadership in the Jerusalem church.

Knowing this fact, James had the opportunity to observe the Person and life of Jesus firsthand. He saw Jesus in every possible circumstance. He was able to recall just how Jesus reacted to every situation. What he saw in Jesus was wisdom "from above" that he described this way: pure, peaceable, gentle, submissive, full of mercy and good fruits, impartial, and sincere.

It is for that reason that God gave us His Holy Spirit to bear these same attributes in our lives. What a remarkable, supernatural transformation this transaction is. Therefore, we, above everything else, must be focused on our walk with Christ. The Book of James is a book of Christian practicalities, but it is rooted in the reality that wisdom and all of the other virtues mentioned here are "from above." They are those elements that God, for the glory of Jesus, bestows on all who request them! And our God "gives to all liberally" (James 1:5), so ask boldly!

EVENING
Heavenly Father, as my day finishes, I pray that You hasten the day when Your glory covers the earth as the waters cover the sea! Lord, thank You for allowing me to serve You. In Jesus' name and for His sake, Amen.

R. PHILIP ROBERTS, KANSAS CITY, MO

Heavenly Father, I ask for a righteous heart that is worthy of Your praise. Keep me from temptation, and guard me from the wiles of the devil. Allow me to serve and bless You today. Amen.

The wicked is ensnared by the transgression of his lips, but the righteous will come through trouble. A man will be satisfied with good by the fruit of his mouth, and the recompense of a man's hands will be rendered to him.
PROVERBS 12:13, 14

Galatians 6:7 contains a near paraphrase of today's text: "Whatever a man sows, that he will also reap." These two verses reflect a deep truth: if we live and speak righteously, there will be four positive results.

The first is that the righteous man will not be "ensnared by the transgression of his lips." Lies always lead to entrapment. Once the truth is twisted, it will eventually have to be twisted again to cover the first lie. But no trap waits for those who are consistent with all they say.

Second, "the righteous will come through trouble." Once our way is committed to the Lord, He is committed to see us through any difficulty in our path. Proverbs 3:6 reminds us that if we acknowledge the Lord, "He shall direct [our] paths."

Third, the righteous man will be "satisfied with good by the fruit of his mouth." The greatest of all rewards is an upright and righteous character. Consequently, what is earned by truth telling is a righteous character that is the most valuable of possessions.

Lastly, the "recompense of a man's hands will be rendered to him." In other words, what goes around comes around. When we stand in judgment before Christ, our perfect Judge—and we soon shall—all that matters will be to hear Him say, "Well done, good and faithful servant" (Matthew 25:23). May we live in a way that is worthy of His approval!

EVENING

Lord, please grant me a clean heart. May the searchlight of Your Holy Spirit examine my thoughts and actions and reveal any wicked actions, words, or thoughts in my life today. As You bring them to mind, I confess them before You and ask for forgiveness. Thank You for Your promise that if I confess my sins, You will forgive and cleanse me from all of them. In Jesus' name. Amen.

MORNING

Lord, help me to walk in fellowship and communion with You today! Thank You for Your promise to guide my steps and direct my thoughts. Today, Lord, give me an opportunity to tell someone about You! In Your name, Amen.

We also, since the day we heard it, do not cease to pray for you,
and to ask that you may be filled with the knowledge of His will in all wisdom and
spiritual understanding; that you may walk worthy of the Lord, fully pleasing Him,
being fruitful in every good work and increasing in the knowledge of God.
COLOSSIANS 1:9, 10

There is always a danger in emphasizing the importance of good works. The danger is that we forget our utter dependence on the grace of God through Christ for our salvation. The great reformer Martin Luther, who vigorously championed "grace alone" for salvation, said this: "We should be careful that we don't elevate good works to such an extent that faith and Christ become secondary. If we esteem them too highly, good works can become the greatest idolatry."

This reasoning is why the apostle Paul prayed that the Christians in Colosse "be filled with the knowledge of His will in all wisdom and spiritual understanding." It is also why he thanked God for salvation by "faith in Christ Jesus" (Colossians 1:4).

But just as faith in Christ Jesus is at the very root of our salvation, and just as there can be no assurance of heaven without it, so good works are essential as the "fruit" of salvation. Works that please and honor God as a consequence of faith in Jesus should be as assured as the night follows the day. Paul prayed the Colossians would be "fruitful in every good work."

Believer, follower of Jesus, let us pledge together to bear fruit for the Savior knowing that it is He, who loved us and gave Himself for us, who works in us to accomplish His perfect will.

EVENING

Lord, I am weak, but You are strong. I make mistakes, but You are perfect and full of truth. I am mortal, but You are eternal and unchanging. Therefore, Lord, I depend on You. Strengthen my hand to do Your work. Help me to be faithful to You in all that I do. Lord Jesus, I love You! In Your name I pray. Amen.

R. PHILIP ROBERTS, KANSAS CITY, MO

Week 11, Monday

Lord, I do not know what I will face today. Help me to see You in every situation and decision. Lead me to respond to all adversity in faith. Amen.

Behold the proud, his soul is not upright in him; but the just shall live by his faith.
HABAKKUK 2:4

Sometimes it is difficult to believe God's promises for the future because of how we view the past. This verse in Habakkuk contrasts the person of pride with the person of faith. Those who have been saved by Christ have humbled themselves before God, confessed their sin to Him, and depended upon Christ alone for their salvation. The proud see themselves as the source of life and blessing. They do not give thanks to the Lord.

When we move on to the next prayer, the next event, or the next problem without recognizing God's intervention in our lives, we exhibit a form of pride. Gratitude is the key to moving from pride to faith.

Recently, I had an experience that reminded me of this valuable lesson. My wife, Pam, discovered a lump in her breast. She had a biopsy, and the results came back positive. She had cancer. At first, I was overcome with shock, then concern for her. And then I found myself getting angry. After all, we had been serving God faithfully. She had already gone through so many physical trials . . . and now this. My anger grew as I realized I might lose her.

After twenty minutes of silent seething, God spoke to my heart. He had given me the sweetest and most wonderful person I have ever known to be my wife for twenty-nine years. She was far more than I ever deserved. Instead of being grateful for the twenty-nine years He gave me, I was feeling entitled to a future with her as well. Only as I was able to give glory to God for the past was I able to have peace about the future. A key to living by faith is to be grateful to God for the blessings of life.

EVENING

Teach me to give thanks in all things. Help me to be grateful for all Your wonderful blessings in my life. In every situation, guide me to forge ahead in faith, remembering Your faithfulness in my past. Amen.

Lord, help me give all my concerns to You today. Help me trust in You and remember that there is nothing You cannot do. Amen.

> *Now if God so clothes the grass of the field, which today is, and*
> *tomorrow is thrown into the oven, will He not much more clothe you,*
> *O you of little faith? Therefore do not worry, saying, "What shall we eat?"*
> *or "What shall we drink?" or "What shall we wear?"*
> MATTHEW 6:30, 31

It's been said that 95 percent of the things we worry about never happen. Then why do we worry? One of our biggest problems is that we worry about what we own. However, if you truly believe God owns all you have, your worry quotient will greatly diminish.

A few years ago, three men from my church took me to a football game in Gainesville, Florida. Since I was scheduled to preach the next morning in a nearby town, I decided to drive my car. On our way, we stopped at a Burger King in Ocala to have lunch. I decided I would leave my car in the parking lot and ride the rest of the way with my friends.

When we returned to the Burger King, my car was gone—it had been stolen. We made the necessary phone calls and filed a police report, and after a two-hour delay, we started to head home. My mind was racing. How I would get back to preach the next day? Just then our driver said, "Oh boy." There it was—another Burger King on the same side of the road two miles from the one we had just left. There was my car, exactly where I had left it. What a relief—but how embarrassing!

One of the men with me observed that throughout the ordeal he did not see me get rattled or angry. This would not have been my normal reaction, but God had been teaching me about ownership and worry. Realizing the car was God's helped me to keep things in perspective. Whatever you own can become your worry, so give it all to God and let Him worry about it.

EVENING

Lord, help me surrender ownership of all the things You have given me. May I only worry if there is something in my life that will hinder me from knowing and loving You more. Amen.

DR. DWAYNE MERCER, OVIEDO, FL

Lord, help me to live a life of worship and to see You in every circumstance today. Amen.

Jesus said to them, "Because of your unbelief; for assuredly, I say to you,
if you have faith as a mustard seed, you will say to this mountain, 'Move
from here to there,' and it will move; and nothing will be impossible
for you. However, this kind does not go out except by prayer and fasting."
MATTHEW 17:20, 21

We are not only saved by faith, but we live by faith. One aspect of having faith in Christ is believing we are better off following God than going our own way. By faith we resist temptation because we believe following God is better than committing sin. This faith leads us to make wise decisions, receive answers to our prayers, and cling to Him in the midst of suffering and trial.

The disciples recognized the value of faith and asked Christ to help them increase it. There are many ways we can grow our faith. One way is to worship God. As we praise and thank God, we are reminded of who He is and what He has done in our lives. Another way is to study God's Word. Romans 10:17 teaches, "So then faith comes by hearing, and hearing by the word of God." As we build Scripture into our lives, we become closer to God and know Him better. The better we know trustworthy people, the more we will trust them. A third way we can grow our faith is to exercise our faith. I believe that Dr. Charles Stanley once said, "Faith must act in order to develop and produce." We may begin with little faith, but as we act on the faith we have, faith grows. Fourth, we should pray. First John 5:14 says, "Now this is the confidence that we have in Him, that if we ask anything according to His will, He hears us." God desires for our faith to grow. Ask God to increase your faith, and He will.

The mustard seed is a very small seed, but it grows to be large and produces fruit. Increase your faith, and see what great things God will accomplish through it!

EVENING
Lord, increase my faith. I see the value in developing my faith. Help me to read Your Word more and to use the faith You have given me. Amen.

Lord, help me to see others through Your eyes. May I never be ashamed of Your gospel. Help me to be faithful to share it with someone today. Amen.

I am not ashamed of the gospel of Christ, for it is the power of God to salvation for everyone who believes, for the Jew first and also for the Greek. For in it the righteousness of God is revealed from faith to faith; as it is written, "The just shall live by faith."
ROMANS 1:16, 17

In this verse, Paul wrote about sharing the gospel with the world. He said that he was not "ashamed" of the gospel. Shame comes from embarrassment. Sports figures who are caught using steroids or living immoral lifestyles bring shame upon themselves. Paul said, "No one will ever come to me and say, 'I tried this gospel and it doesn't work.'" He was never embarrassed because he knew the gospel would work every time.

Paul's confidence was based upon two things. First, the gospel is "the power of God to salvation." The word for power in the original language is *dunamis*, which is where we get our word *dynamite*. Dynamite needs no other explosive to aid it. The power is within the dynamite itself. Likewise, the gospel needs no assistance; it has power within it. Second, the gospel is "the righteousness of God." The gospel is the fact that the righteousness of God will come into the believer's heart through the Holy Spirit at the moment of salvation. Not only are our sins forgiven, but God's imputed (put-in) righteousness changes our lives today, giving us hope, peace, and love.

Paul said that all who call on the Lord and place their faith in Him will be saved (Romans 10:13). It works from faith to faith, from one person's faith to the next. We will never have to apologize for the gospel. It will never embarrass us; it works every time. As we share the gospel, we can do so with great confidence. What has worked for you will work for everyone.

EVENING
Lord, thank You that the same faith that saved me sustains me. Help me to rest in You as I rest my body tonight. Father, help me to trust You with my life the way I have trusted You with my soul. Your Word works every time. Amen.

DR. DWAYNE MERCER, OVIEDO, FL

Lord, teach me to be thankful today. Show me Your grace in my life. Help me to see Your hand in all my circumstances and Your blessings even in the midst of adversity. Amen.

> *We conclude that a man is justified by faith apart from the deeds*
> *of the law . . . since there is one God who will justify the circumcised by*
> *faith and the uncircumcised through faith. Do we then make void the law*
> *through faith? Certainly not! On the contrary, we establish the law.*
> ROMANS 3:28, 30, 31

The human mind could never have conceived a plan of salvation like God's. Every other religion in the world can be characterized by the word "do." In order to please the deity, one must do something. In Christianity, it has all been done.

This passage explains that believers are justified, which means that we are declared not guilty for our sin. We are justified by our faith, not by our works. Why? First, if we earned our own salvation by what we do, we would receive the credit. We could brag about our salvation. When we believe God's Word and trust His character for our salvation, we bring glory to Him. Second, God is all about relationship. Before sin, churches, or religion, God desired a relationship with Adam. Now He desires an intimate relationship with you. Faith or trust is the glue of any relationship. Whether it is marriage, parenting, or following a leader, trust holds relationships together. Since the entire Christian life is built upon trusting God, salvation is the beginning point of that trust.

So why do we have the law? It was given to set a standard for right and wrong. It reveals our sinfulness and our need for Christ. Christ fulfilled the law on the Cross, and we fulfill it as Christ gives us the power to obey Him. We are saved by faith through grace in order to live a life of obedience (Ephesians 2:10).

No human mind could have conceived of such a plan of salvation. Begin or continue to build a trust relationship with God today by placing your faith in Him and following Him.

EVENING

Lord, I ask You to forgive all my sins. Come into my heart and help me to trust You with my life on earth and the life to come. Amen.

Lord, even in Your presence, I do not always enjoy the blessings You offer me. Help me to live this day enjoying You. Help me demonstrate to others the peace and hope You give. Amen.

> *Having been justified by faith, we have peace with God through*
> *our Lord Jesus Christ, through whom also we have access by faith into*
> *this grace in which we stand, and rejoice in hope of the glory of God.*
> ROMANS 5:1, 2

If the Christian life is so victorious, then why do so many Christians act so defeated? Many Christians still act as if they're searching, when all they need is found in Jesus Christ and the fullness He brings to their lives. These verses give us an introduction to the blessings God offers daily. We have peace, hope, growth, and love, and we are saved from wrath through Jesus Christ. These blessings would make any life more fulfilling!

The key to receiving these blessings is to be justified, through Christ, by faith—being forgiven of our sins based on Christ's death on the Cross (Romans 5:9). Christians are not only forgiven, but are also given access to God. In the Old Testament, only the high priest could go behind the veil in the temple once a year. When Christ died on the Cross, God tore the veil in the temple in half, signifying that people could have complete access to Him through Christ. This means we always have the opportunity to receive the blessings described in Romans 5.

When I was in college, I had a summer job in a local factory. I had an opportunity to share the gospel with a man who had a reputation of being indifferent to Christ. When I finished, he looked at me and said, "I have everything I thought I would ever want, but you have something I don't have—peace. I have no real hope for my future." Here was a man who desperately wanted what only Christ offers. We must never forget that victorious Christian living always involves enjoying the peace and fullness found in Christ alone.

EVENING

Lord, thank You that all I could ever want is available as a result of having a loving relationship with You. Help me to sense the peace of Your presence and the joy of my salvation. Amen.

DR. DWAYNE MERCER, OVIEDO, FL

Week 12, Monday

Father, I worship You for being a God who speaks through Your Word. Thank You for leading me to Jesus. Create opportunities for me to share how You've changed my life, and give me the compassion and boldness I will need to serve as a channel of Your grace. Protect me from apathy and make my heart sensitive to the prompting of Your Spirit as I encounter those who need You. Increase my confidence in Your Word. Compel me to be Your witness in this world. In Jesus' name I pray. Amen.

Faith comes by hearing, and hearing by the word of God.
ROMANS 10:17

Telling others about Christ is often intimidating, even for the most committed Christian. Yet reducing evangelism to nothing more than being a good example is a dangerous tendency that circumvents God's primary means of sharing His grace with others. Family members, neighbors, co-workers, friends, strangers, and people around the world need to hear the gospel to experience the transforming grace of Christ that we enjoy.

Though originally spoken about the nation of Israel, Paul's insight in Romans 10 reminds us that God's Word is powerful—it changes lives! When sinners call upon the name of the Lord, God supernaturally saves them. But they cannot call upon a God they have never heard of, and they cannot hear unless we tell them. This sacred privilege bears the weight and responsibility of eternity. Christ-followers are not only held accountable to God for believing His Word, but also for sharing it with others. Surely this is why Jesus instructed believers to be His witnesses in Jerusalem, Judea, and Samaria, and to the end of the earth (Acts 1:8). Faithfully share God's Good News and live as a strong witness for Him today.

EVENING

Lord, as I end this day, I praise You for the privilege of sharing Your truth with others. Forgive me for the times I failed to point people to You. Continue breaking my heart for those who are lost and increasing my faith in Your ability to save. Thank You for being a merciful God who makes His grace available to all people. Help me to be a faithful messenger as I continue experiencing the depths of Your love personally. Amen.

MORNING

Father, I worship You for being a merciful God. I recommit myself to living in a way that honors the tremendous sacrifice You made on Calvary's Cross. My greatest desire is to walk within the parameters of Your will. Give me wisdom to think and live as a Christian fully surrendered to You. Amen.

> *I beseech you therefore, brethren, by the mercies of God, that you*
> *present your bodies a living sacrifice, holy, acceptable to God, which*
> *is your reasonable service. And do not be conformed to this world,*
> *but be transformed by the renewing of your mind, that you may prove*
> *what is that good and acceptable and perfect will of God. For I say,*
> *through the grace given to me, to everyone who is among you,*
> *not to think of himself more highly than he ought to think,*
> *but to think soberly, as God has dealt to each one a measure of faith.*
>
> ROMANS 12:1–3

How should we respond to the mercy of God? We offer ourselves as living sacrifices on the altar of God's grace. Placing the totality of who we are in the hands of our Savior is the only sufficient response to the Cross. If Jesus Christ died for us, we ought to be willing to live for Him.

We are also told to "be transformed by the renewing" of our minds. No concern plagues believers more than discerning God's will for their lives. What they need to know is that it is more about thinking correctly than finding a mysterious path. It's about how we make decisions, not just what we know. When God renews our minds, His direction is readily apparent because we have the ability to think God's thoughts. Rather than pleading with God to unveil what seems like His secret will, learn to reason with the spiritual compass of heaven. With Scripture, prayer, and discussion with other Christians as guides, you will not only find the will of God, but you will also prove it be good, acceptable, and perfect.

EVENING

Lord, thank You for the grace and direction You gave me today. Help me continue to see the privilege of living for You in light of the sacrifice You made for me. Transform my mind so that I will recognize Your will as it unfolds. Amen.

ADAM DOOLEY, CHATTANOOGA, TN

Father, I recognize You as the source of every good and perfect gift in my life. Thank You for the freedom I enjoy in Jesus Christ and the relief of resting in Your grace. Increase my capacity to love fellow believers as an expression of worship to You. As a living sacrifice, I gladly forsake anything that would bring reproach upon Your name. Amen.

It is good neither to eat meat nor drink wine nor do anything by which your brother stumbles or is offended or is made weak. Do you have faith? Have it to yourself before God. Happy is he who does not condemn himself in what he approves. But he who doubts is condemned if he eats, because he does not eat from faith; for whatever is not from faith is sin.
ROMANS 14:21–23

Freedom, rights, self-preservation . . . unfortunately, when people become Christians, these tendencies don't disappear immediately. This struggle is clearly seen in the issue of Christian liberty. Within the diversity of God's kingdom, believers often disagree about what is permissible and what is forbidden in "gray areas." Though our temptation is to defend of our point of view, Paul reminds us to operate within the boundaries of edification. In other words, Christians should never demand their rights to the detriment of other believers.

To the contrary, we are most like Christ when we willingly forfeit our liberties so that others will not stumble. Life is about more than what we eat and drink, and we should never let things in the "gray areas" become stumbling blocks for those who are weak. Where the Bible isn't explicit in pronouncement or principle, Christians must exercise sanctified flexibility that displays compassion and love for others. With our conscience as our guide, we must value every member of God's family by seeking the good of our neighbor before our own (1 Corinthians 10:24).

EVENING

Lord, help me forsake my rights and privileges to help unify Your body. Forgive me if I've made another believer stumble and then defended my right to do so. Empower me to live a gentle life, considering the needs of others before my own. Thank You for being more patient with me than I am with others. Help me to be more like Jesus. Amen.

Father, thank You for satisfying my sin debt on the Cross of Calvary. Forgive me for behaving like the work of my hands could add anything of value to Your sacrifice. Help me rest in Your acceptance more than others' approval. Protect me from thinking that those around me need Your grace more than I do. In Jesus' name, Amen.

We who are Jews by nature, and not sinners of the Gentiles, knowing that a man is not justified by the works of the law but by faith in Jesus Christ, even we have believed in Christ Jesus, that we might be justified by faith in Christ and not by the works of the law; for by the works of the law no flesh shall be justified.
GALATIANS 2:15, 16

Gaining salvation by grace through faith alone is the foundation of Christianity, yet Christians often add requirements to the gospel. When they do, they don't end up with a varied expression of the *same* gospel, but rather a *different* gospel altogether.

Paul rebuked Peter for propping up the Cross with pseudo means of pleasing God. Peter took part in marginalizing Gentile believers for being uncircumcised, and he insinuated that they needed both grace and circumcision to be saved. Paul's message clearly demonstrates that social impropriety was not the issue; the gospel itself was at stake. Both Jews and Gentiles, regardless of circumcision, had to depend upon the grace of God, not their works, to be saved.

We often glory more in what we do for God than in what He does for us. While Christian baptism, church attendance, prayer, Bible study, and good deeds are proper responses to the grace of God, they are poor substitutes for it. Attempting to earn God's favor is not only theologically amiss, but it is also blasphemous. Grace, by definition, means that God will not share His glory with anyone. Renew your commitment to the only true gospel so that others might see His grace in your life.

EVENING

Lord, Your grace is always sufficient, and my heart overflows with love and gratitude toward You. Thank You for the security that is mine in Christ. Forgive me for exalting my works and diminishing my need for Your grace. Continue to sanctify my life as a testimony to Your work in me and through me. Amen.

ADAM DOOLEY, CHATTANOOGA, TN

Father, I realize I cannot live the Christian life by myself, and I praise You for giving me resurrected life and power. Grant me strength to forsake my agenda and to yield to You today. Make the crucified life a reality in my actions and attitudes. Protect me from my old way of life so that Your name will be honored through me. I dedicate this day to You. Amen.

> *I have been crucified with Christ; it is no longer I who live, but Christ lives in me; and the life which I now live in the flesh I live by faith in the Son of God, who loved me and gave Himself for me.*
> GALATIANS 2:20

Though we often celebrate Christ's death for us, we seldom master the daily death He requires from us. Identifying with Christ means more than believing that He died on the Cross for our sins. Crucifying the person you used to be is the prerequisite to spiritual resurrection and new life. You will never live for Jesus Christ until you ruthlessly put to death the person you were without Him.

God does not rehabilitate His children; He resurrects them! God has no desire to change you; He wants your sin nature to die so He can live through you. As strange as it may sound, the key to the Christian life is death. Because Jesus died for us, we must be willing to die to ourselves. Do you have any bad habits that need to die? Are you holding on to a dream that dishonors Christ? Is there any part of the person you were before you became a Christian that you refuse to kill? The greatest evidence of living in Christ is repeatedly dying to self. Do this, and you will walk in newness of life and display the riches of God's grace.

EVENING
Lord, thank You for living in me and through me throughout this day. I worship You for the privilege of serving as Your ambassador on this earth. Forgive me if I was unwilling to crucify the things in my life that dishonor You. Help me put to death the person I used to be in order that my commitment to You will be obvious to the people around me. Thank You, God, for Your patience and love. Amen.

MORNING

Father, You are holy. Thank You for revealing Your holy standard to me and leading me to the Cross. Thank You for loving me in spite of my iniquities. Empower me to live in gratitude for the salvation You provide rather than in guilt for the sin that held me in bondage. Help me give grace to others just as You give grace to me. In Jesus' name. Amen.

> *The Scripture has confined all under sin, that the promise by faith in Jesus Christ might be given to those who believe. But before faith came, we were kept under guard by the law, kept for the faith which would afterward be revealed.*
> GALATIANS 3:22, 23

If Scripture teaches that grace is the only means of salvation, why did God give so many commandments in the Old Testament? What purpose could they possibly serve? Some erroneously insist that obeying the law was a means of salvation before Jesus came, but Paul said God designed the law for the opposite reason. The commandments confine, or secure, people under the bondage of sin because they confirm what people's consciences whisper. God has a standard that we can never reach or maintain. This awareness magnifies the beauty and hope that we find through the grace of Jesus Christ. The very commandments that highlight our separation from God are also the most powerful means of pointing us to His Son (Galatians 3:24).

Grace is never contrary to the holiness of God—quite the opposite. We will never fully appreciate and value how merciful God is until His holiness breaks our pride. Allow Him to use His law in your life continually, protecting you from sin and guiding you in becoming like Him in holiness.

EVENING

Lord, I would be lost apart from Your grace. Seeing my sin through Your eyes is painful, but I rejoice that You turn my weeping into joy. Thank You for setting me free to live under the cloud of Your grace. Forgive me for the times I've treated Your grace as a license to sin. Protect me from arrogance and self-righteousness. I rejoice that in Christ, You not only reveal Your holiness, but You also empower me to live accordingly. Amen.

Week 13, Monday

Heavenly Father, I come to You this morning confessing my tendency toward anxiety. Perhaps the hardest assignment You gave us is to wait on You. I am an impatient person serving a patient God. Keep me from the pitfalls of hurry and the sin of worry. You are always good, and right on time. My prayer for today and this week is that I will be conformed to Your timetable and that I will pursue becoming more like You. Amen.

We through the Spirit eagerly wait for the hope of righteousness
by faith. For in Christ Jesus neither circumcision nor
uncircumcision avails anything, but faith working through love.
GALATIANS 5:5, 6

Have you noticed how we make a way to pass the time when we're doing something difficult, boring, or dreadful? I work out at a local gym and have been doing so for a very long time, but it is still a chore to get up and go. The best part of it is walking back to my car after the workout is over. Just about everyone in there has music or some kind of motivation playing in their ears. It makes the time pass more quickly.

How do we make time pass more quickly in our workout toward spiritual maturity? Paul wrote that our wait for righteousness is made less tedious by the eagerness of the Spirit within us. We will not experience the perfection of righteousness until the fulfillment of our hope, Christ's return. Even though life is a vapor, the length of time it takes to mature spiritually seems long, and will not fully come until we are in the presence of Christ. Regardless, the music of the Holy Spirit playing within us enables us to wait in eager faith for our perfection in Jesus Christ at His coming!

EVENING

Dear Father, tonight I rest my body from the work of the day. At Your pleasure I will arise tomorrow to a day of working, watching, and waiting. With Your direction I will serve You, regardless of my occupation. I will watch for You with the expectancy that You will soon return for me and for all who have faith in Jesus. With the eager music of Your Spirit playing songs of faith, hope, and love within me, I will long for Your perfection. Good night, my Lord!

It is Tuesday, my Lord, and as I requested last night, I want to hear Your music in my heart today, that I might continue this race without growing weary. When I face discouragement or frustration, help me to depend on Your enabling power to complete the race and finish strong. Today is Yours, Father. I live to serve You and bless Your holy name! Amen.

> *Let us not grow weary while doing good, for in due season we shall reap if we do not lose heart. Therefore, as we have opportunity, let us do good to all, especially to those who are of the household of faith.*
> GALATIANS 6:9, 10

The Bible tells us that it is unwise to compare ourselves with others, but when I read that the apostle Paul included himself in a group that struggled with giving up and throwing in the towel, I take a little comfort in it. For me, it is like watching golf on television and seeing one of those high-dollar guys fly one into the woods, landing their ball behind a tree in a clump of weeds with a hornets' nest dangling above it. It does my heart good!

These verses from Galatians 6 encourage us to keep doing good for as long as we can for the right reasons. This concept reminds me of stories about "paying it forward." God gives each of us opportunities to touch everyone around us, especially our spiritual family, with His goodness. We pay His mercy and love forward! God is pleased to watch and bless us as we do this and to give us in the coming harvest more than we could ever imagine. We cannot lose! Dedicate this day to trying to benefit others in a way that glorifies God and magnifies His church.

EVENING

This has been a great day, dear Father. Thank You for every opportunity You gave me to bless others. I need my rest tonight and the gift of sleep. Wake me in the morning refreshed and mindful of the lessons I've learned about finishing strong and paying forward Your grace and mercy. Watch over me tonight. I pray in Jesus' name. Amen.

Heavenly Father, I want to be a team player. In a world fighting to get ahead and claiming rights, I want to be different. Even when I can have my way, help me to determine if my way is what You desire. In Jesus' name I pray. Amen.

> *There is one body and one Spirit, just as you were called in one hope of your calling; one Lord, one faith, one baptism; one God and Father of all, who is above all, and through all, and in you all.*
> EPHESIANS 4:4–6

———————— ⟞⟝ ————————

A friend of mine gave me a gift that made quite an impression on me—an American flag. It is so special that I had it framed and placed in one of the hallways of our church. The uniqueness of this flag is that it is a printing of the names of the almost three thousand people who died in the attacks that took place on September 11, 2001. Individually, they are names, but collectively, they are the stars and stripes.

The Bible teaches that believers are many individuals making up one whole body. We are different colors, ages, and genders, but still we are one. Today's passage shows that "one" is a key in much of our spiritual understanding. Look closely and you will count seven ingredients of unity in the church held together by the united front of the Trinity of God.

The fact of oneness does not make unity automatic; we have to work at it. There is much to divide us, but the seven points of our unity are more powerful than any point of our division. We are in the picture, but we are not the picture! Today, look for ways you can be a unifier and a blessing, and take joy in being a part of the body of Christ.

———————— ⟞⟝ ————————

EVENING

Dear Father, I acknowledge the importance of fitting in with Your church, not with the world. Thank You for allowing me to fit into the plans You have for Your people. Help me to remember that Your plan for me is not more important than Your will for those around me and certainly not greater than Your Great Commission. As I go to sleep, cradle me in Your everlasting arms, and let me rise in the morning in harmony with You. Amen.

Thank You, Father, for another day to live this life and serve You. I want to have courage today. Prepare me for whatever You may bring or whatever the Wicked One may throw my way. Someone I meet may need to hear Your words of truth, so make me aware of Your divine appointment and help me obey. When the opportunity is before me, remind me of my prayer of the morning. With this prayer, I am reporting for duty in the service of my King!

> *Stand therefore, having girded your waist with truth, having put on the breastplate of righteousness, and having shod your feet with the preparation of the gospel of peace; above all, taking the shield of faith with which you will be able to quench all the fiery darts of the wicked one.*
> EPHESIANS 6:14–16

O ne of the highlights at North Florida Christian School, a ministry of our church, is watching the middle school football players wear their uniforms the first time. From my office I can see them going to the practice field, following in the footsteps of junior varsity and varsity players. Sometimes those young ones are so small that they look like a helmet with shoes! The beauty of the comedy is in knowing that most of them will grow into the helmet and become valuable members of our high school team someday.

Every believer must don the uniform of the Christian soldier and grow into the role. From the waistband of truth to the shield of faith, every piece of armor has a purpose. It's not just a uniform; it's a lifelong preparation that begins today. Jesus is the truth, so we surround ourselves with things that are of Him. We have no righteousness of our own, so that, too, must be His. The gospel is our sure footing that allows us to walk in confidence. To fend off the attacks of the Wicked One, we rely on our faith in Christ. Put on the armor and start growing into it today!

EVENING
Heavenly Father, thank You for the experiences of the week thus far. If I failed You in making the most of any divine appointment You brought my way, forgive me and give me another chance tomorrow. As Your soldier and servant, I want to be ready always to defend the faith or claim new territory under Your leadership. Amen.

RANDY RAY, TALLAHASSEE, FL

Week 13, Friday

Lord, it is Friday, the day You designed to lift our spirits from the routine of the week. I don't want to just finish today, but finish strong. In my walk, my work, and my life, may this day be filled with a sense of completion. I am truly thankful for what You began in my heart, saving me from my sin. My desire is to be transparent enough that others can see You in me. For the task ahead, strengthen me. For a fruitful life, establish me. I am Your vineyard. In Jesus' mighty name, Amen.

> *As you therefore have received Christ Jesus the Lord, so walk in Him,*
> *rooted and built up in Him and established in the faith, as you*
> *have been taught, abounding in it with thanksgiving.*
> COLOSSIANS 2:6, 7

Isn't it true that everything in life is either coming or going? Church members are coming or going, getting closer to the heart of the church or drifting away. It isn't likely that the ones who just sit there are really just sitting there. There is a drift in one direction or another. You can make so many applications, but the reality is much the same. Life is a journey bringing us into or taking us away from any number of important relationships.

When we receive Jesus Christ as Savior and Lord, the journey of the Christian life begins. We have new strength and stability, and we are ever learning and rejoicing. Isaiah 40:31 says that we can run and not be weary, walk and not faint. That is amazing! The only way to continue making steady progress in our walk of faith is to rely on the One who gives us life. We have no more power to continue in Christ than we did to be born again into Him—it is the power of God that establishes, enables, and enriches us. Flourish in your faith today!

EVENING

Heavenly Father, I want to end my journey coming toward You, not going away from You. If life is a tide, my desire is to finish on a high-water mark. As You gave me life, help me to live it fully. God, I want to be a force, not a fizzle! With the week behind and the weekend ahead, give me joy for the journey. Teach me Your ways! Amen.

Lord, I will be with many of my Christian friends this weekend. It will be good to see them, but it will be even better to see You! I am humbled by You and confident in You. With You there is no pretense about who I really am; You know me better than I know myself. In spite of my flaws, use me for Your purposes, and I will bless and glorify Your holy name. Amen.

> *Do not cast away your confidence, which has great reward.*
> *For you have need of endurance, so that after you have done the*
> *will of God, you may receive the promise . . . Now the just shall live*
> *by faith; but if anyone draws back, my soul has no pleasure in him.*
> HEBREWS 10:35, 36, 38

I do not like to admit that I have ever had a "quitter" mindset, but when God called me to preach, my first fear was that I might quit His calling. However, there is something I have learned and am continuing to understand better: there is a big difference between "self-confidence" and "God-confidence." Self-confidence is fragile and temporary, but God-confidence is solid and eternal. As I depend on Him, any measure of success I have in life and ministry is from Him. Then, enjoying successes is an act of faith and worship.

Do not throw your confidence away; redefine it. Find your God-confidence and enjoy the rewards of it. One thing is for sure: you must have some holy grit to stick with God's will in your life. There are so many ways to be knocked off your feet, but getting up again is an act of faith. God never promised we would have glassy seas and smooth sailing, and sometimes it can be rough. But there is reward ahead for the believer who lives by faith and walks in the confidence of the Lord!

EVENING

Heavenly Father and God of all ages, give me more confidence in You. I am grateful for the abilities You have given me, but I'm more grateful for Your calling and power at work in my life. Whenever arrogance or self-sufficiency creeps in, remind me that You are the source and the reward. With Your faithful hand to guide me, I rededicate my life to follow You and never retreat! In Jesus' name, Amen.

RANDY RAY, TALLAHASSEE, FL

Father, help me to trust You and seek You with all of my heart today. I am so grateful to You for always guiding me through the good times and the bad. You are my rock and my strength. Give me the wisdom to please You in all I say and do. In Jesus' name, Amen.

They made war with the Hagrites, Jetur, Naphish, and Nodab. And
they were helped against them, and the Hagrites were delivered into their hand,
and all who were with them, for they cried out to God in the battle. He
heeded their prayer, because they put their trust in Him.
1 CHRONICLES 5:19, 20

These verses give an account of one of Israel's battle victories. Consider the role the Israelites played in this victory. Verse 20 says "they cried out to God in the battle." Earlier in the chapter we learned the Israelites had a large army of skilled warriors with capable weapons. Did they rely on their own strength and abilities? No, they cried out to God.

How did God answer? "He heeded their prayer, because they put their trust in Him." Now, I don't believe that prayer is a bunch of magic words or a guarantee that God will do what we think He should do. Sometimes God says yes, sometimes He says no, and sometimes He tells us to wait. However, in this case, the Bible says that God answered the Israelites' prayer because they put their trust in Him. Remember when the Israelites crossed the Jordan River to enter the Land of Promise in Joshua 3? The priests had to step into the water and get their feet wet before God stopped the water and allowed the people to walk across dry land. Sometimes God wants us to trust Him even before we see Him move.

Do your prayers demonstrate your trust in God as your first and best hope, or do you pray only as your last resort? The difference could make all the difference in His answer.

EVENING
Lord, teach me to trust You, cry out to You, and then leave the results in Your more-than-capable hands. Please help me put feet on my prayers by trusting You in every step I take. Amen.

Lord, help me remember that I can get through anything that happens today because You are with me. Whenever I feel afraid, I will trust You. You are my strength and the song I will sing throughout this day. Amen.

As for God, His way is perfect; the word of the LORD is proven; He is a shield to all who trust in Him. "For who is God, except the LORD? And who is a rock, except our God?"

2 SAMUEL 22:31, 32

David, reflecting back on his life, was grateful for God's provision and knew that God's way, though rocky and scary at times, is always perfect. We need God plus nothing to make it through the worst life can throw at us. God is our rock, and He will deliver us. He can be trusted and is worthy to be praised.

Our second child, Shelby, was almost three when she insisted on having a pair of roller skates. Reluctantly, we bought her skates, and the kitchen floor became her skating rink. It was terrible. She had one tumble after another. Finally, she pulled off the skates, handed them to me, and said, "Go buy me some skates that won't fall!"

In life, all of us want deliverance from falls and failures, but that is not what God tells us to expect. God did not deliver David *from* his trials but *through* his trials. God tells us that in this life, we will have trials and struggles. Expect them. Learn from them.

When our girls were preschoolers, we helped them memorize Psalm 56:3. It says, "Whenever I am afraid, I will trust in You." When they were in middle school, they told us they had found a verse that they liked even better—Isaiah 12:2, which says, "I will trust and not be afraid; 'For YAH, the LORD, is my strength and song; He also has become my salvation.'"

Although you don't know what's ahead of you, God does, so keep going. Keep trusting. Ahead there will be a way through. You will never go wrong in trusting the One who died for you.

EVENING

God, thank You for making a way through this day. You are the only One worthy of my praise. Help me to trust You even more tomorrow. I thank You that You are already there waiting for me. In Jesus' name, Amen.

FRED LOWERY, BOSSIER CITY, LA

Father, I know that You will walk with me through this day. Thank You for being my shield and protection from anything that Satan might try to use to hurt me. I will trust in You. In Jesus' mighty name, Amen.

The LORD is my rock and my fortress and my deliverer; the
God of my strength, in whom I will trust; my shield and the horn of my
salvation, my stronghold and my refuge; my Savior, You save me from violence.
2 SAMUEL 22:2, 3

Oswald Chambers said, "A saint's life is in the hands of God like a bow and arrow in the hands of an archer. God is aiming at something the saint cannot see." In our darkest days, God is up to something good. He wants to bless us, not blast us. His desire through adversity is never to make us bitter, but always to make us better. So we can trust Him!

Saul chased David for years and tried to kill him several times. Fortunately, God was David's GPS. He told him where to go and when to go so that David was able to stay one step ahead of Saul's wrath. God doesn't remove our trials, but He does walk through them with us.

David called God his rock. God is strong, trustworthy, and unchanging. David trusted God and called Him his shield because he knew that his protection and deliverance from his enemies came from God Himself. In our verses for today, David praised and thanked God for His character and His works.

What should we do when we are drowning in a sea of problems? We should cry out to God and trust Him to give us what we need when we need it. Such trust is not based on who we are, but who God is. David, a man of prayerful trust, depended on the Lord for wisdom, strength, and deliverance, and the Lord never failed him. What God did for David, He will do for you. Trust Him.

EVENING

Lord, I am grateful for another day to live for You. Please give me the strength I need to do what You want me to do tomorrow. Thank You for never leaving me or forsaking me. Amen.

Lord, I come to You this morning because You are merciful and because You have said You will hear the cries of my heart. I will be joyful today because my trust is in You, and I know that You already know what this day holds. I celebrate another day to give You glory. Thank You for hearing me. In Jesus' name, Amen.

Let all those rejoice who put their trust in You; let them ever shout for joy, because You defend them; let those also who love Your name be joyful in You. For You, O LORD, will bless the righteous; with favor You will surround him as with a shield.
PSALM 5:11, 12

Wouldn't you love to read a page out of David's quiet time journal? Well, in a way, we can. The psalms are full of his private thoughts and heart cries and contain pieces of his intimate conversations with God.

At the beginning of Psalm 5, David seems discouraged. He asks God to consider his sighing and to hear his cry for help. Can you relate? Do you ever need to be encouraged? I don't think I have ever met anyone who overdosed on encouragement. But later in his prayer, in verses 11 and 12, David says that if we put our trust in God, we should be encouraged! Be joyful! Celebrate! Shout for joy! Why? Because God defends, blesses, and protects those who love Him. Since God is absolutely trustworthy, those who put their trust in Him have every reason to rejoice.

Life's unexpected trials should teach us not to trust in our own strength, our own wisdom, or our own ability, but to depend on and trust the Lord, who alone knows what is best. We will still struggle, but we will also find joy and peace as we move by faith from trial to triumph. And when we put our trust in God, we stop focusing on our own feelings and problems. Our struggles seem insignificant when we view life from our Father's perspective and the shelter of His arms.

EVENING

Father, thank You for providing everything I needed to get through this day. Thank You for encouraging me and for giving me reason to be joyful. I will sleep in peace knowing You surround me as a shield. Amen.

FRED LOWERY, BOSSIER CITY, LA

Week 14, Friday

Lord, today I trust You to be my rock, my fortress, my deliverer, my strength, my shield, my salvation, and my stronghold. You are worthy to be praised. In Jesus' name, Amen.

The LORD is my rock and my fortress and my deliverer; my God, my strength, in whom I will trust; my shield and the horn of my salvation, my stronghold. I will call upon the LORD, who is worthy to be praised; so shall I be saved from my enemies.
PSALM 18:2, 3

David used seven attributes in today's verses to describe the God he trusted. David knew that God alone had rescued him, and he wanted to praise and thank Him.

During World War II, King George of England ordered an evacuation of children from the bomb-torn areas of London. Imagine the fear and anxiety of the precious children as their heartbroken parents put them on a train, not knowing when they would see them again.

As a mother and father waved a tearful goodbye to the train as it left the station, their little girl turned to her brother and cried, "I'm scared. I don't even know where we're going!" Holding back his own tears, her brother put his arms around her and said, "I don't know where we're going either, but the king knows, so we don't need to worry."

At some point, most of us have felt alone and afraid of what might be around the next curve. David certainly did. He ran from Saul and his army for about ten years. He didn't know what cave he would sleep in each night, or if he would even live to see the next day. But David trusted God's leading, and God delivered David from all his enemies and made him the king of all Israel. Why did God wait ten years to deliver David? More than likely, God used the severe trials in David's life to make him the great leader He'd created him to be.

The safest place on earth is in God's will. In all circumstances, we can take refuge in the Lord. We may not always know where we are headed, but our King knows, so we don't need to worry!

EVENING
Father, even though I may not know what's around the corner, I can rest in perfect peace tonight because You do—and I trust You. Amen.

Week 14, Weekend

MORNING

Father, thank You that Your way is perfect and Your Word is true. You don't need to prove anything to me, yet daily You provide me with more than sufficient evidence to show that You are trustworthy. I thank You for being my shield and my strength. In Jesus' name, Amen.

> *As for God, His way is perfect; the word of the LORD is proven;*
> *He is a shield to all who trust in Him . . . It is God who*
> *arms me with strength, and makes my way perfect.*
> PSALM 18:30, 32

Dwight L. Moody once said, "True faith is man's weakness leaning on God's strength. When man has no strength, if he leans on God he becomes powerful."[4] Truly, it is God who arms us with strength for the journey.

My grandson Hudson has a tall tree house in his backyard. One day I was in the yard watching him play in his tree house, and he walked out to the edge and looked down at me. I held up my arms and said, "Jump to me, Hudson, and I'll catch you!" He paused for a moment and then looked down at me again and said, "Go get my daddy!" This three-year-old boy was not about to jump into the arms of anyone but his daddy. Why? He had learned to trust his daddy's strength.

As a believer, you have a heavenly Father whose strength is sufficient for your every need. I call it "trouble grace." When you get into trouble, God gives you the grace (strength) to handle the trouble. In Isaiah 26:4 we read, "Trust in the Lord forever, for in YAH, the LORD, is everlasting strength." Always remember that it is impossible to break God's promises by leaning on them.

EVENING

Lord, thank You for being more trustworthy than even the best earthly father. Thank You for being my shield and the source of my strength. Help me let go of my fear and jump straight into Your strong, waiting arms. Amen.

FRED LOWERY, BOSSIER CITY, LA

85

Week 15, Monday

Lord, help me to delight myself in You and focus on Your faithfulness, not the faults of others or the fallen world. I commit my way to You on the basis of the trust I have in my Savior, Jesus Christ. Amen.

Trust in the LORD, and do good; dwell in the land, and feed on His faithfulness.
Delight yourself also in the LORD, and He shall give you the desires of your heart.
Commit your way to the LORD, trust also in Him, and He shall bring it to pass.
PSALM 37:3–5

In this one sentence, "Trust in the LORD, and do good," the psalmist gives a recipe for a great life. As a psychologist, I have counseled hundreds of people with serious problems. After much time and discussion, the answer is usually that I don't have an answer to their problems. I don't know how they can stop their kids from doing drugs or get their spouses to return to them. I often have people put their hands over their hearts and repeat this pledge: "I, being of sound mind, do hereby acknowledge that I have not, nor have I ever, nor will I ever, control the universe. Therefore, I resign as general manager."

The fact is, you can't control most of what is happening. The issue is whether you do what is right in the midst of circumstances that you can't control. If we trust God, we have the power to do that. That choice is something no one can take away from you. I was once given the good advice to do what is right and leave the consequences to God, which is really a paraphrase of these verses in Psalm 37. No matter what others say or do, trust the Lord and do good.

I admit I followed that advice many times in a self-righteous and resentful spirit. My attitude was, "It's not fair, but I'll do the right thing." I was just one verse short of joy. Today's passage says to "delight yourself" in the Lord. Focus on His promises, not others' performances, and His desire for your life will come to pass.

EVENING
Father, thank You for Your faithfulness. May Your righteousness be a rudder to focus my heart's desires. I pray that my desires will be birthed from the heart of Your will. Amen.

Week 15, Tuesday

Lord, I commit my way to You. I put my trust in You. Forgive me for not trusting You in the past. Forgive me for making things that I can see my rock and my refuge. I know of Your righteousness and Your justice, and I put my confidence in You. I know that Your commandments are for my good and Your glory. In Jesus' name, Amen.

> *In You, O LORD, I put my trust; let me never be put to shame. Deliver me in Your righteousness, and cause me to escape; incline Your ear to me, and save me. Be my strong refuge, to which I may resort continually; You have given the commandment to save me, for You are my rock and my fortress.*
> PSALM 71:1–3

When our oldest daughter turned fifteen, the state of Texas believed that she was competent to drive. That would not have bothered me if the state of Texas had allowed her to drive a state vehicle—then it would be their problem! I love her, but I had a hard time giving her the keys. I recommended that she start out by just driving around the neighborhood, or driving on a Sunday when there wasn't much traffic. I didn't want her operating a vehicle in the real world, because I didn't trust her driving ability.

In a way, my view of my fifteen-year-old daughter is similar to how we think about God. We know God is with us, but we don't want Him to take the keys. We don't want Him in the real world, just in the church. We don't trust God enough to allow Him to dominate our lives. People are naive to think they aren't dominated by something. They say they just want to be free. If we say we want to be free from brushing our teeth, we will be free from the toothbrush but dominated by cavities. Life is full of choices, and we decide what dominates us. Trust God with your life and allow Him to dominate your thoughts, and He will be your rock and fortress.

EVENING

Father, help me see You for who You are. Give me confidence to call on You for help because You are a helping God. I ask You to manifest Your Spirit in my life, for You are my strong refuge. Amen.

CHARLES LOWERY, PH.D., PILOT POINT, TX

Week 15, Wednesday

Lord, I make my secret place under the shadow of the Most High. Allow me to abide in the power of the Almighty. Teach me to focus on the good, but not be naive about the bad. Deliver me from faults and foes as I take the upward path, walking hand in hand with You. In the wonderful name of Jesus I pray. Amen.

He who dwells in the secret place of the Most High shall abide under the
shadow of the Almighty. I will say of the LORD, "He is my refuge and
my fortress; my God, in Him I will trust." Surely He shall deliver you from
the snare of the fowler and from the perilous pestilence.

PSALM 91:1–3

John Bradshaw tells a story in *Reader's Digest* about a lady who went on a mule ride through a canyon. It was a steep ride—she could see the cliffs and the rocks that plummeted down into the valley—and she was afraid. The woman managed to cover her fear until she saw one of the guides nod to her mule as he said to another guide, "I thought we had retired old Stumblefoot." That's when she broke down in fear. She'd been feebly putting her trust in old Stumblefoot, but he wasn't trustworthy!

We often look for something or someone to trust in uncertain situations, but we always face disappointment. The history of humanity proves that when we put our trust in others, we will find that the world is full of old Stumblefoots. Pastors, family members, and friends are all imperfect; at some point, they will let us down. Even marriage partners will let us down. Some of us have pledged, "Till death do us part," only to have our spouses abandon us. Our scripture today assures us that He, the One who dwells in the secret place of the Most High, will never let us down. His shadow is more secure than the Stumblefoots of this world. Put your trust in the Almighty!

EVENING
Father, thank You for being my rock of refuge and my fortress of defense. I confess that I am afraid and need Your confidence. Deliver me from my fears and give me a life of faith. May the coin of my heart read, "In God I trust." Amen.

MORNING

Lord, I look forward to this day of walking arm in arm with You. Help me to grow in trusting You. Strip away my arrogant self-reliance, which drains my faith. Help me to acknowledge You in all my ways. In the name of Jesus I pray. Amen.

Trust in the LORD with all your heart, and lean not on your own understanding;
in all your ways acknowledge Him, and He shall direct your paths.
PROVERBS 3:5, 6

The word in this text that jumps out to me is "all." It says "all" your heart and "all" your ways. Most Christians trust God for eternal life—we know that we don't have a chance dealing with a six-foot hole. It never crosses our minds to tell God that we understand death better than He does. It is in the "all our ways" part that we tend to lean on our own understanding. There is usually one area of life where we end up thinking that we know better than God. But consider the wise words of Solomon: "There is a way that seems right to a man, but its end is the way of death" (Proverbs 14:12).

Life is like a parade. We see what is in front of us, but God sees the whole parade. He has a greater perspective than we have. My favorite football team hired a great coach and paid him millions of dollars. When we watch him on the sidelines, he has a headset on and is listening to another coach up in the box. Why? He knows that the other coach has a greater perspective. Allow God to direct your path, knowing that He has a better perspective. Trust His promise for eternal life in heaven and practice His principles for a great life on earth.

EVENING

Father, thank You for Your principles as well as Your promises. Thank You for eternal life in heaven and abundant life in earth. I acknowledge that You alone are the One with the power and understanding to direct my path. Teach me to acknowledge You in all my ways. Amen.

CHARLES LOWERY, PH.D., PILOT POINT, TX

Lord, help me not to miss a word of Your wisdom today. Allow me to take it all in and grasp its meaning. May Your wisdom not just be a platitude to quote but a principle to practice in my life. Show me how to apply Your wisdom in my walk, work, and worship. In Jesus' name I pray. Amen.

> *Incline your ear and hear the words of the wise, and apply your heart to my knowledge; for it is a pleasant thing if you keep them within you; let them all be fixed upon your lips, so that your trust may be in the LORD.*
> PROVERBS 22:17–19

Words of wisdom are the divine design for life, and they are available to all people. The phrase "fixed upon your lips" in Proverbs 22 implies that the words of our mouths should be the words of Christ, the embodiment of wisdom.

A pastor who was recovering from surgery was going to miss seeing his son run in the state championship meet. He asked his brother to go in his place. Since he could not be there to see his son run, he wanted his brother to be there to yell and cheer for his son, since his voice sounded nearly identical to the father's voice. His brother agreed, and the son ran a strong race.

His brother, also a pastor, discerned a theological lesson in the situation. He did what God wants us to do—to make our best effort to sound like Him. God's people are running a race, too, and He wants us to be there for them, making our voices sound like His. Do your best to have God's wonderful, wise words of life on your lips!

EVENING

Father, thank You for sharing Your wisdom with me. Build Your life and Your speech into me. Today I celebrate and embrace Your words. Make me not only a listener but also a teacher. May my love for others involve teaching Your lessons. Thank You, Jesus, for Your beautiful words of life. Amen.

MORNING

Lord, as I open Your Word, open my eyes that I might see the wondrous things that You want to teach me. May Your living water hydrate my soul. Thank You that You have given me a map of Your plan for my life in Your Word. Amen.

Every word of God is pure; He is a shield to those who put their trust in Him. Do not add to His words, lest He rebuke you, and you be found a liar.
PROVERBS 30:5, 6

These verses underscore the reliability of what God has said to His people. His Word is pure, unmixed with any error. It is strong like a mighty shield to protect us from the world's teachings and temptations. This Word will be a light to our path if we don't mingle it with our own imaginations, traditions, and family dysfunctions.

The great divide between Christianity and other religions is not that they lack truth, noble standards, gracious teachings, or gifted leaders. It is the fact that the Word became flesh. In other religions, a word stays a word. They are good standards of morality, but they are just words, so those religions become dry. Because the Word became flesh, Christianity is not merely words but a relationship with Jesus Christ.

E. Stanley Jones tells of a time he got so lost in a jungle in India that he had to pay a guide to lead him out. The guide used a sword to cut through brush and bushes, but Jones could see no path. It looked as if they were heading further into the jungle. Eventually he stopped his guide and asked him to point out the path they were taking. His guide turned and said to him, "Sir, I am the path."

Christianity is powerful because it is personal. Jesus said, "I am the way, the truth, and the life" (John 14:6). He is our path! Live on the path of Christ and of God's written Word today.

EVENING

Father, teach me to invest in Your Word. Teach me to carry Your Word in my heart so that I will have a shield in difficult times. Keep me rooted in You and Your Word. Thank You that my stability is in You and Your will. In Jesus' name, Amen.

CHARLES LOWERY, PH.D., PILOT POINT, TX

Week 16, Monday

Good Morning, Holy Spirit. Thank You that throughout the night You protected me. Thank You that I could rest and be refreshed. You are in total control today of all that is happening around me, and I want to learn how to trust You more. Help me to hear Your voice as I study Your Word and follow Your guidance throughout this day. I pray in Jesus' name. Amen.

> *"Behold, God is my salvation, I will trust and not be afraid; 'For YAH, the LORD, is my strength and song; He also has become my salvation.'"*
> *Therefore with joy you will draw water from the wells of salvation.*
> ISAIAH 12:2, 3

———— ◦◦◦ ————

The part of this passage that speaks of drawing water from a well points to a practice done in ancient times. After people heard God speak, they would often dig a well and give it a name. As a result, whenever they took water from it, they would remember God's words and goodness.

Believers can walk in confidence and not live in fear because they belong to a mighty God. Do you need something like a well to remind you of this reality? There are times I do! Fear has been a battle in my life. For the last ten years, God has been showing me His truth and helping me overcome my fears. As I look back, I can see significant moments when He worked powerfully in my heart, replacing my unwise thoughts with His wise thoughts and setting me free to live a life of faith and worship. A friend challenged me to write down my memories of those moments in a journal, so I could go back and read about the goodness and protection of God in my life. It's been amazing to see how God has used those journal entries to remind me of His truth and trustworthiness and to help me remain in His peace and strength.

Make your own "well" to remind yourself of God's Word and to encourage you to walk in obedience, fully dependent on God. He is your strength, your song, and your salvation!

———— ◦◦◦ ————

EVENING

Holy Spirit, thank You for Your protection and guidance today. Please help me to rest tonight and remember that You hold all things together! I love You! Amen.

MORNING

God, I am grateful to be in Your presence and to have the privilege of prayer. Help me to live this new day in a way that pleases You. Lord, I completely surrender myself to You. Make me more like Jesus. Show me the areas of my life where I'm holding on too tight and not trusting You. I love You, and I need You today. I pray this in Jesus' name. Amen.

Who among you fears the LORD? Who obeys the voice of His Servant?
Who walks in darkness and has no light?
Let him trust in the name of the LORD and rely upon his God.
ISAIAH 50:10

Trusting in the name of the Lord means trusting in His character. He is the Almighty God, righteous and pure, merciful and loving, wise and perfect. He is the Creator, Sustainer, and Owner of all things. He is the source of all goodness and beauty, and He has the power to do anything we could imagine. This is His nature, and He never changes!

Human character traits develop over time and can even change from day to day, but God is eternal. Long before our lives began, He has been keeping all of His promises to people and bringing glory to Himself through His works. His character is not dependent on our emotions or circumstances. While we go through the highs and lows of life's difficulties or of our own feelings, He is steadfast.

We can't begin to understand the depths of how true His name is until we learn to rely on Him. As long as we think we can solve the issues in our lives, we won't rely on Him. Are you trusting in your own character and abilities, or in God's? Saturate yourself with the knowledge of God's character from His Word. Dwell on the One who is trustworthy, and then trust Him! Ask Him to show you the step of faith you need to take that will compel you to rely totally on Him today.

EVENING

Thank You, Holy Spirit, for revealing truth to me today. Show me the step of faith You want me to take. I want to be a radical follower of Jesus and not grow stagnant and cold. Thank You for life today! I love You. Amen.

BRAD WHITE, TAMPA, FL

Father, thank You for life today. My heart is open to You, and I want You to change me. I want to learn how to lean on You and trust You with everything You've given me. It is in Jesus' precious name I pray. Amen.

> *He who heeds the word wisely will find good, and whoever*
> *trusts in the Lord, happy is he. The wise in heart will be*
> *called prudent, and sweetness of the lips increases learning.*
> PROVERBS 16:20, 21

I learn by leaning. The more I lean on God, the more I learn about His character. Leaning on God is resting in God! Some people ask how they can possibly do that when they feel like their lives are out of control. In my life, I have identifed three ways.

First, lean on God's character. Research the names of God and memorize them—each name is a character description, an aspect of God you can cling to and depend on. Understanding the One in whom you are putting your trust will give you great confidence in Him. Second, lean on what He has done in the past. You are alive in this moment because God has taken care of you. You are able to read these words because He has given you sight. Take a moment and remember all the circumstances that were involved in God bringing about goodness in your heart and life. Third, lean on what God has said. Spend time looking at life from His perspective and listening to His wisdom. Search for God's promises in His Word and then claim each one as yours.

Our passage today says that as you trust and obey Him, you will "find good" and be "happy"—the result of abiding in the One who is the source of goodness and happiness! Devote yourself to Him, and see what blessings He has in store for you.

EVENING

God, I want to learn how to lean on You. I have been leaning on my own strength and chasing my own ambitions. They don't bring me rest; they only make me restless. Help me to live out this truth and to rest in You! Thank You for having complete control over my life. I love You. In Jesus' name, Amen.

Good Morning, Holy Spirit. What a beautiful day it is to be alive! It is beautiful because it was made by You and for You. Thank You again for the privilege of life and of serving You. Thank You for allowing me to experience Your incredible story today. I pray this in the name of my Lord and Savior, Jesus Christ. Amen.

> *He who is of a proud heart stirs up strife, but*
> *he who trusts in the LORD will be prospered.*
> *He who trusts in his own heart is a fool,*
> *but whoever walks wisely will be delivered.*
> PROVERBS 28:25, 26

Trusting God is an authority issue. God is my authority, and if He tells me to do something, I am to be obedient. When I choose not to trust, I am struggling with authority. This bleeds over to a struggle with authority in other areas of my life and reveals pride in my heart. As a pastor, I have encountered people over the years that stir up strife, and they typically struggle with authority. They claimed their issue was with the church or pastor, but in truth it was with God.

No one is exempt from the battle with pride. When have you seen the pride of your heart revealed? Has it shown up in your relationships with family or friends? Children of God are to do nothing out of "selfish ambition or conceit," but in humility esteem others better than ourselves (Philippians 2:3). We're called to have the same mindset as Christ, who "humbled Himself and became obedient to the point of death, even the death of the cross" (v. 8). Jesus modeled submission perfectly while He was on earth, and He is our example to follow.

"God resists the proud but gives grace to the humble" (James 4:6). When we submit to His authority and to the authority He places in our lives, we will prosper. Bring joy to Your Father and receive His blessing by having a heart that trusts and submits to Him.

EVENING

You are my authority, God, and You are always right. Even when where You lead seems crazy to me, I believe that You are right on target. I will trust You regardless of whether I understand You. I want to be centered on Your purpose and plan. I love You. In Jesus' name I pray. Amen.

BRAD WHITE, TAMPA, FL

Lord, thank You for coming to live inside me and for guiding me. You have gone before me into every part of this day. You have a purpose and plan in all of it. Help me to be aware of Your presence and what You want me to do. In Jesus' name, Amen.

Our soul waits for the LORD; He is our help and our shield.
For our heart shall rejoice in Him, because we have trusted in His holy name.
Let Your mercy, O LORD, be upon us, just as we hope in You.
PSALM 33:20–22

There is freedom and joy in trusting God. When we depend on Him as our help and shield, we don't have to be anxious or try to figure everything out on our own. When we view Him as the sovereign God who is carrying out His perfect will, we can wait on Him in worship. When we glory in His holiness and might, we rejoice that He is our God and offer Him all we can.

But our natural tendency is not to trust Him. We'd rather trust what we understand and trust our own control. God calls us to lay it all on the line and hang on to Him instead of doing our own thing, yet many Christ-followers shy away from that kind of trust. Do we lose sight that it is the almighty God, our gracious Father, calling for our trust? Our response ought to be: "You own me and all I possess, and I gladly surrender it back to You." Sure, we might be nervous about the unknown. But we can also be excited about discovering what great new wonders God might work in our lives as a result of our obedience.

As a pastor, I have loved the seasons when our entire church has sacrificed together to do more for God. In those seasons, the church was so happy and excited. Why? They were doing what was right; they were trusting God! Begin a new season of trusting God more in your life, and your heart will rejoice in Him.

EVENING
It has been so much fun to serve You today, God. Thank You for choosing to use me. I lay all the requests of my heart at Your feet. I trust You! Amen.

Good Morning, Holy Spirit. Thank You again for a new day and a fresh start. What do You want me to see and hear? What do You want to say to me? Lord, I'm listening, and I want to obey. In Jesus' name, Amen.

> *Blessed is the man who trusts in the LORD, and whose hope is the LORD.*
> *For he shall be like a tree planted by the waters, which spreads out its roots*
> *by the river, and will not fear when heat comes; but its leaf will be green,*
> *and will not be anxious in the year of drought, nor will cease from yielding fruit.*
> JEREMIAH 17:7, 8

You cannot out-give God—it's impossible! The more openhandedly you live, the more God gives to you. A preacher once said, "If God can get it through you, He will get it to you." We must be willing to receive something from God and not hold it with a tight grip, thinking it is something we rightfully own.

God desires to pour out His blessings on His children, but we are often not in a position to be blessed. We are in that position when we bring God the first in our lives—the first in our finances, the first in our schedules, the first in our relationships. When you have been faithful with "the first," God will bless you and lead you.

Every resource imaginable is God's. He has resources we do not even understand! Never put more trust in the Federal Reserve than in your faithful God. Honor Him and trust Him. If you do, you'll be positioned to receive God's blessing when seasons of drought come. Are there areas of your life where He is not first? Surrender to Him fully today.

EVENING

Father, You created everything, and You own everything. I am just a manager of a few things for a few years. Thank You for trusting me with these resources. I will bring You the first in every area of my life. Break the manacles of materialism from me, and help me live with open hands. Thank You for the freedom that is found in trusting You! I love You. In Jesus' name I pray. Amen.

BRAD WHITE, TAMPA, FL

Father, I acknowledge that without You I can do nothing, yet I can do all things through Christ who strengthens me. I confess that the truth is in Jesus. I am grateful that You have empowered me by the Spirit of truth. Amen.

> *If you love Me, keep My commandments. And I will pray the Father, and*
> *He will give you another Helper, that He may abide with you forever—the*
> *Spirit of truth, whom the world cannot receive, because it neither sees Him*
> *nor knows Him; but you know Him, for He dwells with you and will be in you.*
>
> JOHN 14:15–17

As believers, we are to heed Jesus' words. Our love for God is not exhibited by how well we talk or how loudly we shout, but by how obedient we are. Three times in John 14, Jesus said that those who love Him will keep His commandments (vv. 15, 21, 23). It is apparent that this message is very important! Jesus said the commandments were *His* commandments. He personally owned them, so when we reject them, we reject Him. Many have been deceived, thinking that we will be pleasing to God when we simply know Christ's commandments. But Jesus didn't say, "If you love Me, *know* my commandments." Biblical knowledge is vital, but it is not the ultimate test of your love for God. Knowledge is a means to an end; the end is obedience.

As believers, we receive help from the Holy Spirit to keep Christ's commandments. Jesus knew we would need it! We are prone to wander. Our spirits are often willing, but our flesh is always weak. He prayed to the Father and promised to send us "another Helper." The word "another" implies that the next Helper would be like Jesus, who was the first Helper. Jesus is the embodiment of truth, and the Spirit is the empowerment of truth. The Spirit indwells every disciple of Christ. So be filled with the Spirit, walk in the Spirit, and do not quench the Spirit.

EVENING

Heavenly Father, I have known Your presence today by Your indwelling Spirit. I thank You for the Spirit's strength and protection as I travel this dark world. He is a faithful Helper, and I have depended upon Him so heavily today. Amen.

Holy God, faithful and true, may I join You, Your Son, and Your Spirit in believing the truth, living the truth, and sharing the truth today. I am so prone to drift into trivial matters of the world that I let eternity skip right by. May Your truth and Your Spirit so consume me that I spend the day on mission to take the truth of Jesus to others. Amen.

> *When the Helper comes, whom I shall send to you from the Father, the*
> *Spirit of truth who proceeds from the Father, He will testify of Me. And you*
> *also will bear witness, because you have been with Me from the beginning.*
> JOHN 15:26, 27

The Father sends the Holy Spirit, and since God the Father is true, the Spirit must also be true. Paul instructed the Ephesians that the truth is in Jesus (Ephesians 4:21). The Spirit is the "Spirit of truth" because He testifies of Jesus who is the truth (John 14:6).

The Spirit testifies of Jesus so that we will testify about Jesus. The acid test of being filled with the Spirit is not speaking in an unknown tongue, but speaking God's clearly-revealed gospel! Jesus told the disciples that when the Spirit came, they would receive power and become His witnesses (Acts 1:8). Jesus didn't say that they *might* become witnesses, but that they *would* become witnesses. The same is true for modern-day disciples!

Think about what concerns you most. Does it concern God? Are your concerns eternal or temporal? Jesus taught these truths in John 15 in the context of telling His disciples that the world would hate them and persecute them. Later that same evening, Jesus was betrayed by Judas and arrested. The very next day He was crucified.

May our witness today be as bold and unashamed as that of the Spirit of truth! We do not charge hell with a water pistol; we charge with the gospel, for it is the power of God unto salvation!

EVENING

I thank You, Oh great missional God, that I could join You today on Your mission to see the world repent and come to faith in Christ. Your Spirit of truth has helped me to confront the deceptions of Satan, the father of lies, and to bear witness to Jesus. I now rest in the comfort of Your Spirit. Amen.

ALLAN TAYLOR, WOODSTOCK, GA

Week 17, Wednesday

Father, I am overwhelmed by the ministry of the Holy Spirit. For through Him I know Your truth, and by Your truth I am sanctified as a child of God. May Your Spirit burn Your truth into me today. Amen.

> *When He, the Spirit of truth, has come, He will guide you*
> *into all truth; for He will not speak on His own authority, but*
> *whatever He hears He will speak; and He will tell you things to come.*
> JOHN 16:13

What's so important about the truth? Well, do you want me to tell you the truth? If you didn't know the truth, you might gargle with antifreeze instead of mouthwash. You might pet a rattlesnake instead of a poodle. You might believe in a false god and be forever separated from the one true God. The knowledge of truth is imperative, because without it we die. This is the case both in the natural and supernatural worlds.

What if God withheld the truth from us? We would be eternally doomed. What if the Father spoke the truth to the Spirit, but then the Spirit revealed something else to us? We would be without hope. Truth must be trumpeted if it is to triumph, and this is the work of the Spirit of truth. The Holy Spirit is in the truth business. Where the Holy Spirit is at work, truth is at work; where falsehood and deception are, the Spirit is not.

The Spirit energized the Old Testament authors with the truth (2 Peter 1:20, 21) and prompted the Gospel writers, too (John 14:26). Jesus told His disciples that He had many things to say to them, but they couldn't bear to hear them at the time (John 16:12). The Spirit of truth would continually guide the apostles to give us the written Word of God we have today. The Spirit of truth will never guide in a way contrary to Scripture since He is the One who gave us the Scripture. Praise God for His agent of truth, the Holy Spirit! Rely on Him to learn God's truth and to live according to it.

EVENING

Father, Your Son taught us to pray, "Your will be done on earth as it is in heaven" (Matthew 6:10). I am grateful that I can do Your will because Your Spirit has revealed Your will. Amen.

MORNING

Father, I awaken ready for a spiritual breakfast to start my day. I am hungry for Your Spirit to guide me in Your Word so I may taste it and be filled, nourished, and satisfied. In Jesus' name, Amen.

The Helper, the Holy Spirit, whom the Father will send in My name, He will teach you all things, and bring to your remembrance all things that I said to you.
JOHN 14:26

A good teacher not only gives students answers but also gives them an appetite for learning. This was certainly true of Jesus, and it is also true of the Holy Spirit. As our teacher, He answers many things about truth, Christ, and the one true God, and He also gives us an appetite for truth, Christ, and our Father. The author of Hebrews wrote that those who were "partakers of the Holy Spirit" had "tasted the heavenly gift" and "tasted the good word of God" (Hebrews 6:4, 5). The apostle Peter put it this way: "As newborn babes, desire the pure milk of the word" (1 Peter 2:2). Where does such an appetite come from? The Spirit, who is constantly feeding us so we can "taste" the Word and goodness of God. So how's your appetite? Are you showing up for your spiritual meals? If you taste what the Spirit has served up, you will want a second helping!

The Heavenly Teacher's job is to give us answers and an appetite for the truth so we will accept the truth. Today, many are confused about Jesus and the teaching of the Bible. We live in a day much like Isaiah's; he said that some called "evil good, and good evil" (Isaiah 5:20). But "God is not the author of confusion" (1 Corinthians 14:33), and the Godhead is not misaligned. The Spirit has been sent by the Father and speaks of the Son. Truth abides in all three Persons of the Trinity. Therefore, the Spirit will never teach us anything that conflicts with the Father, His Word, or His Son. Accept the truth and nourishment that the Spirit brings today!

EVENING

Father God, my spiritual mealtimes today have been so nourishing. As Your child, I am grateful Your Spirit has fed me and led me into Your truth. I go to bed tonight with the good taste of the Word of God in my mouth. Amen.

ALLAN TAYLOR, WOODSTOCK, GA

Most Holy God, I confess that You are greater than all, so I commit myself to You. I depend on Your strong hand to hold me, knowing that nothing can pluck me from it. Amen.

Where can I go from Your Spirit? Or where can I flee from Your presence?
If I ascend into heaven, You are there; if I make my bed in hell, behold, You
are there. If I take the wings of the morning, and dwell in the uttermost parts
of the sea, even there Your hand shall lead me, and Your right hand shall hold me.
PSALM 139:7–10

God is everywhere. There is no place that He is not. When you consider the collective immensity of all the galaxies, you start to get a peek at the size of almighty God. He is in every square inch of all space. If you were to go to the moon, God is there. If you travel to Neptune, He is there. "V12" is the name given to the most distant star known to humanity and is 10.4 million light years away in the galaxy "NGC 4203." If you travel there, God will be waiting for you. You cannot flee from God, for He is omnipresent. You cannot hide your sin from Him, for He was there when you committed it. Hebrews 4:13 says, "There is no creature hidden from His sight, but all things are naked and open to the eyes of Him to whom we must give account."

Where are you going today? God will be there. In any location or circumstance, the Spirit of God will be with you. God's strong hand is always ready to hold you up and lead you. Wherever you are, He has already been there. Whatever may befall you, He already has it under control. You have nothing to fear today, child of God. All you have to do is take His hand and let Him lead you.

EVENING
Heavenly Father, I have found Your Word to be true today, for I have not been anywhere that I did not sense Your presence. And even now as I lie down to sleep, I close my eyes in peace, knowing the presence and protection of the Great One is mine. In Jesus' name I pray. Amen.

MORNING

Father, I know from Your Word that the battles awaiting me today are not against flesh and blood but against spiritual rulers and wickedness. Strengthen me to walk in Your Spirit. Protect me from the wiles of the devil and receive glory from my life. In the mighty name of Jesus I pray. Amen.

I say to you, every sin and blasphemy will be forgiven men, but the blasphemy against the Spirit will not be forgiven men. Anyone who speaks a word against the Son of Man, it will be forgiven him; but whoever speaks against the Holy Spirit, it will not be forgiven him, either in this age or in the age to come.

MATTHEW 12:31, 32

No warning in the Bible is as grave as this one. Jesus' sobering message is that whoever commits the sin of blaspheming the Holy Spirit will not be forgiven in this temporal age or in the eternal age to come. When I read it, I say, "Wow." And then I say, "Woe." People can "resist" the Spirit (Acts 7:51), "grieve" the Spirit (Ephesians 4:30), and "quench" the Spirit (1 Thessalonians 5:19)—and still receive forgiveness. But when people blaspheme the Spirit, they have crossed a line from which they can never return!

What is the sin of blasphemy against the Holy Spirit? There are many thoughts about this, but I think it is speaking out against the Holy Spirit. First, that interpretation fits the context of Jesus' discourse. He went on to discuss how the words we speak reveal our hearts and will have consequences, whether good or bad (Matthew 12:34–37). Secondly, verse 32 seems to interpret verse 31. Jesus said that anyone who "*speaks against* the Holy Spirit" will not be forgiven (emphasis added). Thirdly, the Greek word *blasphemia* means "to vilify, to speak evil of, to rail against." I do not believe that born-again believers can commit this sin because they are indwelt (Romans 8:9) and sealed (Ephesians 1:13) by the Spirit. Our God is worthy of reverence. Thank Him for His holy presence in your life and honor Him with your words and actions today.

EVENING

Abba Father, thank You for Your divine Helper who steered me clear of spiritual danger today. By His guidance I have escaped every trap of the Evil One. Thank You for preserving me until the day of Christ's return. Amen.

ALLAN TAYLOR, WOODSTOCK, GA

Week 18, Monday

Gracious heavenly Father, thank You for the precious gift of eternal life You have given me through Your Son, the Lord Jesus. I am so grateful for all the blessings of life today, and I am mindful that outside of You I have nothing and am capable of nothing. Please help me to live for You today and grant me the wisdom to make decisions that are pleasing to You in every way. I pray this in Jesus' name. Amen.

> *If Christ is in you, the body is dead because of sin, but the Spirit is life because of righteousness. But if the Spirit of Him who raised Jesus from the dead dwells in you, He who raised Christ from the dead will also give life to your mortal bodies through His Spirit who dwells in you.*
> ROMANS 8:10, 11

Life can bring some tough times. I wish I could offer a burden-free life to my children, but I cannot. On the other hand, life can bring many wonderful joys and blessings. In the good times and the bad times, God's children can trust completely in His plan for them. The exact moment Jesus came into your heart and life, He took up residence in you and, in a sense, unpacked His bags! This means you can rely on His presence and power working in you at all times, including when you face challenges. Jesus will never leave you at any time or for any reason—even when you pass from this life to the next. Because He is alive and living in you, He guarantees you safe passage into heaven, where you will live forever!

Aren't these truths that can make the darkest day bright? Thank the Lord Jesus! Take joy in His presence and remain in the power and hope that He brings.

EVENING

I thank You, Lord Jesus, for all You have done for me today. I began this day with a prayer in my heart and now come to the end of this day with a prayer in my heart. You are true to Your word and I know You have lived "in" me throughout the day. I want You to know that I love You. Amen.

Dear heavenly Father, I am so glad to begin another day with You in my heart. Thank You for loving me and helping me to handle all that will come my way today. I am totally dependent on You for wisdom and grace, and I celebrate Your presence in my life. Amen.

You have an anointing from the Holy One, and you know all things . . . But the anointing which you have received from Him abides in you, and you do not need that anyone teach you; but as the same anointing teaches you concerning all things, and is true, and is not a lie, and just as it has taught you, you will abide in Him.

1 JOHN 2:20, 27

The world is searching for truth in a day and age where information flows from every source imaginable. Mass communications and modern technologies are no longer relegated to libraries but are readily available with just the push of a button. Most people question whether they can truly rely on what they hear. So much information comes from gifted and capable individuals, but the task to sift through it all and identify truth remains.

In this passage, God affirms the work of His Holy Spirit in the lives of all believers. Essentially, He does two things for us. First, He guards us from error and false teaching. This means Jesus has placed a hedge of protection around us so that Satan's lies can be destroyed before they reach us. Second, He guides us into truth. This means God alerts us to truth. What wonderful care the Almighty gives to His children! Remember that you have been anointed by God through His Holy Spirit and that God shields you from the lies of the world.

EVENING

Precious heavenly Father, thank You for this day. So much has gone on in my life today, but I have tried to be conscious of Your abiding presence, even when I least felt like it. I have tried to live for You. I confess my sin and failures to You before I turn in for the night. Thank You for guarding me from error and for guiding me into truth. In Jesus' name I humbly pray. Amen.

Most gracious and loving heavenly Father, I bow before You at the beginning of this new day. How I need You in my life. Your presence is my source of strength, and Your Word is my light. I will live for You today. In Jesus' name I pray. Amen.

> *You did not receive the spirit of bondage again to fear, but you received the Spirit of adoption by whom we cry out, "Abba, Father." The Spirit Himself bears witness with our spirit that we are children of God.*
> ROMANS 8:15, 16

In anticipation of the dreadfulness of war, Franklin D. Roosevelt, during his first inaugural address in 1933, said to the American people, "The only thing we have to fear is fear itself." He was trying to rally our nation with a sense of courage so the enemy could be defeated. While so many paid the ultimate sacrifice, some say this war was won before our troops left our shores. They knew who they were and were proud to be Americans.

In this passage, Paul reminds God's army of believers that they should have absolute confidence in God regardless of the Enemy they face. All believers have been adopted into God's family, thereby making it possible for every Christian to approach the throne of God without fear. The word *Abba* refers to God as our Father and serves to remind us that He provides for us as His own sons and daughters; He meets our every need. For an adoption to be legally binding in Roman culture, seven reputable witnesses had to be present. They verified the legality of the adoption. Here Paul reminds us that the Spirit of God is the One who confirms our adoption into God's family, thereby making available to us all that God has for His own Son, the Lord Jesus Christ! Never forget that you are a child of the King and a vital part of His holy army. Charge!

EVENING

Father God in heaven, You are my Abba and I am Your child. Thank You for saving me and adopting me into Your family. As I go to bed tonight, I do so with a renewed sense of Your presence and power in my life. Grant me a good night's rest and allow me to serve You again tomorrow. With thanksgiving in my heart and humility in Your presence, Amen.

MORNING

Dear heavenly Father, thank You for allowing me to wake up today. I never want to take my life for granted, and I want every minute to count for You. I confess all my sins to You. Help me remember today that You are with me every step I take. In Jesus' name I pray. Amen.

> *The kingdom of God is not eating and drinking, but righteousness and peace and joy in the Holy Spirit. For he who serves Christ in these things is acceptable to God and approved by men.*
> ROMANS 14:17, 18

My wife, Karyn, and I are the proud grandparents of four young boys. I dearly love my children and grandchildren, and I want to live in a way that blesses them. But even more than that, I want to live in a way that is pleasing to the Lord. This Bible passage reminds us that eating and drinking are the non-essentials of a life that counts in God's eyes. We are exhorted to major on the things that really matter to God and to our fellow man. The Lord tells us where to set our sights and focus our energy.

At first glance, the three spiritual attributes listed in this passage look impossible. But they are attainable because the Holy Spirit can make each of them take root in our hearts and become the hallmarks of the legacy we leave behind. Righteousness is simply living in a holy and obedient way. Peace is having a loving and tranquil attitude toward others. Joy is having spiritual contentment regardless of circumstances. You and I cannot do these things, but Christ can do them as He lives in us! By submitting to Him and growing these spiritual attributes into your character, you will be pleasing to God and a blessing to those around you.

EVENING

Dear God, please help me to be all You desire for me to be. I cannot do this on my own. I get so distracted, and my sin is ever before me. Please forgive me tonight of all my sins and help me live out righteousness, peace, and joy in my daily life. I pray this prayer in Jesus' name. Amen.

DON WILTON, SPARTANBURG, SC

Dear heavenly Father, as I begin this day I turn to You because You alone are the Lord of my life. I worship You and exalt Your name above all. Thank You for saving me from my sin and writing my name in the Lamb's Book of Life. In Jesus' name I humbly pray. Amen.

As it is written: "Eye has not seen, nor ear heard, nor have entered into the heart of man the things which God has prepared for those who love Him." But God has revealed them to us through His Spirit. For the Spirit searches all things, yes, the deep things of God.

1 CORINTHIANS 2:9, 10

Knowing God is a lifetime pursuit. When we see Him face-to-face in heaven, we'll realize that even after spending our lives continually knowing Him more, we could only know our great and awesome God to a limited extent on earth. Of course, it will not matter then!

Perhaps you learn great things from gifted pastors and teachers, yet you grapple to really understand God's nature and ways. Perhaps you discipline yourself to study and learn on your own, yet never seem to arrive at a final point of spiritual understanding. Take heart, my friend! God's wisdom is not of this world, and the vast treasure He has in store for all who believe in His name is beyond human understanding. But the Holy Spirit opens the eyes of our limited human minds and allows us to see the vast extent of God's grace, the wide scope of His love, and the glorious majesty of His heavenly home. God has not only prepared these things for us, but has appointed His Holy Spirit to search out the deep things of His nature and reveal them to us.

So do not be dismayed by the apparent blindness of a world without Christ, for they cannot see and cannot know truth without the indwelling presence of God Himself. Take joy in the fact that you have received God's Spirit and that He can open your eyes to catch a glimpse of God's glory and majesty.

EVENING

Tonight, I echo the words of an old hymn: "Thank You, Lord, for saving my soul; thank You, Lord, for making me whole! Thank You, Lord, for giving to me Your great salvation, so rich and so free!" I worship You in Jesus' name. Amen.

Most gracious and loving heavenly Father, I want to go through this day knowing You better than ever before. I need You in my life and believe You will guard my heart and guide my actions. Amen.

> *Beloved, do not believe every spirit, but test the spirits, whether they*
> *are of God; because many false prophets have gone out into the world.*
> *By this you know the Spirit of God: Every spirit that confesses that Jesus*
> *Christ has come in the flesh is of God . . . We are of God. He who knows*
> *God hears us; he who is not of God does not hear us. By this we*
> *know the spirit of truth and the spirit of error.*
>
> I JOHN 4:1, 2, 6

False prophets are everywhere it seems! They write books, preach in churches, have television shows, enjoy large crowds, knock on neighborhood doors, teach Sunday School classes, and promote great causes. Sadly, we have increasingly become Christians who know our Savior but who cannot discern God's truth from Satan's deception.

There are two major ways to determine if a person is of God. First of all, keep a general rule of not immediately believing everything you hear. Make a commitment to the Lord to have a healthy skepticism that will drive you to find out if truth is being spoken. Second, test what you hear directly with the Bible—and only God's Word! When you do, you'll be carrying out the two tests given in this passage that identify false prophets. First, does this person believe that Jesus has come in the flesh? It's not just an issue of believing that He has come; the full humanity and full deity of Jesus is an ultimate test of genuineness. Second, does this person speak the doctrine of the Bible as preached by the apostles? If not, this person is preaching and teaching a false doctrine. Be warned and be careful because the devil is a roaring lion, seeking whom he may devour. Cling to God's Word, and you will steadily stand on truth.

EVENING

Dear God, my heavenly Father, thank You for Your Word. I desperately want to know You more and ask that You would fill me with Your Holy Spirit. Help me to be strong in my faith. I humbly pray this in Jesus' name. Amen.

DON WILTON, SPARTANBURG, SC

Week 19, Monday

Lord, I thank You that the strength of my life comes from the source of my life—Your Spirit. The spirit of this world is dark, weak, and deceiving, but You have given me Your Spirit of light, strength, and truth. Today, I want to walk in the Spirit and live in the Spirit, reflecting Christ in all things. Empower me to live for Your glory. Amen.

The fruit of the Spirit is love, joy, peace, longsuffering, kindness,
goodness, faithfulness, gentleness, self-control. Against such there
is no law. And those who are Christ's have crucified the flesh with its
passions and desires. If we live in the Spirit, let us also walk in the Spirit.

GALATIANS 5:22–25

Life is draining. Whether it's investment in a relationship or responsibility on the job, our roles and daily tasks are demanding and often depleting. When we seize a new opportunity or start serving in a ministry, life often demands even more. When we face disease, distress, and disappointment, we need spiritual fuel. Yet many believers try to live on just the "fumes" within their souls rather than on the true source of strength, God's Holy Spirit. The Spirit is often neglected and forgotten in the daily grind of life.

On occasion, I've made it a practice to pause as I refuel my car and use my "pump time" to think about the "fuel" of my faith, God's Spirit. How prone I am to live near empty rather than to live in the fullness of God's grace found in the work of His Spirit! My father always said, "It's just as easy to drive around with a full tank as it is to drive with one that's nearly empty." Why do we live on fumes when God has promised to fill us and enable us through His Spirit?

Temptation, adversity, and conflict quickly draw our attention to our need for more fuel. Yet we often face such moments unprepared, not relying on the Spirit's power. God has provided all you need for life's demands today—His Spirit.

EVENING

Lord, thank You for Spirit-strength and Spirit-truth in my life. I close this day reliant upon the truth and assurance of Your Spirit's all-sufficient work in me. May I awaken to be renewed and refueled by Your Spirit. Thank You that whatever tomorrow holds can be faced and embraced in Your Spirit. Amen.

Week 19, Tuesday

Lord, give me clarity today. I live in a world where darkness rules, sin pervades, and deceit hinders. Help me to see Your truth. Give me sensitivity to Your Spirit; let my heart remain in tune with Your voice. As I travel the path You have established for me, let me hear Your voice saying, "This is the way, walk in it" (Isaiah 30:21). May Your Spirit be my strength and Your strength my security as I walk through this day. Amen.

Now we have received, not the spirit of the world, but the Spirit who is from God, that we might know the things that have been freely given to us by God. These things we also speak, not in words which man's wisdom teaches but which the Holy Spirit teaches, comparing spiritual things with spiritual.

1 CORINTHIANS 2:12, 13

The city of Augusta, Georgia, is known for its beauty and tradition. It is called "The Garden City," and it is the host site of The Masters® Golf Tournament. Each year, the world's greatest players and fans from all over the globe converge for the tournament. The event is planned to coincide with the arrival of spring with its beautiful array of colorful blossoms.

Recently, prolonged winter weather collided with a sudden increase of spring warmth during the tournament, creating an explosion of pollen that blanketed buildings, lawns, and even guests with a hazy, dusty, yellow residue. This overshadowed the opening days of the tournament and created havoc for many people with allergies.

We live in a world that bears the "pollen residue" of sin—every person on the planet is affected by its presence. It hinders our vision, stains our lives, and touches everything. But we can have clarity, purity, and wisdom when the Spirit of God is at work in us. Apart from Him, we live without discernment or discretion, reflecting the spirit of the world. Depend on God's Spirit to give you clear vision and to lead you in truth.

EVENING

Lord, I reflect on Your truth and grace as I close my eyes in sleep. Oh, the delight of knowing You and the joy of communion with You in my heart! May Your wisdom guide me, Your truth guard me, and Your power uphold me. I rest in You. In Jesus' name, Amen.

DAVID MCKINLEY, AUGUSTA, GA

Week 19, Wednesday

Thank You for the gift of Your Holy Spirit, Lord Jesus, and for the confidence and encouragement He brings. Thank You for the Spirit's help in prayer, service, and grace. Thank You that He works for my good and Your glory in all things. Fill me with Your Spirit and guide me throughout the day. In Jesus' name, Amen.

Ask, and it will be given to you; seek, and you will find;
knock, and it will be opened to you . . . If you then, being evil,
know how to give good gifts to your children, how much more will
your heavenly Father give the Holy Spirit to those who ask Him!
LUKE 11:9, 13

Have you every failed to deliver on a promise? Recently, I pulled a practical joke on some friends. I promised to get tickets to an important event, but then—knowing how much my delivery mattered—sent a note telling my friends that I had a change of plans and that I'd sold the tickets because I received an "offer I could not refuse." Under my signature, I wrote: "P.S. April Fools' Day . . . gotta have fun!" Sadly, my friends did not read carefully beyond the "change of plans" part of my note. At the end of the day, I was apologizing rather than laughing at my own hoax.

God does not fool His children. His wisdom and love keep us from every hoax played by the Enemy of our souls, the devil. God is faithful, gracious, and steadfast in His love. He provides all we need for life and godliness! God gives us not just what we request and hope for; He gives us His Spirit. Psalm 84:11 says, "No good thing does He withhold from those who walk uprightly." With the Spirit of truth in us, we live a life of promises fulfilled.

EVENING

I rest tonight in Your goodness. You are my sun and shield by day. You are my rock and fortress by night. You are my delight and my desire. Thank You for promising to give me my heart's desires when I delight myself in You. I bring all of my striving and desire and place it at Your feet. I know I can trust Your Spirit to supply my every need and fulfill every yearning. Amen.

Lord Jesus, I lift my eyes to You. I give thanks for the Good News of Your death, burial, and resurrection. Thank You for the grace, mercy, and love that have transformed my sinful heart and delivered me from the kingdom of darkness. Thank You for the power and permanence of the Cross. Thank You for the renewal and regeneration of the Holy Spirit. Thank You for the gift of the Spirit, who secures my salvation and guarantees an imperishable inheritance. Amen.

> *"Let all the house of Israel know assuredly that God has made this Jesus, whom you crucified, both Lord and Christ." Now when they heard this, they were cut to the heart, and said to Peter and the rest of the apostles, "Men and brethren, what shall we do?" Then Peter said to them, "Repent, and let every one of you be baptized in the name of Jesus Christ for the remission of sins; and you shall receive the gift of the Holy Spirit."*
> ACTS 2:36–38

The Holy Spirit testifies to the truth concerning Jesus Christ: Messiah, Redeemer, Son of the living God. He proclaims that Jesus Christ is the way, the truth, and the life and that no one comes to the Father except through Him (John 14:6). Apart from the active work of God's Spirit through the gospel, we cannot know God or the hope of eternal life. The Spirit convicts, calls, and converts weak and wayward people to live for a new purpose: to honor, serve, and magnify the Lord Jesus Christ. This work of grace begins when we recognize that we are without hope apart from Christ. Repentance leads to the peace and freedom of grace. We confess our disobedience and turn away from our stubbornness. We cast ourselves wholly on the work of Christ for us, acknowledging its sufficiency, and we are saved! Praise God that His Spirit reveals truth to us and glorifies Christ in our lives!

EVENING

Thank You for the Cross, Lord. Thank You for the costly, yet complete work of salvation. Thank You that repentance and faith are met with forgiveness and peace. Thank You for so great a salvation. Help me remember the Spirit of Christ lives in me. I am secure in Your love and sustained by Your Spirit. I can sleep in peace and face the morning with fresh confidence. Amen.

DAVID MCKINLEY, AUGUSTA, GA

Lord, I know that I am not my own. I belong to You, and I want to live this day to glorify You. Keep me from indulgence, lust, and laziness in my body. Guard me from anger, pride, and bitterness in my spirit. I ask You to fill me with Your Spirit and to preserve my spirit, soul, and body throughout the day. I am Yours. Be glorified in me! In Jesus' name, Amen.

Do you not know that your body is the temple of the Holy Spirit who is in you,
whom you have from God, and you are not your own? For you were bought
at a price; therefore glorify God in your body and in your spirit, which are God's.
1 CORINTHIANS 6:19, 20

The human body is a living organism made up of nearly fifty trillion cells, ten distinct operative systems, and five unique senses used for interaction and experience. While diverse in design and distinct in function, the body is intricately correlated to work as a whole. It is natural in its relationship to the world, spiritual in its design, and intended to function for the glory of God.

Each day we open our eyes, roll back the covers, and move into the activities ahead of us. We also renew the engagement of conflict, temptation, and struggle common to every human body. The possibilities of sinful indulgence and dishonoring God with our bodies confront us. For this reason, we must pause each morning to remember and affirm, "We are not our own."

The title deed of your life is not in your hands, but in God's hands. You were bought at a price. Christ's redemption defines you today. His Spirit inhabits you so that your body may be used for the praise of His glory. You are His temple, and He is your triumph over the weakness of the body. Surrender all you are to Him for His service and His purpose.

EVENING

Lord, thank You for my body and that I am fearfully and wonderfully made. In weakness and weariness, I cast every care upon You. I thank You for the strength You gave me today. It is time for rest, so I relax and rejoice that You give Your beloved sleep (Psalm 127:2). Be glorified in my sleep even as in my service, oh Lord. Amen.

"Let the words of my mouth and the meditation of my heart be acceptable in Your sight, O LORD, my strength and my Redeemer" (Psalm 19:14). These words of the psalmist shape my prayer today. May my words help others and honor You. I confess I am quick to speak and become angry, slow to listen and give grace. Deliver me from a critical, poisonous tongue and help me speak truth in love. I pray this in Jesus' name. Amen.

Let no corrupt word proceed out of your mouth, but what is good for necessary edification, that it may impart grace to the hearers. And do not grieve the Holy Spirit of God, by whom you were sealed for the day of redemption.

EPHESIANS 4:29, 30

The only way to describe some interactions with our spouses, children, co-workers, and friends is *grief*! Agitating remarks are often the cause. And let's be honest—our own comments and criticisms probably give them grief as well. The power of the human tongue for good and evil is amazing.

The Bible says your tongue can bring grief not only to those in your sphere of influence, but also to God's Spirit. God intends for you to minister grace, not grief. How do you do this? Consider the following things before you speak: Is it **T**rue? Is it **H**onest? Is it **I**mportant? Is it **N**ecessary? Is it **K**ind? **T-H-I-N-K** before you speak and your words can bring grace, not grief.

God's Spirit of truth enables you to speak truth in love to build up others in faith instead of tearing them down in criticism. You can bring others hope, not despair. THINK about your words. Are you the cause of grief in someone's life? Your family? Your friends? God's Spirit?

We grieve God's Spirit when we ignore His redeeming and renewing work in us. The Spirit is the seal of our redemption. With His help, our words can be transformed from weapons that destroy into God's instruments that minister grace. Thank God for the enabling and enduring ministry of the Spirit of truth!

EVENING

Lord, in the silence before my sleep, may I hear Your voice of correction. Cleanse me. Let me experience Your grace. When I awake, may I rise to impart grace to others through the work of the Spirit. Amen.

DAVID MCKINLEY, AUGUSTA, GA

Week 20, Monday

Heavenly Father, You truly are an awesome God! As I behold the majestic handiwork of Your creation, I'm reminded of Your sovereignty and glory. Thank You for establishing a personal relationship with me, even though Your ways and thoughts are always above me. Thank You that I can call You my God and know You as my heavenly Father. In the name of the Lord Jesus Christ, I give You praise. Amen.

The law of the LORD is perfect, converting the soul; the testimony of the LORD is sure, making wise the simple; the statutes of the LORD are right, rejoicing the heart; the commandment of the LORD is pure, enlightening the eyes; the fear of the LORD is clean, enduring forever; the judgments of the LORD are true and righteous altogether.

PSALM 19:7–9

In this psalm, David expresses wonder at how God reveals Himself through creation and through His Word. Creation reveals God as the mighty Creator with infinite power, but the Word reveals God as One who enters into covenant relationship with His people. The cosmos bears witness to His awesome glory and power; His Word reveals His love and grace. Note that David uses the name LORD, which means "Yahweh" and is an expression of the personal covenant name for God.

As he did in Psalm 119, David gives a litany of characteristics to describe God's Word. He says it is perfect; it is free of error, both in historical fact and in spiritual truth. It is sure; it is immutable and steadfast, never changing. It is right; it contains the best principles for daily living, and we'll be blessed when we obey it. He also says it is pure; it exposes the depravity of human nature. It gives true and righteous judgments; God has infinite knowledge of all things and makes perfect judgments. David also presents four wonderful ministries of God's Word: converting the soul, making the simple wise, rejoicing the heart, and enlightening the eyes. Praise God for reaching down to humans in grace and revealing Himself to us through His works and His Word!

EVENING
Lord, God Yahweh, I am in total awe of You! I can rest tonight in complete peace, knowing Your Word promises that my life is in Your hands. Amen.

Week 20, Tuesday

Lord, thank You for giving me the opportunity to behold the glorious beauty of Your creation! Help me not to get so caught up in business that I overlook the little things You have orchestrated for me along life's journey. So often I take simple blessings like sight for granted. Please remind me today that You created all things by Your marvelous hand and that You give them to Your children to enjoy. Thank You, Lord God, for making a brand new day! In Jesus' name I pray. Amen.

The LORD your God is God of gods and Lord of lords, the great God, mighty and awesome, who shows no partiality nor takes a bribe. He administers justice for the fatherless and the widow, and loves the stranger, giving him food and clothing.
DEUTERONOMY 10:17, 18

We all can be stubborn and cold-hearted. We desperately need for our Father God, the Great Physician, to take His righteous hand and merciful scalpel and graciously perform surgery on our calloused hearts. We, like the Israelites, sometimes view our relationship with God as through physical circumcision, as if it were a symbol of a merely *outward* covenant of *religion*. God teaches us that true circumcision must be of the heart as an *inward* covenant of *relationship* with God.

The apostle Paul stated that a man is a Jew if he is one inwardly; "circumcision is that of the heart, in the Spirit, not in the letter" (Romans 2:29). By God circumcising our hearts, we recognize that God the Father loves all His people unconditionally, without partiality. No one is excluded from His operational mercy and grace.

In Deuteronomy 10, Moses seems to be overwhelmed by the awesomeness of God's justice and mercy toward the outcasts of society. The fatherless, the widows, and the aliens are socially powerless; there is no one to protect or take care of the poor and the weak. Yet our great and awesome God loves them more than the sparrows, for whom He provides. As God's child, rely on Him to provide for you physically and spiritually, and minister that same unconditional love to others, treating them the way the Father has treated you.

EVENING
Father God, thank You for loving me and caring for me and for sending Jesus to die for me. You truly are an awesome God! Amen.

DUSTY MCLEMORE, ATHENS, AL

Father, thank You for a restful night and a beautiful new day. I pray that You will enable me today to walk in the Spirit and not yield to my flesh. I desire so much to please You, heavenly Father. I never want to become a reproach upon Your name or an offense to Your church. I love You, Father, and thank You for blessing me with Your lovely Son, Jesus. Help me seize every opportunity to be a witness for Your glory and honor. I devote myself anew to You this day. In Jesus' name, Amen.

Our God, the great, the mighty, and awesome God, who keeps covenant and mercy: do not let all the trouble seem small before You that has come upon us, our kings and our princes, our priests and our prophets, our fathers and on all Your people, from the days of the kings of Assyria until this day.
NEHEMIAH 9:32

Nehemiah acknowledged Israel's persistent sin and praised God for His righteous judgments and forgiving mercy. He saw that God honored His covenant with His people in spite of their failures. The covenant merits God's divine justice; God will not tolerate impurity. He doesn't dismiss sin as if it never happened—sin always warrants consequences. But the covenant also reveals God's infinite compassion. God is just in administering His punishment and in showing mercy.

The climax of God's love and mercy is in the sending of His Son, Jesus Christ. For in Christ, God took the full punishment for all the sin of humanity and placed it upon His sacrificial Lamb, Jesus. Second Corinthians 5:21 says, "He who knew no sin became sin that we might become the righteousness of God in Him." Express reverence for God's justice and gratitude for His compassion today. Pour out praise to the great, mighty, awesome God of your salvation!

EVENING

Dear God, at the close of another day, I want to pause and give You thanks for Your great love and mercy. I thank You for having such compassion upon me, a sinner, and for sending Jesus Christ to die for my sins. I'm thankful that even though my sin merits consequences, You covered my sin with mercy. I'm grateful to be called a child of the King! Amen.

MORNING

Heavenly Father, as I approach a new day, I do so with a song in my heart. Your name is majestic in all the earth, and I ask for Your blessings upon me as I represent You today. Direct my steps and guard my paths that I might not sin or bring a reproach against Your holy name. I desire to honor You and let people know just how awesome You are. I pray this in the name of my Savior and King, Jesus Christ. Amen.

> *He comes from the north as golden splendor; with God is awesome majesty. As for the Almighty, we cannot find Him; He is excellent in power, in judgment and abundant justice; He does not oppress. Therefore men fear Him; He shows no partiality to any who are wise of heart.*
>
> JOB 37:22–24

W hen God appears to be distant and we feel discouraged, we must always remember He is with us, He is powerful, and He is good! As God's children, we can never escape the strong hand of the Almighty.

Today's verses are in the context of Elihu rebuking Job and his three friends. Chapters 36 and 37 present Elihu's reflection upon God's great goodness and creative majesty. He said, "God thunders marvelously with His voice" (Job 37:5). He described God's excellent power: "By the breath of God ice is given and the broad waters are frozen" (v. 10). He pointed to God's control over storms and seasons when he said, "He comes from the north as golden splendor" (v. 22). Elihu ended his speech by acknowledging that fearing God involves recognizing His supremacy and humanity's inferiority. We should never question God's justice or challenge His sovereignty, because His ways are beyond human understanding (Isaiah 55:8, 9).

Elihu assured Job that God's dealings with him were not to oppress or oppose him, but to reveal that He is just and mighty in His words and works. Whatever your circumstances, take comfort in the truth that God is in control and that He is right in all He does.

EVENING

Father, thank You for revealing Your might through Your awesome creation. As I behold a golden sunset or hear the breaking of the ocean waves, I'm reminded of how amazing You truly are. May I be constantly mindful of Your majesty. Thank You for surrounding me with Your beauty. Amen.

DUSTY MCLEMORE, ATHENS, AL

Good morning, Lord. I bow before You as my God and King. I come to this special place each morning to acknowledge Your presence and to worship You as my heavenly Father. I cannot begin a single day without seeking Your guidance. I desperately need You! I ask You to fill me this day with Your Spirit and Your power. Mold and shape me for Your great glory. Speak to my heart throughout the day. Help me walk in Your Spirit and know Your will. Teach me Your ways that I may teach and lead others to You. Help me to be a godly influence and have an attitude of worship as I live out this day. I love You, Father! In Jesus' name, Amen.

> *Oh, clap your hands, all you peoples! Shout to God with the voice of triumph!*
> *For the LORD Most High is awesome; He is a great King over all the earth.*
> *He will subdue the peoples under us, and the nations under our feet.*
> PSALM 47:1–3

I love to worship the Lord! A Spirit-filled worship service leads God's people into His presence and prepares them to hear His Word proclaimed. Our God desires for His people to worship and praise Him! Psalm 45:11 instructs us, "Because He is your Lord, worship Him." Psalm 48:1 reminds us, "Great is the LORD, and greatly to be praised."

The majority of the psalms written by King David were songs of praise and worship. Of all the kings and leaders of Israel, no one loved to praise and worship the Lord like David. In Psalm 57:7, he said, "O God, my heart is steadfast; I will sing and give praise." David was not ashamed to praise the Lord before the peoples! He said, "I will praise You, O Lord, among the peoples; I will sing to You among the nations" (Psalm 57:9). We should worship God freely and earnestly, shouting from our hearts with a voice of triumph! For the Lord Most High is an awesome, great King and worthy to be praised!

EVENING

My Father and God, You truly are worthy of my worship. Before I lie down to rest, I praise You that You are not only my heavenly Father, but You are also my life! And I'm so grateful to be called a child of the King! In the name of Jesus I pray. Amen.

MORNING

Lord, I come to give You praise this morning. Thank You for watching over me throughout the night. I praise You for a new day and new opportunities to serve You. Strengthen me for the tasks at hand. Help me to walk in Your Spirit and not fulfill the lusts of my flesh. I thank You that I can call out to You at any time and You will hear my prayer. I praise You for sending Your Son so I might receive eternal life. Amen.

Make a joyful shout to God, all the earth! Sing out the honor of His name;
make His praise glorious. Say to God, "How awesome are Your works! Through the
greatness of Your power Your enemies shall submit themselves to You. All the earth
shall worship You and sing praises to You; they shall sing praises to Your name."
PSALM 66:1–4

The writer of this psalm invites all peoples of the earth to unite in joyful praise to God. That's the way it will be in heaven—all tribes and tongues gathered around the throne, worshiping the Lord in one accord and singing a new song. What an awesome day that will be! The psalmist declares what the Lord had done for His people, and that is the basis for his invitation to the world to praise God with shouting and singing. Because of God's awesome works, even His enemies submit to His awesome power.

In verse 6 the writer speaks of two of God's mighty water miracles—the escape from the Egyptian pharaoh after crossing the parted Red Sea and the entrance into Canaan after crossing the parted Jordan River. We, too, are to celebrate and praise God for the miracles of the Cross of Calvary, the resurrection of our Lord, and the gift of eternal life through Jesus Christ. We as God's people are to join the psalmist in declaring to the world that our God is awesome in His works and mighty in His great power. Let us honor His name as we shout to the Lord and make His praise glorious!

EVENING

Lord, You are a miraculous God. The very air I breathe is a gift from You! May I always be found with praise upon my lips and gratefulness in my heart. I love You and thank You for saving my soul! Amen.

DUSTY MCLEMORE, ATHENS, AL

Father, throughout this day, help me to focus not on circumstances or difficulties, but on You. I confess that You are God and I'm not. Many people in the world don't know You. Use my life to point them to You. Amen.

> *Come and see the works of God; He is awesome in His doing toward*
> *the sons of men. He turned the sea into dry land; they went through*
> *the river on foot. There we will rejoice in Him. He rules by His power*
> *forever; His eyes observe the nations; do not let the rebellious exalt themselves.*
>
> PSALM 66:5–7

Come and rejoice. Not everyone in the world has a reason to rejoice, but the redeemed of the Lord do! Our God is an awesome God! He still works miracles today! Sure, we go through tests along the journey of life, but God knows what we are ready for and how much we can handle. He can even cause us to rejoice in the midst of difficult times.

Come and remember. Do you feel like your back is up against the wall? Nothing takes God by surprise. God has brought you to this very spot. God sees what is ahead and will go before you. He still parts the Red Sea. There are those who do not believe the miracles of the Bible. They try to explain them away by saying it was the Reed Sea and a marshland they tiptoed across. That would not explain away the miracle, but would make it even more amazing. Pharaoh's army would have drowned in an inch of water! Someone has said, "Life is filled with obstacles and opposition, but to God they are only opportunities to show His omnipotence." God is bigger than your problems! He will go before you and make a way.

Come and repent. Pharaoh is a reminder that God resists the proud, but gives grace to the humble (James 4:6). Most people think much of themselves and little of God. May we think much of God and little of ourselves!

Meditate on today's verses. Has it ever occurred to you that nothing ever occurs to God? Trust Him. He oversees all and overlooks none.

EVENING

As I come to the close of this day, forgive me of all my sins. I don't want anything in my life that is a hindrance in my relationship with You. Amen.

God, I worship You in Your holiness. Create in me a clean heart and renew a right spirit within me. Help me to think pure thoughts and have a pure heart. In Jesus' name, Amen.

O God, You are more awesome than Your holy places. The God
of Israel is He who gives strength and power to His people. Blessed be God!
PSALM 68:35

———— ✦ ————

There are some breathtaking places on earth. Can you imagine how beautiful heaven must be? However, God Himself is more awesome than the places He created. He demonstrated how much He cares for us by leaving heaven and coming to this earth. The Son of God became the Son of Man so that the sons of men might become sons of God. Wow! When we could not come to where He was, He came to us. Psalm 68:5 says, "A father of the fatherless, a defender of widows, is God in His holy habitation." Even though there may be times when we feel like no one cares, we can be assured that God sees and He cares.

One way we can see God's care for us is in what He gives us. He has given us too many gifts to count, but one of the greatest gifts is His holiness. At the Cross, Jesus took our sin upon Himself and imputed His righteousness to us, meaning God ascribed Jesus' righteousness to us! He also gave us His written love letter, the Holy Bible, and the Comforter who lives inside each believer, the Holy Spirit.

God also gives us His strength and His power. God looks for people through whom He can show Himself strong. When we are weak, He is strong. He makes us strong in the power of His might. We can do all things through Christ who strengthens us (Philippians 4:13). Steven Curtis Chapman wrote, "His strength is perfect when our strength is gone. He'll carry us when we can't carry on. Raised in His power, the weak become strong."[5]

God is able to do exceedingly and abundantly above all we can ask or think—God can do anything! Nothing is too difficult for Him. Live in His resurrection power today!

———— ✦ ————

EVENING
Father, thank You for giving me Your holiness, strength, and power to make it through the day. Lord Jesus, You have the power to forgive sins. Forgive me and make me holy like You. Amen.

GRANT ETHRIDGE, HAMPTON, VA

Week 21, Wednesday

Father, I praise You for Your mighty works. I see You at work in the world, in the church, and in my own life. Work in and through me today. May I accomplish the work that You placed me on this earth to do for Your glory. In Jesus' name, Amen.

The works of the LORD are great, studied by all who have pleasure in them. His work is honorable and glorious, and His righteousness endures forever. He has made His wonderful works to be remembered; the LORD is gracious and full of compassion.

PSALM 111:2−4

⟞⟋⟍⟝

The psalmist glories in the works of God. All work is His work. History is His story. All of God's works are great, but the work of salvation eclipses all others. No other work can compare. No other work brings more glory to God and good to humanity. The Lord's Supper commemorates the greatest work of all, redemption. The song lyrics say it well: "May we never forget the cross and the blood. The price that was paid so that we might live. May we never forget the cost of this love. He'll never forsake us. He'll always forgive. May we never forget."[6]

Salvation is the work of God, not of humans. It is by His grace, not our works, lest anyone should boast (Ephesians 2:9). Our good works could never save our souls. Our works are as filthy rags before a holy God (Isaiah 64:6). We are justified by faith alone. Yet faith and works should not be separated. Faith without works is dead (James 2:17). Faith is the root of salvation. Works are the fruit of salvation. A workless faith is a worthless faith.

What are you doing in the work of God? There is nothing wrong with retiring from a job, but there is something wrong with retiring from work. When you retire from a job, it gives you more time to do God's work. Jesus said, "The night is coming when no one can work" (John 9:4), so make the most of every opportunity to join God's "honorable and glorious" work (Psalm 111:3).

⟞⟋⟍⟝

EVENING

Lord Jesus, thank You for giving me health and strength to serve You. Give me a good night's rest so that I will be ready to walk worthy of You tomorrow. May I be fully pleasing to You and fruitful in every good work. Amen.

God, I thank You that whoever calls on Your name will be saved. Put people in my path today who are ready to receive You. Enable me to be a faithful witness for You. In Jesus' name, Amen.

Oh, give thanks to the LORD! Call upon His name; make known His deeds among the peoples! Sing to Him, sing psalms to Him; talk of all His wondrous works! Glory in His holy name; let the hearts of those rejoice who seek the LORD!
PSALM 105:1–3

The psalmist invites us to do six things today: give thanks to God, call on Him, make Him known, sing to Him, talk about Him, and glory in Him.

Give thanks to God—in all things. This is God's will. We can always find something for which to be thankful. **Call on His name**, and call Him by His name. It matters to which god you pray, because there is salvation in no other name but Jesus. Study His name. The more we know about His name, the more we know Him. Speak His name. There is power, protection, and provision in His name. **Make Him known**. Israel's great commission was to proclaim His name and His works among the nations. It is our unfinished task. **Sing to Him**. Don't just sing about Him, sing to Him. He loves to hear His children sing. He inhabits the praises of His people. Sing unto Him a new song. Fill your world with music that glorifies Jesus. It not only invites the presence of the Holy Spirit but also drives the Enemy away. **Talk about Him**. Don't just talk about the weather, sports, or politics. Talk about spiritual things. When is the last time you talked to someone about the Lord? **Glory in Him**. Celebrate and praise His name. Whatever you do in word or deed should be for His glory. Let your light shine today so that people see your good works and glorify your Father. Brag on Jesus! Don't ever be embarrassed to call on His name.

If you seek the Lord in these six areas, you will have a good day because your heart will be rejoicing!

EVENING
Father, I look back on this day with a grateful heart. You are so good. My soul sings to You, because You are great in all the earth! Amen.

GRANT ETHRIDGE, HAMPTON, VA

Father, You are the God who answers prayer. You are a very present help in time of trouble. Father, You are gracious, You are righteous, and You are merciful. I praise Your name this morning! You set my feet upon the Rock, so I will not be moved. You are my shield, my strength, my shelter, and my strong tower. Amen.

> *Gracious is the LORD, and righteous; yes, our God is merciful. The LORD*
> *preserves the simple; I was brought low, and He saved me. Return to*
> *your rest, O my soul, for the LORD has dealt bountifully with you.*
> PSALM 116:5–7

In today's passage, the psalmist said he was "brought low." Had any low times in life? You may be going through one right now. Remember that God has been faithful in the past. When you thought you would not make it, God brought you through. When you lost it all, God gave it back to you and more. When you lost your job, God provided work. When you thought you were not going to live, God spared your life. The psalmist almost died. He cried out to the Lord, and God saved him. Many people can give this testimony.

Based on God's faithfulness, the psalmist calls his soul to rest. When we were young, we did not like to rest. Parents have to make their children go to bed. Few children run up to their parents and beg to take a nap! But just as children need regular times of rest, so do adults! I read a sign one time that said: "I am planning to have a nervous breakdown. It is mine. I have worked for it. I deserve it. I have earned it and nobody is going to keep me from it." Can you relate? Call your soul to rest. Stop burning the candle at both ends. Be still and know that He is God. Turn off all the noise, and listen for His still, small voice. Jesus welcomes all who labor and are heavy-laden to find rest in Him. Take your burdens to the Lord and leave them there.

EVENING
God, I ask for a healing rest. I place all the worries of the day in Your hands. I cast all my cares upon You because You care for me. Amen.

Father, I thank You that Your mercies are new every morning. Great is Thy faithfulness! May goodness and mercy follow me all throughout this day. In Jesus' name, Amen.

> *Oh, give thanks to the LORD, for He is good! For His mercy endures*
> *forever. Oh, give thanks to the God of gods! For His mercy endures forever.*
> *Oh, give thanks to the Lord of lords! For His mercy endures forever.*
>
> PSALM 136:1–3

Have you ever taken the time to thank the people who influenced your life? Have you expressed appreciation to those who mean the most to you? We take so much for granted. Generally speaking, the more we have, the less grateful we are. It should be the opposite. The more we have, the more thankful we should be. Make an effort to focus on what you have rather than what you don't have. Give thanks for the simple and special things in life.

One of the greatest things we have to be grateful for is God's mercy. A mother once approached Napoleon, seeking a pardon for her son. The emperor replied that justice demanded death. "But I don't ask for justice," the mother explained, "I plead for mercy." "But your son doesn't deserve mercy," Napoleon replied. The woman cried, "It would not be mercy if he deserved it." And he spared the woman's son.

Of all God's gifts, I am most thankful for God's mercy. The worst thing that could happen to us is for God to give us what we deserve. May God deliver us from having an entitlement mindset; God does not owe us anything! Anything that is a notch above hell is better than we deserve. If you feel like you deserve God's mercy, you have a bigger problem than you realize. Remember, when pride walks in, God walks out.

We all need mercy. God's mercy endures forever, so live with an attitude of gratitude!

EVENING

Lord, be merciful to me, a sinner. Thank You for grace that is greater than all my sin. Thank You for the abundance of blessings in my life today, and thank You for Your love. In Your merciful name, Amen.

GRANT ETHRIDGE, HAMPTON, VA

Father, You are my God. I am so grateful that You bought me and that I belong to You. I desire to know You more today. Reveal more about Yourself to me as I live this day. Amen.

> *This is the covenant that I will make with the house of Israel after those days, says the LORD: I will put My law in their minds, and write it on their hearts; and I will be their God, and they shall be My people. No more shall every man teach his neighbor, and every man his brother, saying, "Know the LORD," for they all shall know Me, from the least of them to the greatest of them, says the LORD. For I will forgive their iniquity, and their sin I will remember no more.*
>
> JEREMIAH 31:33, 34

A covenant is a binding legal contract between two parties that is conditional—"If you will do this, then I will do this." This passage is about the New Covenant that God makes with us, and it is fulfilled by the death of Christ on the Cross. Jesus spoke of it when He told His disciples, "This cup is the new covenant in My blood" (Luke 22:20).

The Old Covenant was outward; it was based on the law that was written on stone tablets and delivered by Moses. However, His people were never able to keep it. Its purpose was to show humanity's total inability to meet God's requirements.

The New Covenant is inward; it is based on God's law that is written on our minds and hearts and delivered by the Holy Spirit. It is a covenant that is initiated and activated by God. In the Old Covenant, God continually said, "You shall . . . You shall . . . You shall not . . ." But in the New Covenant, God says, "I will . . . I will . . . I will . . ." It is based on grace!

While the Old Covenant was restricted to Israel, anyone can have a personal relationship with God through the blood of Christ. Israelites knew about God, but under grace, you and I can know Him personally and intimately.

EVENING
Lord, thank You for the precious blood of Jesus that has taken away all my sin. Thank You that because of Your grace my sin will never be brought against me. Amen.

Good morning, Lord. Thank You for the gifts of life and of rest. Thank You for today's opportunities and tests. In whatever I face today, You are with me. Lord, I praise You for Your grace, Your mercy, and Your love. I look forward to experiencing those things today. In Jesus' name, Amen.

> *Who is a God like You, pardoning iniquity and passing over the transgression of the remnant of His heritage? He does not retain His anger forever, because He delights in mercy.*
> MICAH 7:18

It is important not only to know God personally, but to know what God is really like. If we do not, then we may waste our time and energy doing and saying things that He does not want. Micah clearly taught that God hates and judges sin, but he also taught that God enjoys showing mercy to sinners because His love is unchanging.

This is another characteristic that separates the God of the Bible from all the gods of this world. In the Koran there are ninety-nine names for Allah, but one is missing— Love. Our God is the only God who forgives sin. And that is something all of us need. We are desperate to be released from the guilt, the weight, and the wages of our sin.

The Hebrew word for *pardon* means to "lift up, or to relieve a burden." Sin is a heavy burden that weighs us down, but God wants to lift that burden. He not only pardons, but He passes over. We worry about things in our past, but He just passes right over them. When God pardons us, He no longer takes into account our past sin. If God does not dwell on those things, why should you?

You can search all you want, but you will find that there is no God like our God. As Lenny Leblanc wrote, "There is none like You. No one else can touch my heart like You do. I could search for all eternity long, and find there is none like You."[7]

EVENING

Father, I thank You for the tenderness You have shown me today. You have not dealt with me as I deserve, but according to Your mercy. I give You thanks! You are God, and there is none like You! Amen.

Week 22, Wednesday

Lord, thank You for being here before I got here. You are eternal, immortal, invisible, and all-powerful. You alone are God. I praise You as my Creator, my Sustainer, and my Redeemer. Since You made all there is just by speaking Your Word, I know there is nothing I will face today that will be difficult for You. I trust in Your power. Amen.

In the beginning was the Word, and the Word was with God, and the Word was God. He was in the beginning with God. All things were made through Him, and without Him nothing was made that was made. In Him was life, and the life was the light of men. And the light shines in the darkness, and the darkness did not comprehend it.

JOHN 1:1–4

You are not an accident or a coincidence; you are a created being put here for the glory of your Creator. He loves you and wants to enjoy intimate fellowship with you. Intimacy in any relationship is developed by communication, by spending time speaking and listening to each other.

Our great Creator is also our great Communicator. All the idols and gods of this world have mouths, but can't speak; they have eyes, but can't see; they have ears, but can't hear (Psalm 135:16). Our God speaks and He hears. He listens not only to our spoken words, but also to our thoughts. He speaks to us through His Son and through Scripture. These verses tell us that our Lord Jesus is eternally, equally, and essentially God, which tells me He is able.

"In the beginning" are the first three words in our Bible (Genesis 1:1). God said, "Let there be light" (v. 3), and in six days everything that exists came into being. From His Word came light, and with it came life. John begins his book with those same three words, reminding us that the only way we have life and light is through the Word. As you spend time talking and listening to Him, allow the written and the living Word to bring life and light to you today.

EVENING

Father, thank You for leading me by Your Word today. It has been my joy to hear You speak to me and to know You are capable of meeting all my needs. I look forward to listening to You tomorrow. Amen.

Father God, thank You for Your great salvation. You saved me from the wages of my sin. You are saving me day by day from the control of sin from my old nature. Thank You God, that one day You will save me from the hold of death and bring me to live forever with You. I want to bless You today. Amen.

Blessed be the Lord, who daily loads us with benefits, the God of our salvation! Our God is the God of salvation; and to GOD the Lord belong escapes from death.
PSALM 68:19, 20

God has promised that His children will have happiness in spite of heaviness. When the psalmist speaks of how God "loads us with benefits," he is referring to God bearing our burdens. Many translations read "who daily bears our burdens." The daily burdens of family issues, financial concerns, physical problems, and spiritual warfare can weigh us down and cause us to become discouraged.

Our Lord has commanded us, "Cast your burden on the LORD, and He shall sustain you; He will never permit the righteous to be moved" (Psalm 55:22). The greatest burden we have ever had was the enormity of our sin—the guilt and consequences it brings, and our inability to take it away. But when we received salvation, our sins were covered by Christ's death on the Cross. Peter states that Jesus "bore our sins in His own body on the tree" (1 Peter 2:24).

God has also promised hope in spite of horror. Death is a horrible enemy. When Jesus Christ bore the burden of our sin over two thousand years ago, He conquered that enemy. By His resurrection from the grave, He made it possible for us to be freed from the burden of death. In his hymn "Leave It There," Charles A. Tindley, a former slave, wrote, "When your youthful days are gone and old age is stealing on, and your body bends beneath the weight of care; He will never leave you then. He'll go with you to the end. Take your burden to the Lord and leave it there."

EVENING
Father God, You have blessed me with every spiritual blessing in the heavenly realms because I am in Jesus Christ, my Lord. I am not afraid of death, or of life, because of You. Thank You for Your salvation. Amen.

Heavenly Father, thank You for being in control. You are sovereign. You are on the throne. You are unchanging. You are my rock, my fortress, my shield, and my armor. In this unstable world today, Lord, I need Your grace. Thank You for always having Your eyes upon me. You are my security. Amen.

Since we are receiving a kingdom which cannot be shaken,
let us have grace, by which we may serve God acceptably with
reverence and godly fear. For our God is a consuming fire.
HEBREWS 12:28, 29

Have you noticed how many earthquakes are in the news? According to the U.S. Geological Society,[8] earthquakes occur every day somewhere in the world, but most of them are so weak that only sensitive instruments can perceive the seismic activity. However, at least seven hundred quakes each year will cause damage, injury, and death. Our Lord told us that this is one of the signs of the end: "There will be famines, pestilences, and earthquakes in various places. All these are the beginning of sorrows" (Matthew 24:7, 8).

When Jesus said *sorrows,* He used the word for "birth pangs." Mothers understand about birth pangs and the law of contractions; the closer one gets to delivery, the more intense the pangs are and the more frequent they become. Every earthquake is a reminder that we are nearer and nearer to our time of delivery! Jesus said, "When you see all these things, know that it is near—at the doors!" (Matthew 24:33).

Jesus tells the story of two men who built houses and then faced severe storms (Matthew 7:24–27). At the end, the house that stood was the one that was built on the rock. When you not only hear His Word but also obey it and apply it to your life, then you are building your life on the Rock—an unshakable kingdom.

EVENING
God, thank You for giving me stability in such a shaky world today. I know You are always in control, and I bless You for that. I rest in Your grace, Your power, and Your care. I put all my trust in You. Amen.

Precious Father, I bless You and praise You for the mercy You have extended toward me. I bless Your name, Savior, Redeemer, Holy One, and Friend. Thank You for the promise that You will not withhold any good thing from me as I choose to walk in integrity today. For Your glory, Amen.

> *Teach me Your way, O LORD; I will walk in Your truth; unite my heart to fear Your name. I will praise You, O Lord my God, with all my heart, and I will glorify Your name forevermore. For great is Your mercy toward me, and You have delivered my soul from the depths of Sheol.*
>
> PSALM 86:11–13

There is a difference between knowing the works of God and knowing the way of God. Moses prayed, "Show me now Your way" (Exodus 33:13), and the Lord answered his prayer. Psalm 103:7 says, "He made known His ways to Moses." We must remember that His ways are so different from our ways. Our maturity is marked by how willing we are to trust His heart and His motives, without having to see visible actions or results. If we trust His way, then we, like Moses, will obey His truth whether it makes sense to us or not.

As we learn and trust His ways, our hearts should become undivided and totally yielded to Him. It is not our money that He is after; He wants our hearts! Not distracted hearts that notice Him only when we want something from Him. Not divided hearts that love Him among a list of other loves in our lives. No, He desires and deserves devoted hearts.

If He has all of our hearts, it will be evident by our passionate praise of Him. Our purpose in life is to glorify God and to enjoy His presence forever. He has not and will not give us what we deserve; instead, He has given us eternal life. Does He have all of your heart?

EVENING

Lord, thank You for revealing Your way to me. Even when I do not understand so many things that have happened, I trust Your heart and know that You allow them for Your glory and for my good. You are an awesome God, and I willingly give You all my heart. Amen.

DR. MICHAEL CLOER, ROCKY MOUNT, NC

Lord, You have given me ultimate victory. Despite my circumstances, I want to sing praises to You all day today. Help me live a life of worship. Amen.

> *When he had consulted with the people, he appointed those who should sing to the Lord, and who should praise the beauty of holiness, as they went out before the army and were saying: "Praise the Lord, for His mercy endures forever."*
>
> 2 CHRONICLES 20:21

Worship is essential in warfare. Jehoshaphat, King of Judah, found himself and his people in a terrible predicament. The Moabites, Ammonites, and others were coming to attack them. Fear struck the king; he called a fast and began to seek God. He knew God was his only hope of deliverance from their coming enemies. God heard Jehoshaphat and gave him instructions to go out against the enemy with the promise of victory and assurance that He would be with him.

The king appointed singers to "praise the beauty of holiness" as they sang to the Lord. Verse 22 says that as they began to sing and praise, "the Lord set ambushes" against the Moabites and Ammonites.

For us, worship must precede warfare. We are involved in a war that has been won, but still has battles to be fought. The war we are involved in is with the forces of hell. Ephesians 6:12 identifies our Enemy. He fights against us as we advance the gospel of Christ in the world. We come under attack when we live an exemplary life that bears the fruit of the Spirit. Combat often discourages us and causes us to fear and compromise our walk with Christ. We must not fear or compromise—we have victory in Jesus! He defeated the forces of the Enemy on the Cross and by His resurrection.

Like Jehoshaphat, we have been promised victory. Therefore we ought to begin every day with praise to our Lord. We must sing His praises daily. Worship reminds us of our victory. Worship reminds us of how powerful our Lord is. Worship sets an ambush for the Enemy. Sing to the King today!

EVENING

Thank You, Lord, for the victory over sin and the forces of the Enemy. Your victory keeps me singing. May I always have an awareness of Your greatness. Amen.

Father, help me to remember that You are the One in whom I should trust daily. Help me to praise You all day, for it reminds me of Your eternal faithfulness. Amen.

While I live I will praise the LORD; I will sing praises to my God while I have my being. Do not put your trust in princes, nor in a son of man, in whom there is no help.
PSALM 146:2, 3

raise is an essential part of the Christian life. It is something we are to practice despite our circumstances, because we have a secure, eternal inheritance and a promise that everything we experience in life works for our benefit (Romans 8:28). Thus, we praise! God is worthy of all our adoration. We express it with our voices—singing to Him and sharing His praise with others so they may also know His greatness. We express it with our actions—a life lived in obedience to the Lord is a life of worship.

One of the few constants in life is that every possession we have will be gone or left behind someday. People we are close to will leave earth, and some will disappoint us. We know this, but we often still trust in people more than we trust in the Lord. The One who is worthy of our complete trust is the Lord God. He never changes. "Jesus Christ is the same yesterday, today, and forever" (Hebrews 13:8). His plans are always best. His purposes are the most vital. His love is unchanging. He will never leave us or let us down. When we praise Him, we are constantly reminded of His faithfulness. Praise fuels faith.

A figure of speech used to express admiration for people is "singing their praises." It is appropriate to encourage one another, but the One whose praises we are to sing is our worthy and great God.

EVENING
Lord, I will praise You all the days of my life. I put my trust in You—not in the people and things You created, but in You, Lord God. May my praise fuel my faith. In Jesus' name, Amen.

Week 23, Wednesday

Lord, You made me. You have given me purpose. May praise to You always be on my lips. No matter what my circumstances are, may I glorify You through praise. In the name of Jesus, my Savior, Amen.

Let them praise the name of the LORD, for He commanded and they were created. He also established them forever and ever; He made a decree which shall not pass away.
PSALM 148:5, 6

Every created being has the responsibility to praise our Creator, the Lord God. At the command of His creative word, we came into being, and our purpose is to worship Him. Even inanimate objects praise God by fulfilling their created purpose, thus revealing God. The Book of Romans teaches that God reveals His existence to humanity through creation. The result is that everyone is without excuse; no one can say, "God, I didn't know You existed." Creation has declared His glory. When the Lord Jesus arrived in Jerusalem riding on a donkey, people praised Him. The religious leaders didn't like it and demanded that Jesus stop the people from praising Him. Jesus answered, "I tell you that if these should keep silent, the stones would immediately cry out" (Luke 19:40).

The psalmist said that all of creation is to praise the Lord. All of God's elect angels praise Him (Psalm 148:1). The sun, moon, and stars praise Him (v. 3). These celestial creations of God glorify Him by producing their light. Throughout the psalm, all created things are described as producers of praise.

We, as redeemed people, have more reason to praise God than any other created beings, even the angels of heaven. We are the recipients of His grace. He has established us forever. And after this life is over, we will experience an eternity with God that cannot be fathomed by the finite mind. We have every reason to praise Him, so take joy in praising Him today and every day!

EVENING
Heavenly Father, I praise You for giving me a place to lay my head tonight and for the assurance of knowing that You watch over me. Thank You for giving me life and for every good thing You've graciously given me. Amen.

Lord, help me to praise You when I'm at church as well as when I'm going about daily life. Remind me every day that I was made to worship You. Amen.

Praise the LORD! Praise God in His sanctuary; praise Him in His mighty firmament! Praise Him for His mighty acts; praise Him according to His excellent greatness . . . Let everything that has breath praise the LORD. Praise the LORD!
PSALM 150:1, 2, 6

One of the simplest yet most profound truths we need to grasp is that we were made to worship, so we will always worship something. If we don't worship the one true God, we will find a false god. Idolatry comes in a variety of forms, but essentially it is worshiping anyone or anything other than the one true God. The Lord God is the only One worthy of genuine worship. To worship Him is an extremely high purpose, and a meaningful and satisfying one. Many people don't experience life to the fullest and consequently sense a missing component in life. This emptiness is caused by the absence of a worthy object of worship, and the only way to fill it is through the salvation Christ accomplishes and the new life of worship He enables.

The redeemed know the joy of worshiping God daily. We praise Him with our lips. We give Him credit for all that is good in us. We live obediently to His Word so we can worship Him with our lives. We reflect on God's mighty acts, and that motivates our worship. We remember His powerful deeds that are recorded in Scripture and can still be seen in our own lives, primarily in the miracle of justification. Then we praise Him because He is great. There is nothing on this earth or in this vast universe greater than the Lord God. He is superior to all! Therefore we praise Him, and it is fulfilling to do so.

If you feel that something is missing in your life, consider the possibility that it might be regular worship of the Lord. Start today. Praise Him all day!

EVENING
Father, may Your mighty deeds always be on my mind. I want to praise You always, because You are always worthy of praise. Lord, You are great, and I want You to be the object of my worship always. Amen.

MIKE ORR, CHIPLEY, FL

Week 23, Friday

Lord, I pray that I will have a deep sense of Your work of grace in my life today. Give me an awareness of Your presence. You are my God and King. May I praise You with my whole being. In Jesus' name, Amen.

I will praise You, O LORD, with my whole heart; I will tell of all Your marvelous works.
I will be glad and rejoice in You; I will sing praise to Your name, O Most High.
PSALM 9:1, 2

The psalmist's desire to praise the Lord with his whole heart is based on two things: the works of God and the Person of Christ. David had seen the power of God displayed when God delivered him, as well as Israel, multiple times. Ultimately, God's work of salvation was His greatest work of deliverance for David, as it is in our case.

We must worship with sincerity—with our "whole heart." I fear there is too much mere ritualism involved in the Christian life today. Worship is to be a product of our relationship with God. We have fellowship with Him, the God of all creation. Those of us who are saved have an eternal inheritance. What a privilege! Understanding that privilege should result in an explosion of praise to the Lord! When that happens, we don't go through the motions of worship; we live a life of worship.

If we aren't alert, we will fall into a trap laid by the Enemy called "a sense of entitlement." We can begin to believe that we are entitled to every good thing we experience, or can imagine experiencing. If things don't work out for us as we hope, we react with anger and self-pity.

The fact is, we deserve eternal punishment, but by God's grace, He has given us eternal life. We should always be aware of God's work of grace. Then we can give sincere praise to God. Instead of focusing on ourselves, we will rejoice in God and spend our energy praising Him and telling others about Him.

EVENING

Father, I want to end today with the same thing I've been doing all day: praising You. Thank You for saving me and sanctifying me. You are worthy of all worship. Amen.

MORNING

Lord, may Your praise forever be on my lips despite my circumstances. May my life invite others to worship You. Amen.

I will bless the LORD at all times; His praise shall continually be in my mouth.
My soul shall make its boast in the LORD; the humble shall hear of it and be glad.
Oh, magnify the LORD with me, and let us exalt His name together.
PSALM 34:1–3

There are people in our world who have almost everything humanity seeks after. They have possessions, the latest gadgets, nice houses, and anything else money can buy. Also, many have positions of power. Power enables them to maintain a certain status and to be recognized by people. Having a say in other people's lives gives them fulfillment. but it never lasts. As a matter of fact, having fame and fortune hasn't brought true stability or satisfaction to their lives. A struggle continually brews within them. There is something missing, but they can't quite put their finger on what it is.

We know what it is. It is redemption; it is a relationship with Creator God. Some folks who "have it all" would trade it all to experience real joy, peace, and fulfillment. Those things are only possible through the abundant life provided by the Lord Jesus.

The psalmist proclaims that he will praise the Lord at all times. Genuine worship is not dependent on a person's circumstances, but on a person's position in Christ. As recipients of salvation, we are to be full of praise because we know who owns us and controls us. We are to boast in the fact that our great God guides, delivers, provides, heals, and fulfills a master plan through us. Worship becomes a witness. Others observe a lifestyle that continually honors God and sings His praises, and it makes them glad. It reveals hope and promises to them.

Today we battle over church worship styles and often think if we secularize our singing and praise time, we will be more attractive to the seeking lost world. On the contrary, continual and genuine praise directed toward God has an effect on others. It invites them to worship God. May we practice such continual praise so that others are invited to have a relationship with God and worship Him.

EVENING
Thank You, Lord, that I belong to You. I know You're in control. Amen.

MIKE ORR, CHIPLEY, FL

Heavenly Father, I know that You have not forsaken me, but sometimes the battles of this world get me down. That's not my desire. As I begin this week, I want others to see me praise You even on the darkest days. You are certainly worthy, so I commit to praising You today. Please help me honor my commitment to prioritize praise. Amen.

> *My praise shall be of You in the great assembly; I will pay My vows*
> *before those who fear Him. The poor shall eat and be satisfied;*
> *those who seek Him will praise the LORD. Let your heart live forever!*
> PSALM 22:25, 26

When was the last time you praised God "in the great assembly"? In other words, when was the last time you praised Him publicly? Public praise and worship is a vital characteristic of the devoted Christ-follower. While our faith is personal, it was never intended to be private.

The psalmist not only chose to praise God publicly, but he also chose to praise God in spite of what he was facing. Perhaps you have let the circumstances of life keep you from praising God. Be careful. Praise and worship must never be circumstantial. We must determine to praise Him regardless of what each day brings. Praise should never be a response to what we experience, but *who* we've experienced. If we truly seek Him, we will praise Him.

King David could not have given a more dire depiction of circumstances. In fact, the words he used in Psalm 22 refer to the Passion narrative of our Lord. He describes a dark and depressing day. Yet as this chapter comes to an end, the tone turns from private pain to public praise.

Praise always changes your outlook. There is resurrection power in praise. It revives the heart and gives new life to the darkest of days. Are the circumstances of this day getting you down? Is your heart heavy with the burdens of life? Start this week by giving God an offering of praise. Find your satisfaction in Him. It will do your heart good!

EVENING
Jesus, thank You for enduring the Cross so I might know that You "feel my pain." Thank You for rising from the grave so I might experience resurrection power. Thank You for the opportunities to praise You today. My heart lives forever in You! Amen.

Week 24, Tuesday

Jesus, I praise You today! For what You've done, I praise You. For who You are, I praise You. Please use my life today to encourage others to praise Your name. You are worthy and I am grateful. In the wonderful name of Jesus I pray. Amen.

> *Let the peoples praise You, O God; let all the peoples praise You. Then the earth shall yield her increase; God, our own God, shall bless us. God shall bless us, and all the ends of the earth shall fear Him.*
> PSALM 67:5–7

Y ou have probably heard that statement before, "You are blessed to be a blessing," but have you ever really stopped to think about it? How can our blessings from God become blessings for others?

God deeply desires your praise. In fact, more than anything else, God wants you to give glory to Him. You and everything you see exists to bring glory to God. But that's not the end. God knows that when you praise Him, others see you, and ultimately they see Him. As you praise Him, He will bless you. But you must never forget that when God blesses you, He is doing so with the intent of prompting all the earth to worship Him. God has blessed you with life, eternal life, and in many cases, abundant life, for one primary reason: so that you might be a blessing. Your praise is part of God's plan for making Himself known to His world. In other words, praise is a central component of missional living.

When God blesses you, make the most of His gift—be a blessing. Today, thank Him for His many blessings, and praise Him simply for who He is. Let God use your praise to draw others to Him today.

EVENING

Father, thank You again for Your many blessings in my life, and thank You for the opportunities I have had to be a blessing today. May Your praise continually be in my life and on my lips, so that this world might see You in me. In Jesus' name, Amen.

PAUL PURVIS, FORSYTH, MO

Good morning, Lord. This is the day You have made, so I will rejoice and be glad in it! Give me faith today to trust what I do not see. I want to praise You no matter what comes my way. I look forward to joining heaven and earth in praising You in Jesus' name. Amen.

> *Let heaven and earth praise Him, the seas and everything that moves in them. For God will save Zion and build the cities of Judah, that they may dwell there and possess it. Also, the descendants of His servants shall inherit it, and those who love His name shall dwell in it.*
> PSALM 69:34–36

D o you ever take time to praise God for what He is going to do in your life? It's easy to offer prayers of thanksgiving and praise when things are going great, but it's a whole different matter to praise Him in the storms. Are you facing a financial, relational, emotional, or spiritual storm? Have you given Him praise?

"I'll praise You in this storm and I will lift my hands, for You are who You are no matter where I am."[9] These words written by Mark Hall could have been written by King David as he concluded Psalm 69. After crying out to God in desperation, he found hope in his present situation based on his confidence in God's future provision. That is faith-based praise! Praise should never be based solely on what God has already done. We must also praise God for who He is and for what He is going to do.

In order to be full of faith in your praise, you must learn to rest in assurance of who God is. When you accept that God is who He is "no matter where you are," you will willingly join heaven and earth in praising Him for what He will do.

Determine to worship God today, no matter where you are. Then, reap the benefits of praise as you dwell in the place He has prepared for you.

EVENING

Thank You, Father, for the gift of this day. You demonstrated Your faithfulness in everything I faced. I praise You in advance for what You will do tomorrow. You are great and worthy of my praise. It is a privilege for me to join heaven and earth in praising Your name. Amen.

Heavenly Father, as I begin this day, I do so with Your praise on my lips. Help me also to praise You with my life. Help me avoid the temptation of making this day all about me. I desire to live this day for You. Thank You in advance for what You are going to do in and through me today. Amen.

Know that the LORD, He is God; it is He who has made us, and not we ourselves; we are His people and the sheep of His pasture. Enter into His gates with thanksgiving, and into His courts with praise. Be thankful to Him, and bless His name.

PSALM 100:3, 4

All of life is all about God! It's usually at this point in the week that we begin to lose focus. Fight the temptation! Don't get sidetracked by your problems, your burdens, or your temptations. It's not about you; it really is all about Him. As today's passage says, "He is God"! When you remember that core spiritual truth, it should relieve a great deal of stress in your life. Why? And how?

You didn't get yourself into this—He is your Maker. You don't have to get yourself out—you are one of His people. Think about these words: "We are His." When children declare that something is "theirs," we usually think they are being possessive and perhaps selfish. When God declares that you are His, He is being possessive in a righteous way. God cares about you so much that He made you His own.

What does this mean? It means that your life must look different from those who are not His. It means you should serve Him with gladness, thanks, and praise! When you do these things, everyone around you sees that you are His, and they begin to see it's all about Him. When you don't act like someone who belongs to Him, He grieves and wants you to return to Him.

God desires your attention, and He deserves it, too. Remember who He is, praise Him with your life, and be faithful to Him.

EVENING

Jesus, thank You for another day of life. I realize it is You who made me and gave me the gift of another day. Thank You for making me Yours. Help me to find my rest in You tonight. I give You thanks. Amen.

Week 24, Friday

Good morning, Jesus. Thank You for this moment. I am grateful that I can begin this day giving You praise. I recognize today is unique. I will only have one opportunity to live for You this day. Please help me make the most of it. Help me hear Your voice as I seek to honor You. Amen.

Oh come, let us worship and bow down; let us kneel before the LORD our Maker. For He is our God, and we are the people of His pasture, and the sheep of His hand.
PSALM 95:6, 7

By nature, we tend to procrastinate; we think that tomorrow would be a good time to do whatever we need to do. Consequently, we miss out on many of the blessings we would have received if we had heard His voice *today*.

God's Word consistently challenges us to take advantage of today. Exodus 32:29 says, "Consecrate yourselves today to the Lord that He may bestow on you a blessing." Deuteronomy 30:15, 16 says, "See, I have set before you today life and good, death and evil, in that I command you today to love the Lord your God, to walk in His ways, and to keep His commandments." God's Word makes it clear that He desires our worshipful obedience today. Why are we so hesitant to give God our total, heartfelt worship? Could it be that we have hardened and rebellious hearts? We battle the same problems His followers have fought for centuries. That's why Christ-followers must regularly hear and respond to the call of the psalmist to worship God today!

Now is always the right time to bow your head and bend your knee in reverence to your Maker. Do not harden your heart. Take advantage of this moment and give God your worship. He is worthy of your praise today!

EVENING

Timeless God, thank You for *this* day. My prayer has been that I would redeem the time You've given me. Thank You for giving me Your grace both when I succeed and when I fail. As I prepare to spend another night in Your hands, I recognize You as my Maker. If You give me another day to honor You, grant me a tender and responsive heart to know and do Your will. I love You *today* and forever. Amen.

MORNING

Heavenly Father, thank You for the week You have given me. You are an awesome God, worthy of my attention. Help me honor You in these closing days of the week. Please continue to give me opportunities to worship You sincerely, both privately and publicly. I look forward to my times with You. Amen.

The hour is coming, and now is, when the true worshipers will worship the
Father in spirit and truth; for the Father is seeking such to worship Him.
God is Spirit, and those who worship Him must worship in spirit and truth.
JOHN 4:23, 24

Are you a true worshiper? Jesus clearly stated that the Father seeks true worshipers. If God Himself is seeking worshipers, we had better understand what He wants! Worship has been defined in many ways: "to honor or give reverence," "to regard with great or extravagant respect," "to practice the presence of God," "to bring pleasure to God," and "to celebrate God's worth" are just a few.

Jesus, however, characterized worship with these words: "spirit and truth." What did He mean? Our tendency is to make worship all about a particular time and place, but Jesus said that those things are not what define worship. Tony Evans wrote, "If you limit worship to where you are, the minute you leave that place, you will leave your attitude of worship behind like a crumpled-up church bulletin."[10] Evans' words line up with what Jesus explained in today's passage: true worship is spiritual. It takes place when you are real with God—when deep in your spirit, you are truthful to God about who you are.

We make worship a show, but to God, worship is demonstrated by our sincerity. Worship takes place when you surrender who you are to who God is. Your heart connects to God's heart and you experience true communion.

Worship Him in spirit and truth this weekend!

EVENING

Good evening, Lord. As this week draws to a close, I lay myself bare before You. All that I am, I surrender. All to You I freely give. I want to be Your true worshiper. Take my life as an offering of worship to You. May You find pleasure in my attitudes and actions, and may others see You in me. I pray all this in Your name. Amen.

PAUL PURVIS, FORSYTH, MO

 *Week 25, Monday*

Father, I praise You that I do not have to face this day alone because I have the promise of Your presence. I am grateful that You care for me and You know all that awaits me. I ask You to speak to me today and guide me in Your ways. In Jesus' name. Amen.

> *Give to the LORD, O families of the peoples, give to the LORD glory*
> *and strength. Give to the LORD the glory due His name; bring an offering,*
> *and come before Him. Oh, worship the LORD in the beauty of holiness!*
> 1 CHRONICLES 16:28, 29

———————————— ⌇ ————————————

In 1 Chronicles 16 the ark of the covenant was finally home in Jerusalem. Three chapters earlier in 1 Chronicles 13, we read that the ark was placed in the home of Obed-Edom for three months, and "the Lord blessed the house of Obed-Edom and all that he had" (v. 14). Upon hearing the news, David made a second—and successful—attempt to bring the ark to Jerusalem. Why did David want the ark in Jerusalem? Because he knew that having the ark meant having the presence of the Lord, and the presence of the Lord meant security and victory. This understanding caused David to erupt into a psalm of thanks to God for His presence among His people.

Friend, what was true for Obed-Edom, Jerusalem, and David is now a reality for all who belong to Christ. Each one of us is a temple of the living God (2 Corinthians 6:16). His presence resides not just around us, but in us. What does that mean? It means that every promise that God offers to the believer is available to us! In every struggle or challenge you face today, remember that you have God's presence right there with you and He will see you through (Proverbs 3:5, 6). May this truth create in you, as it did in David, a psalm of thanks to our great God!

———————————— ⌇ ————————————

EVENING

Lord, thank You for the work You are doing in my life. I realize I do not always see where You are working or what You are doing. However, I know You love me and You desire what is best for me. I love You and I bless Your name. In Jesus' name. Amen.

Week 25, Tuesday

Father, You are a faithful God and I will praise You. I need Your strength and Your presence desperately as I face this fallen world. May You guide my steps and comfort and guard my heart with Your truth. In Jesus' name. Amen.

> *Then Job arose, tore his robe, and shaved his head;*
> *and he fell to the ground and worshiped. And he said:*
> *"Naked I came from my mother's womb, and naked shall I return there. The LORD*
> *gave, and the LORD has taken away; blessed be the name of the LORD."*
> JOB 1:20, 21

Pain is something that none of us want but all of us get. One of Webster's definitions for *pain* is simply "a nuisance." But the important—and difficult—question is: "What do we do when it comes?" Our answer should be, "PRAISE!" What? Even on paper it is a challenging, even disturbing, thought. And that is exactly what we see in today's passage. "The Lord gave, and the Lord has taken away; blessed be the name of the Lord," says Job. He lost his children and wealth in one day and his response was, "Praise the name of the LORD." Job further demonstrated this kind of response when he said, "Though He slay me, yet will I trust Him" (Job 13:15).

There are times in life when there are no words, no explanations, no understanding, and no visible way out. Reason cannot help, past experiences offer no advice, and even prayer brings no comfort. Only one option remains: you must put your life into the hands of God and trust Him. You must turn your full attention to God! Allow your confidence to be in His promises and His faithfulness. Know that the One who saved you is faithful (Hebrews 10:23), and praise Him!

EVENING

Lord, I acknowledge my need for You. You are my hope and my salvation. I am nothing without You, my Creator. I praise You for another day of life. May Your peace and Your truth guard my mind and heart as I rest tonight. In Jesus' name. Amen.

CHRIS DIXON, DUBLIN, GA

Father, this morning I praise You, for You are my salvation. Apart from Your grace I have no hope. You have erased my debt, and You have met my greatest need. Today, help me to trust You with all that I am because You are faithful. In Jesus' name, Amen.

> *In that day you will say: "O Lord, I will praise You; though You were*
> *angry with me, Your anger is turned away, and You comfort me.*
> *Behold, God is my salvation, I will trust and not be afraid; 'For Yah,*
> *the Lord, is my strength and song; He also has become my salvation.'"*
>
> ISAIAH 12:1, 2

I magine with me someone who is burdened by a crushing weight of debt. He tries everything he can think of, but every attempt fails. There are too many mortgages and too many liens against him. He continually goes deeper and deeper into debt and faces failure. It is only a matter of time before he loses everything. Then, one morning, he discovers that he is the sole beneficiary of the last will and testament of a billionaire who has died, making him the heir and inheritor of all the billionaire owned. Who wouldn't want to be the person in this story?

This is precisely what has happened to us! We are the spiritual heirs of the Lord Jesus Christ, who died for our sins, leaving us, in His last will and testament, every spiritual blessing. Our massive debt of sin and our spiritual bankruptcy are gone!

Never, ever get over what Jesus Christ has done for you. We owed a debt we could not pay; He paid a debt He did not owe. May that truth always stir in us the same response to God found in today's passage: "O Lord, I will praise You"!

EVENING

God, I praise You that I can rest my head tonight in perfect peace because You have saved me. My life has been changed by the power of Your Cross. I praise You, my Lord. Amen.

MORNING

Lord, thank You for providing salvation through Jesus Christ and for pursuing me when I did not deserve to be pursued. Give me the courage to share the great work You have done in my life. In Jesus' name, Amen.

[God has] predestined us to adoption as sons by Jesus Christ to Himself, according to the good pleasure of His will, to the praise of the glory of His grace, by which He made us accepted in the Beloved. In Him we have redemption through His blood, the forgiveness of sins, according to the riches of His grace.
EPHESIANS 1:5–7

Did you catch Paul's central theme in these verses? GRACE! Grace is unmerited favor. It is getting something we don't deserve. I want to give you some bad news, some worse news, some good news, and the best news. The bad news is we are all sinners in need of a Savior. The worse news is there is nothing we can do to save ourselves. The good news is we don't have to do anything to get this salvation. The best news is, Jesus has done it all for us, and all we have to do is accept it. That is grace. No strings are attached. We can do nothing to earn it; it is a gift (Ephesians 2:8). Grace is the unconditional favor of God to an undeserving sinner.

Many people want to spell salvation D-O. They think there are things you must do to be saved, such as joining a church and helping the poor. Others want to spell salvation D-O-N-T. They believe if you don't do certain things, like murdering, lying, and stealing, you will be saved. But God's way of spelling salvation is D-O-N-E. You are saved by grace through faith in the work of Christ.

What a tragedy it would be if God had revealed Himself to be a God of infinite power, infallible wisdom, and inflexible holiness, and yet a God empty of compassion for a lost and ruined world. How we should praise Him for His compassion toward us and for the riches of His grace!

EVENING

Father, create in me a heart that longs for You. You are my salvation, and my hope is found in You. May I wake up in the morning with a deep desire to meet with You. Amen.

CHRIS DIXON, DUBLIN, GA

Father, I surrender every moment of this day to You. Help me to see each and every opportunity to worship You in word and deed. All that I am and all that I have is Yours to use. May Your Spirit direct each step I take and help me to respond in obedience. I pray all this in the name of Jesus, my Savior. Amen.

By Him let us continually offer the sacrifice of praise to God, that is,
the fruit of our lips, giving thanks to His name. But do not forget to
do good and to share, for with such sacrifices God is well pleased.
HEBREWS 13:15, 16

Matt Redman wrote a wonderful song titled, "The Heart of Worship." Here is the chorus: "I'm coming back to the heart of worship, and it's all about You. It's all about You, Jesus. I'm sorry, Lord, for the thing I've made it, when it's all about You. It's all about You, Jesus."[11] What is the heart of worship? The answer is one simple word: surrender.

The writer of Hebrews challenges us to "offer the sacrifice of praise to God." If you know anything about a sacrifice, you know that it represents surrender. Once you put a sacrifice on the altar, you lose total control of it and you never get it back. The heart of worship, then, is found in surrender. When you surrender your time, your talents, your treasures, and your testimony, that offering of surrender is an act of worship.

L. B. Cowman, a former missionary and author of *Streams in the Desert*, wrote, "Life is not wreckage to be saved out of the world but an investment to be used in the world."[12] Make your life useful in bringing glory to God by surrendering to Him and living with a worshipful heart.

EVENING

God, create in me a heart of worship. Help me to be sensitive to Your Spirit and always be willing to respond in obedience. Thank You for the awesome privilege of serving the King of kings and Lord of lords. May my life sing praises to You. In Jesus' name, Amen.

Father, I come to You with a grateful heart this morning. Thank You for the grace and mercy You have shown in my life. May my lips give testimony to Your goodness and faithfulness! May my time with You this morning create in me a new song for all to hear. In Jesus' name I pray. Amen.

> *Praise the LORD with the harp; make melody to Him with an instrument of ten strings. Sing to Him a new song; play skillfully with a shout of joy. For the word of the LORD is right, and all His work is done in truth.*
> PSALM 33:2–4

On November 27, 1994, God started a new work and put a new song in Chris Dixon. That is the day that Jesus Christ became Lord of my life. I love the last phrase of today's verse: "All His work is done in truth." His plans are always right. What a wonderful promise! No matter what the problems or circumstances of life may be, I must realize that it has first passed through God's faithful plan before it gets to me. The Bible teaches in Philippians 1:6 that "He who began a good work in you will complete it until the day of Jesus Christ." Because of this, even when the noise and distractions of this world seem to drown out the song that God has placed in my heart, I can still sing—not because of the pain or hardship, but because I know that God is faithful and He will bring good out of it (Romans 8:28).

L. B. Cowman[13] wrote about keeping faith in God during hardship:

Don't let the song go out of your life.
Although it sometimes will flow in a minor strain,
It will blend again with the major tone you know.
Although shadows rise to obscure life's skies, and hide for a time the sun,
The sooner they'll lift and reveal the rift, if you let the melody run.

God is always working out what is best; all He does is true, good, and faithful to His promises. Praise the Lord in every way in every season!

Father, I pray that I will never let songs of faith and praise to You be absent from my life. Keep me clean and close to You. In Jesus' name, Amen.

CHRIS DIXON, DUBLIN, GA

Week 26, Monday

Father, as I begin the day that You have made, help me to rejoice in You, my Maker, my Redeemer, my Lord, and my King. You have blessed me; let me seek to bless others today. As I encounter those who are hurting and despondent, let me speak a word of encouragement to them. May they leave my presence having been blessed by the Holy Spirit that abides in my heart. Make me sensitive to each opportunity You bring so others may experience Your life-changing touch in their lives. In Jesus' name, Amen.

> *I will make you a great nation; I will bless you and make your name great;*
> *and you shall be a blessing. I will bless those who bless you, and I will curse*
> *him who curses you; and in you all the families of the earth shall be blessed.*
> GENESIS 12:2, 3

Abraham received a special call from God to separate himself from the life he had known and to follow God. God promised to bless Abraham and make him a blessing to others if he obeyed.

All of us want God to bless our lives and to make our lives bless others. The difficulty that most people have is understanding the precepts that predicate those blessings. Just as Abraham followed God's commands and went where God told him to go in order to receive blessings, so must we.

Blessings from God come as we seek to obey Him with our lives. The truth is that most of us want the blessings to come before the obedience. We say, "Lord, if You will bless me, then I will tithe." God says, "Tithe, and then see if I won't open up the windows of heaven" (see Malachi 3:10). Remember that obedience precedes blessings in all spiritual matters.

EVENING

Lord, I thank You that You spoke into my life today, guided me with Your loving hand, and allowed me to serve You with my time and talents. I am blessed to know that You love me and have a plan for my life. In that plan, let me bless others in the name of Jesus. Amen.

MORNING

Father, Your grace is beyond my ability to comprehend, much less articulate. For me to start my day with the deep, settled security that You have forgiven me of so much brings tears of gratitude to my eyes. Search my heart and reveal to me anything for which I need to extend forgiveness, for I have been forgiven of so much. Show me the ways I have wronged others. Let my earthly relationships convey how much I want to be right with You. In Jesus' name, Amen.

> *Blessed is he whose transgression is forgiven, whose sin is covered. Blessed is the man to whom the LORD does not impute iniquity, and in whose spirit there is no deceit.*
> PSALM 32:1, 2

D o you remember the last time that you and someone else honestly dealt with personal differences and restoration occurred? Do you remember the wonderful feeling of being released from guilt and bitterness? Harboring the pride that kept you in bondage was a horrible experience, wasn't it? Afterwards you probably asked yourself, "Why did I wait so long to make this right?"

It is amazing that we have to learn that lesson over and over again! When we refuse to deal with our sin and let it linger in our lives, that sin creates a painful emotion of guilt. We, in our proud human nature, would rather carry that around than admit our sin before God, forsake it, and receive His forgiveness, which is His eternal covering and gift of righteousness. Yet the Lord says we are "blessed" when we do. What a tremendous blessing it is to have God's joy in our lives as He takes away the guilt, exchanges our sin for His righteousness, and promises never to hold it against us ever again! Hallelujah, what a Savior!

We will find true happiness only when we continually experience God's joy in our lives. That joy will be like a well of living water, springing up in our lives as we seek to be clean with our family, friends, and Savior.

EVENING

Heavenly Father, let me not sleep tonight until I have done my best to refresh all my earthly relationships, beginning with my family. May I extend and receive forgiveness with everyone who may need it. I want my life to be clean and pure before You every day. Wash me, purge me, cleanse me. Amen.

MIKE WHITSON, INDIAN TRAIL, NC

Week 26, Wednesday

Father, what a blessing and joy it is to wake up with the assurance in my heart that I am Yours, You are mine, and we will be together for all of time and eternity. I am overwhelmed that while I was a sinner, You died for me. I am eternally grateful that my soul has been saved by Your grace and that I am part of Your divine family. What a blessing You are! Amen.

> *Blessed is the nation whose God is the LORD, the people He has chosen as His own inheritance. The LORD looks from heaven; He sees all the sons of men.*
> PSALM 33:12, 13

Isn't it fun to read church bulletin bloopers? Outdoor church signs may also contain some humorous announcements. You may have seen the funny caption that says, "I am their leader! Which way did they go?" I wonder if Yahweh God may be asking that of America today. For decades, this nation that was founded on Christian principles stayed true to the Word of God and looked to it as her guide for decision making. To a great degree, Americans are blessed with the pleasures and freedoms of a great land as a result of this heritage of honoring and depending on God. Leaders proclaimed their trust in God. Citizens cherished their religious freedoms. Laws protected those rights.

Is Yahweh still America's God today? Has He been replaced with cheap substitutes that will never bring the joy He promises? Could it be that success is our god? Has money become our priority? Pleasure seems to be the driving force of many lives. Has an inordinate preoccupation with sex perverted God's wonderful plan for us? Often the desire for power and fame obscures the Light of the World.

"Which way did we go?" Consider the way you are going today. Choose obedience, and pray that God will help others do the same.

EVENING
Father, You insist that if we as Your people would humble ourselves, seek Your face, and turn from our wicked ways that we would once again experience the joy of basking in the blessing of having You as our God. Please restore to our nation the joy that comes only when people surrender to You as King. May revival begin in my heart and spread to others. I ask this, and all my prayers, in Jesus' name. Amen.

Father, it is with great expectation that I begin my new day with You. As I make my way through the hours ahead, I ask that You would make me sensitive to each opportunity You bring, so I might be a blessing to others. I trust Your promises. Your Word is true, and I cherish the dependability of Your name. Amen.

> *Blessed is he who considers the poor; the LORD will deliver him in time of trouble. The LORD will preserve him and keep him alive, and he will be blessed on the earth; You will not deliver him to the will of his enemies.*
> PSALM 41:1, 2

If anyone ever knew that God is faithful to deliver the poor, David did. This passage speaks of someone who has slipped or let things go. David went through a time in his life when he turned away from the Lord and slipped in his walk with Him. But God didn't leave him to wander aimlessly in that spiritual condition. He opened David's eyes to see what horrible things he had done.

David wrote this psalm from a spiritually-restored position and knew full well what it was like to be astray and then receive forgiveness and restoration to a fruitful life. David said that God's people will be blessed when they have mercy on those who may not be on track spiritually. The fact is, if we want to be delivered in our times of trouble and experience the stabilizing hand of the Lord when we are struggling, then we must extend that same mercy to others along life's way.

Join God in His work of delivering the poor in spirit, and remember that He blesses us when we extend His lovingkindness to others in His name.

EVENING

Lord, You have been so merciful to me. When I have slipped and missed the mark, You have been faithful to forgive me and restore me to a right relationship with You. Help me never miss an occasion to be used by You to help restore someone to a life of faith, not simply to gain Your favor and blessings, but to help that person experience Your forgiveness and cleansing. In Jesus' name I pray. Amen.

Week 26, Friday

Heavenly Father, would You empower me to walk according to Your Word and not according to the world today? I confess that Your ways are so much better than any substitute. Please don't let me be allured by the cheap imitations of this life. I have tasted of Your goodness and nothing compares to Your abiding presence in my life. I am truly blessed, and I give You thanks in Jesus' name. Amen.

Blessed are the undefiled in the way, who walk in the law of the LORD!
Blessed are those who keep His testimonies, who seek Him with the whole heart!
PSALM 119:1, 2

A young man in his late twenties was recently arrested for drug possession. His older brother, a faithful servant of Christ, spoke to him while he was in jail about the importance of turning to Christ. This drug-addicted, incarcerated young man replied, "That is a waste of time." His brother asked, "What have your recent choices brought you? Are you happy with your life?" Somewhere along the way, this young man became confused, and then he became defiled as he turned to drugs to make him happy.

True happiness has its roots in the joy produced by the Holy Spirit, who indwells believers after they are saved by grace. Notice that this passage from Psalms says that we will be blessed, or happy, as a result of keeping the commands of God's Word. In other words, we can be happy about seeking to be more like Christ as He is revealed through the living Word of God.

It was fun to watch my grandchildren learn to walk. For a while, I thought they would be permanently damaged from repeatedly falling down and getting up . . . until one day, they walked! You may stumble and fall again and again, but one day you will learn to walk by faith according to God's Word. And guess what? God promises that when you do, you will be blessed!

EVENING

Father, thank You for allowing me to walk in Your Spirit today. Thank You for giving me the strength to reject the world's cheap imitations of Your joy and happiness. May Your Word always be my source of guidance. In Christ's name I pray. Amen.

MORNING

Dear heavenly Father, I am Your child, and You are my Father. With Your help, I will seek to live according to Your Word today. I pray that Your Word will be a lamp unto my feet and a light unto my path. As You make the way clear, enable me to walk in it. I pray this in Jesus' name. Amen.

> *Blessed is every one who fears the LORD, who walks in His ways. When you eat the labor of your hands, you shall be happy, and it shall be well with you.*
> PSALM 128:1, 2

A locomotive is most effective and efficient as it moves within the boundaries of the tracks on which it was created to run. When that powerful engine jumps the tracks and moves outside the realm for which it was intended, it bogs down, mires up, and ceases to function as a locomotive.

We were created by God to live within the guidelines of His holy Word. As we do so, we have the promise that we will be blessed. Unfortunately, we forget sometimes that happiness can only be discovered within those parameters. So we turn to other things, like people, money, drugs, sex, and other synthetic sources. But true happiness cannot be experienced apart from God and His plan for our lives. His promise is that blessings will come to those who fear Him and that we can enjoy the fruit of our labor when we've walked in His ways. He will supply all your needs according to His glory by Christ Jesus. Praise God that as you submit to Him in every area of your life, "it shall be well with you"!

EVENING

Father, Your Word is so clear as it tells me how I should live. Forgive me for departing from the guidelines that You have set for my life. I have experienced Your love and blessing from living my life in obedience to You. I have never been happier than when I trust You and obey Your will for me. Thank You for Your blessings. In Jesus' name, Amen.

MIKE WHITSON, INDIAN TRAIL, NC

Father, as I step into this new week, help me understand how to live a life that will reflect who You are to others. I want to be a blessing to others, and yet I don't always know how to do that. Help me to depend on You as I do the things You have taught me to do. Lord, help me to believe You in every circumstance of life. You alone are my sufficiency. I pray this in the name of my Lord and Savior, Jesus Christ. Amen.

Jesus said to him, "Thomas, because you have seen Me, you have believed. Blessed are those who have not seen and yet have believed."

JOHN 20:29

We have all heard the phrase "seeing is believing." However, Jesus reverses the order: "Blessed are those who have not seen and yet have believed." Most of us have probably thought about what it would be like to see Christ—to touch Him, hear Him teach, and ask Him questions. Like Thomas, we sometimes long for His physical presence. The truth is, while we cannot experience Jesus' physical presence right now, He is always with us. He has given us the Holy Spirit to be with us always.

Everything we need in order to believe, serve, and live for Jesus we have in His Spirit and His Word. Our responsibility is to believe and obey. If we are not acting on what we know, then we should not claim to believe. James exhorted believers to be not only hearers of the Word, but also doers of the Word. He said that if we don't do what we know is right, then we sin (James 1:22–25). Today, ask yourself this question: "Based on the way I live my life, do I really believe Him?"

EVENING

Father, today I have thought about what I say I believe and how I live my life. I pray that You will continually mold and shape me into the person that You desire for me to be. I want to bless others, but I understand that will happen only as I conform to Your image. Thank You for a good day, and thank You for giving me all I need to serve You. In Jesus' name, Amen.

MORNING

Father, help me live with sensitivity to Your Spirit and to the people I will meet today. Prepare me to be a blessing, whether physical, emotional, or spiritual. Please help me live according to the power of Your Spirit, and keep my focus on You and on Your desire to use me for Your glory. In Jesus' name I humbly pray. Amen.

> *I have shown you in every way, by laboring like this, that you*
> *must support the weak. And remember the words of the Lord Jesus,*
> *that He said, "It is more blessed to give than to receive." And when he*
> *had said these things, he knelt down and prayed with them all.*
> ACTS 20:35, 36

We live in a world that is all about getting and not much about giving. Unfortunately this is almost as true for the Christian church as it is for the secular world. Today we are told that most believers give about 2.5 percent of their income to kingdom causes. Let that sink in for just a moment. This lack of compassion would be foreign to the early church. The apostle Paul worked as a tentmaker in order to support the weak and become an example to others in matters of compassion.

Jesus' statement that "it is more blessed to give than to receive" is not recorded in the gospels, but it must have been well known to the early believers. Certainly the larger body of Scripture teaches the importance of having a compassionate heart and a commitment to bless others. Maybe there is no other area in life that is as revealing about our commitment to Christ as our bank accounts. How is your heart in this area? Would you say you are growing in the area of compassion? Or have you been caught in the snare of selfishness? Become a blessing by learning to give with a heart of gratitude.

EVENING

God, You have given me so much. When I look at the world around me and see the poverty of so many, I am at a loss for words. Please help me to grow a heart of compassion for the world and to give that which You have entrusted to me. I am thankful for every blessing of life, and I want to become a blessing to other people. In Jesus' name. Amen.

RICK WHITE, FRANKLIN, TN

Week 27, Wednesday

Lord, today I want to trust You with all my needs. I find myself saying that I will trust You for all eternity, but my struggle seems to be in trusting You for daily provisions. Help me to take You at Your word, do what You want me to do, and receive from Your hand all that I need for life. Thank You for Your love and provision. In Jesus' name. Amen.

> *"Bring all the tithes into the storehouse, that there may be food in My house, and try Me now in this," says the LORD of hosts, "If I will not open for you the windows of heaven and pour out for you such blessing that there will not be room enough to receive it."*
>
> MALACHI 3:10

In God We Trust appears on our currency, but do we actually believe that? In our passage for today, the Lord says that we are to "try" Him to supply the needs of our lives. Why is it that we can trust Him with our souls for all eternity, something our finite minds cannot grasp, yet we have so much trouble trusting Him to provide for our daily needs? If we are to please God and become a blessing to others, it will only happen as we learn to trust God in every area of life, including our finances.

When we return a tithe to the Lord, we are acknowledging His lordship in our lives. We are declaring that everything we have comes from His hand and that we are simply stewards of His provisions. God desires to bless us in every area of life, and yet when we fail to trust Him with the tithe, we are basically saying that He is not trustworthy to take care of us. This is not a theology of "health and wealth," but rather of love and obedience. Don't miss out on the blessings of God. Try Him and trust Him in this area of your life. He wants to bless you so that you can be a blessing.

EVENING

Father, thank You for meeting all my needs. Help me to always remember to trust You in all things. Help me to be a better steward of all that You give me. I want to be faithful in returning Your tithe and generous with all that You entrust to me. In Jesus' name, Amen.

Week 27, Thursday

Father, help me guard my speech today so that what I say only builds up others and never tears them down. I realize the power of words for both good and evil, and I want to use my words only for good. Help me to listen before I speak and to make sure that my speech is in line with Your instructions. In Jesus' name, Amen.

> *The lips of the righteous feed many, but fools die for lack of wisdom.*
> *The blessing of the LORD makes one rich, and He adds no sorrow with it.*
> PROVERBS 10:21, 22

It has been estimated that the average person speaks about thirty thousand words a day. That is a lot of talking! Have you ever thought about how much of what we say is actually remembered by others? Or have you ever considered the power and influence of our words?

The Bible says that the lips of the righteous actually serve people in a positive way. We have all been the recipients of encouraging words and of hurtful words. When we speak with wisdom (which means knowing how to apply God's Word to life), we help, build up, and encourage people; we feed them. When we do not speak with wisdom, we either tear them down or just contribute to the noise of life.

How many times have you heard a celebrity giving advice and counsel to the masses through the media without any qualifications whatsoever? Talking has become a big business in American entertainment. There is a little children's song that says, "Be careful little tongue what you say, for the Father up above is looking down in love." That is great guidance for everyone, regardless of age. Ask God for wisdom to speak the truth in love.

EVENING

Lord, would You bring to my mind the words I have spoken today and how they impacted others? Show me how I could have said something differently that would have helped someone in a positive way. Forgive me for speaking words that are not pleasing to You and hurtful to others. Let the words of my mouth and the meditations of my heart be acceptable in Your sight. Amen.

RICK WHITE, FRANKLIN, TN

Week 27, Friday

Father, thank You for saving me through Your Son, Jesus Christ. Thank You for making me part of the body of Christ. I am grateful that today I am part of Your church. Help me bless others in the body. Remind me that I am not on this spiritual journey alone. I am one member of the body, and each member is important to the others. Help me to respect and bless all my brothers and sisters in Christ and keep me from being a stumbling block to any. In the name of Jesus, Amen.

I speak as to wise men; judge for yourselves what I say. The cup of blessing which we bless, is it not the communion of the blood of Christ? The bread which we break, is it not the communion of the body of Christ? For we, though many, are one bread and one body; for we all partake of that one bread.
1 CORINTHIANS 10:15–17

Jesus says that when we come to the Lord's Supper, we are to remember what He has done for us. Remembering is a powerful thing when we do it right. When we eat the bread and drink the cup, we remember His life, death, burial, resurrection, and the promise of His coming again. But we also need to remember something else: we are not doing life solo. We are part of the body, which involves both privileges and responsibilities.

None of us would intentionally hurt our physical bodies. How foolish it would be in a moment of rage to direct that anger at any part of our body. We all know from experience that when there is pain in one part of the body, the whole body has to endure it. Yet so many times we are careless in our attitudes and actions in Christ's body. The next time you eat the bread and drink the cup, let the practice serve as a reminder to be a blessing to the body of Christ.

EVENING

Lord, help me always to bless Your body. I do not want to do anything that would bring my brothers and sisters in Christ pain or embarrassment. Every time I come to Your table, help me to remember Your body that was given for me and for Your body, the church. May we be salt and light to the world. In Jesus' name. Amen.

MORNING

Father, today as I go about my day, help me to remember all the blessings that are mine in Christ. When I am tempted to whine or feel sorry for myself because of adverse circumstances, remind me of all that I have in Christ. Make me a blessing to those around me because of Your presence in me. Thank You for loving me and purchasing my redemption through the blood of Your Son, Jesus. In Christ's name, Amen.

> *Blessed be the God and Father of our Lord Jesus Christ, who has blessed us with every spiritual blessing in the heavenly places in Christ, just as He chose us in Him before the foundation of the world, that we should be holy and without blame before Him in love.*
>
> EPHESIANS 1:3, 4

Blessed be the God and Father of our Lord Jesus Christ! This is our instruction to give Him praise, to speak well of Him for all He has done for us. God alone is worthy of our praise and worship. All that we have is because we are "in Christ." This phrase or its equivalent occurs twelve times in Ephesians. It is a reminder of our unity with Christ and with each other. We are a blessed people simply because we are in Christ.

We are declared justified; we have no condemnation because of our sin. We have been set free in Jesus. We have eternal life and the promise of a resurrected body. We are adopted sons and daughters, and we are His workmanship. The list goes on and on! Maybe you will have time this weekend to take your Bible and just begin to search for all the spiritual blessings that we have in Christ. All of these are blessings in the heavenly places—what a great reminder that this is not our final destination. We have an eternal home in heaven. Don't be discouraged when pressures and temptations show up at your doorstep. He has started a work in you He will finish. You are a blessed person, so bless His name today!

EVENING

God, I honor Your name. You alone are worthy of worship, praise, and glory. You have given me a spiritual inheritance in heavenly places. It is my desire to bless You with my whole heart. Make my life count for Your purpose and for Your glory. In Jesus' name. Amen.

RICK WHITE, FRANKLIN, TN

Week 28, Monday

Father, You are a giving God. You have blessed me with every spiritual blessing in the heavenly places in Christ. Graciously strengthen me to believe all You have said and the promises You have made. In Jesus' name I pray. Amen.

When God made a promise to Abraham, because He could swear by no one greater, He swore by Himself, saying, "Surely blessing I will bless you, and multiplying I will multiply you." And so, after he had patiently endured, he obtained the promise.
HEBREWS 6:13–15

The Bible is saturated with promises of blessings to those who trust God. The writer of Hebrews provides an apt illustration of God blessing a man who trusted Him, then causing that man to become a conduit of blessing for countless others who had faith in Him. God promised Abraham that he would be blessed and become a blessing (Genesis 12:1–3). Abraham believed God, and God delivered on His promise. Abraham fathered Isaac, the child of promise, and through Abraham's lineage, God's children have received the greatest blessing of all, the Lord Jesus Christ.

God loves to bless, and who does not love to be blessed? The key to receiving God's blessings is faith. "Without faith it is impossible to please Him, for he who comes to God must believe that He is, and that He is a rewarder of those who diligently seek Him" (Hebrews 11:6). What promises of God are you depending on today? Do you doubt God will keep His promises? Certainly, God is trustworthy. His very character is truth, and He cannot lie (Hebrews 6:18). The question is not whether God will bless you, but rather, do you trust God for the blessing?

You will bring God the glory He deserves by not only placing faith in Him and receiving His blessing, but also by imitating Him in blessing others. God blessed Abraham so he could bless us. God will bless you so you can bless others. How will you be a conduit of God's blessing today?

EVENING

"Blessed be the Lord, who daily loads us with benefits, the God of our salvation!" (Psalm 68:19). Thank You, Father, for Your multiplied blessings, and most of all, for salvation. Make me a blessing to others, especially to those who do not know You. Prepare me to tell boldly of Your promise to save anyone who will believe. Amen.

Father, thank You for the Bible You have given me. Your words are life to me. Make me now Your instrument so You may impart life and blessing to those You bring into my life today. Amen.

No man can tame the tongue. It is an unruly evil, full of deadly poison. With it we bless our God and Father, and with it we curse men, who have been made in the similitude of God. Out of the same mouth proceed blessing and cursing. My brethren, these things ought not to be so.

JAMES 3:8–10

Words of encouragement are priceless: "You can do it!" "You are a winner." "Great job!" Words of blessing are powerful. Regrettably, out of the same mouth that blesses can come words of cursing. This is an incredible inconsistency for a believer. James lamented that in one breath we can worship God, and in the next, curse the apple of His eye. James must have had in mind all harsh, cutting, slanderous, hurtful, unedifying, or wicked words. He said to believers, "These things ought not to be so."

One sure way of becoming a blessing is allowing God to control our tongues. We cannot overvalue the blessing of godly speech at all times. "A word fitly spoken is like apples of gold in settings of silver" (Proverbs 25:11). Conversely, we must not undervalue the damage harsh words bring. Contrary to old clichés, words do hurt—often deeply.

The heart controls the mouth and tongue (Luke 6:45). Our tongues are unruly, and frankly, we cannot tame them ourselves (James 3:8). People can tame tigers, dolphins, and falcons, but God must tame our tongues by transforming our hearts. The words we speak reveal our hearts, especially when we are under pressure. A change of heart is needed when our words of blessing are waning. Heart transformation begins with confession and repentance. It is followed by obedience to God's Word. Confess and remove unedifying words from your vocabulary regularly. Replace those words with blessings. Today, bless as many people as possible with your words. We have been blessed by our Lord's words, so let us in return be a blessing for His glory.

EVENING
"Let the words of my mouth and the meditation of my heart be acceptable in Your sight, O LORD, my strength and my Redeemer" (Psalm 19:14). Amen.

SCOTT YIRKA, FLEMING ISLAND, FL

Father, Your love is everlasting and unchanging. You loved me first, and You love me perfectly. I love You. May I be a blessing to others today by showing Your love in tangible ways. In Jesus' name, Amen.

Blessings are on the head of the righteous, but violence covers the mouth of the wicked.
The memory of the righteous is blessed, but the name of the wicked will rot.
PROVERBS 10:6, 7

The righteous can give and gain. Solomon wisely pointed out that the one who gives blessings receives blessings. What a beautiful picture he painted: blessings are on the head of the righteous like a crown forever. The blessings the righteous receive are eternal. In other words, it is impossible for you to be a blessing to someone without being blessed with eternal rewards. Nothing you give for the kingdom's sake is ever lost.

While the righteous can give and gain, the wicked may gain for a time, but will eventually suffer loss. The opposite of blessing is taking. Today's passage says the wicked take from others through deception, covering the mouth (v. 6). The wicked will do whatever it takes to gain. Instead of encouraging, they will flatter people, defraud them, and be quick to point out their flaws for selfish gain. They seek to fulfill their own desires instead of others' needs. They will be forgotten, and so will their rewards that appeared to be blessings but instead were only temporary trifles. Their names will rot.

Desiring to be a blessing involves a desire to give whatever is needed. The gift may be a word of encouragement, a note of appreciation, a visit, or some of your time. The blessing may be a material gift or money to meet a need. Our God is a giver. He is the Giver of givers! His name is most blessed, and when we bless others, we imitate our Lord.

EVENING
Father, thank You for Your gifts. Open my eyes to see the ways You want to give through me to others. Make me a blessing regardless of the cost or sacrifice. Deepen my desire to be a blessing for the glory of Your Son and the furtherance of Your kingdom. Amen.

MORNING

Father, You have made it clear that the way to life is Christ. The way to live is Christ. Teach me today to live as Christ lived. I desire to deny myself, take my cross, and follow You in the way You lead and command. Amen.

> *Blessed are the poor in spirit, for theirs is the kingdom of heaven.*
> *Blessed are those who mourn, for they shall be comforted.*
> *Blessed are the meek, for they shall inherit the earth.*
> MATTHEW 5:3–5

In relation to the world, the Christian life is truly upside down. Jesus said that people who are spiritually poor, mournful, and meek are blessed. The word *blessed* could be translated "happy," but our idea of happiness does not go far enough to communicate accurately the blessedness of which Jesus spoke. Our happiness is often based on our circumstances; here Jesus is saying we can be truly happy in unhappy conditions. Christians' blessedness is not based on their subjective feelings, but on God's objective truth. So Jesus is saying the truly blessed are those who understand their spiritual bankruptcy.

These are the first three of eight kingdom beatitudes Jesus taught that surpass the world's attitude toward a happy life and seem paradoxical. But kingdom living is not only blessed living; it is the only right way to live. The world in which we live applauds personal accomplishment, lauds a self-made person, and expects personal ambition to be the driving force toward success. Today's passage says that God blesses people who are driven to Christ because of their spiritual emptiness (v. 3), comforts those who grieve over their sinfulness (v. 4), and raises to greatness people who humbly kneel before Him (v. 5). Don't be a worldly person who errantly pursues happiness through self-exaltation, self-expression, and selfish pleasures. Be a kingdom-minded Christian who exalts Christ, expresses His character, and then experiences joy and blessing as a result.

EVENING

Lord, thank You for the gospel. I know that I was spiritually bankrupt and still would be apart from Christ. I can sleep tonight knowing that You are my righteousness. I am right before You only because You made me right when You saved me and became my Lord. In Jesus' name, Amen.

SCOTT YIRKA, FLEMING ISLAND, FL

God, You are pure and cannot look upon wickedness. Thank You for purifying me with Your blood so that You can look upon me, and one day I will be able to look upon You. Amen.

Blessed are those who hunger and thirst for righteousness,
for they shall be filled. Blessed are the merciful, for they shall
obtain mercy. Blessed are the pure in heart, for they shall see God.
MATTHEW 5:6–8

Becoming a blessing involves becoming more and more like the source of all blessings, Jesus. Becoming like Jesus begins with salvation. Don't miss this step. These beatitudes are inward attitudes only present in a person in whom Jesus is present. If you are not saved, trying to apply these attitudes to your life will not bring blessing, but frustration. Why? Because one of the main points of Jesus' sermon is that we will always fall short of His standards until we receive Him. He teaches these principles not to prompt us to be reformed, but instead to help us realize our need to be transformed by Him. The beatitudes are believers' internal characteristics, not external religious additions. Have you believed on Jesus to save you? If not, pray now to accept Jesus as your Lord and Savior and to receive the gift of eternal life.

Once you are saved, you will desire the thing you never wanted before—a vibrant relationship with God. Today's passage says you will hunger after Him (v. 6) and want to see Him (v. 8). You will desire the true God and not the idol you imagined He was in your heart before you came to truly know Him. This is a blessing. You will desire God more than anything else. Becoming like Jesus is a blessing to you and to others. Our righteous living, mercy extended to others, absence of selfish agendas, and purity of heart are blessings to those around us. Are you beginning to see more clearly how being blessed makes you a blessing to others?

EVENING

Father, You are shaping and forming my heart. Thank You that You are sanctifying me and completing what You started. Make me recognize Your tender hands on the hardened parts of my heart so I can be thankful for Your purifying work in me. I pray this in Jesus' name. Amen.

MORNING

Father, You have been teaching me the importance of becoming a blessing. Open my eyes to truth today so I may be a blessing even to those who are rebels and enemies of Christ. Amen.

> *Blessed are the peacemakers, for they shall be called sons of God.*
> *Blessed are those who are persecuted for righteousness' sake,*
> *for theirs is the kingdom of heaven. Blessed are you when they revile*
> *and persecute you, and say all kinds of evil against you falsely for My sake.*
> MATTHEW 5:9–11

God loves peace, and He is willing to make peace with His enemies. Paul wrote that the Father reconciled "all things to Himself" through Christ, "having made peace through the blood of His cross" (Colossians 1:20). It took the greatest sacrifice imaginable for God to make peace with His enemies. Who were His enemies? We were. Romans 5:1 says, "We have peace with God through our Lord Jesus Christ." Still not convinced we were enemies of God before salvation? Romans 5:10 says, "If when we were enemies we were reconciled to God through the death of His Son, much more, having been reconciled, we shall be saved by His life." We were the enemies of God while we were in our rebellious state of sin. How did God treat us? He treated us with grace and mercy.

We are told that as Christians we will be persecuted. It is not if, but when and how much. Some of our brothers and sisters are suffering greatly for the cause of Christ, but all of us will suffer some. How can we become a blessing to our enemies when we are persecuted for righteousness' sake? How did God treat us when we were His enemies?

Being a blessing is not always easy. It may cost us more than we expect. Being a blessing to those we love is a joyous thought. What about becoming a blessing to those who hate us, revile us, and even persecute us with all kinds of evil? Our Lord demonstrated this final beatitude repeatedly. It is possibly the one beatitude that will carry the greatest witness. Becoming a blessing is for His glory, even among the enemies of Christ.

EVENING

Father, thank You for making peace with me when I was in bondage to sin and Your adversary. I pray this in the name of Christ. Amen.

SCOTT YIRKA, FLEMING ISLAND, FL

Week 29, Monday

Lord, thank You for giving me another day of life. Help me never take for granted the blessings of receiving salvation and having a personal relationship with You. You are a great God! I desire to finish my course and live in such a way that brings You glory. I love You and surrender my will to Yours today. In Jesus' name I pray. Amen.

Seek the LORD while He may be found, call upon Him while He is near.
ISAIAH 55:6

———————

This verse gives an invitation as well as a warning. Today is the day of grace, and everyone is welcome to call upon the Lord. But at some point in the future, the day of grace will be over and God's invitation to know Him will be gone. The opportunity to seek the Lord will not last forever.

What is involved in "seeking the Lord"? For one thing, it means admitting that we are sinners and that we have offended a holy God. It means agreeing with God about the wrongness of our sin, turning away from sin, and turning to the Lord. We must submit to God in faith and believe His promise to pardon us. Repentance and faith go together (see Acts 20:21).

Do not delay in your quest to seek the Lord. The phrase "while He is near" suggests that if we do not take His invitation seriously now, we could lose the opportunity to do so—it could expire while we are delaying. In the parable of the Great Supper, God closed the door on those who spurned His invitation (Luke 14:16–24). Paul wrote, "Behold, now is the accepted time; behold, now is the day of salvation" (2 Corinthians 6:2). Solomon taught that only fools disregard God because His ways are greater than their own (Proverbs 1:20–33).

Do not wait too long. Do not wait until your heart becomes hard and insensitive to the convictions of God's Spirit. God's warning is clear, and it is directed to the entire human race: "Do not wait until it is too late!"

———————

EVENING

Dear Jesus, thank You for calling me to Yourself. You have loved me when I didn't love You in return. May the desire of my heart always be to seek more of You until I see You in the flesh. Thank You for Your Word. Amen.

MORNING

God, thank You for allowing me the privilege to wake up and talk to You. I never want to take Your love for granted. I desire to be teachable and to allow You to change the way I live. Please show me Your face today, and help me to show Your face to others in my words and actions. Help me to be "Jesus with skin on" to everyone I meet. I give You my devotion and praise. I love You so much! In Jesus' name I pray. Amen.

You will keep him in perfect peace, whose mind is stayed on You, because he trusts in You. Trust in the LORD forever, for in YAH, the LORD, is everlasting strength.
ISAIAH 26:3, 4

What does it mean to have perfect peace? Only those who have a personal relationship with Jesus Christ can know it. *Shalom*, the Hebrew word for "peace," means much more than "a cessation of war." It includes blessings such as wholeness, health, quietness of soul, preservation, and completeness. The peace God gives helps one to have a quiet, restful soul and a sense of purpose, contentment, fulfillment, and completion. It delivers a person through all the conflicts, strife, divisions, trials, and temptations of this life. God's peace brings the assurance of present and future security.

Today's scripture says that the way to receive this peace is by keeping our thoughts focused on the Lord. I confess that sometimes I find myself with everything but perfect peace because I have run from the Lord instead of running to Him. Many times I run ahead of Him, and every time I do, I forfeit the peace that comes when I walk with Him. The old hymn "Wonderful Peace" says it best: "Peace, peace, wonderful peace, coming down from the Father above! Sweep over my spirit forever, I pray, in fathomless billows of love!"

EVENING

Lord, thank You for giving me Your peace that passes all understanding. I would be utterly lost without it. May I always be conscious of Your love and grace toward me. Amen.

Week 29, Wednesday

Dear Father, give me the ability to love people with Your love and to treat people the way I want to be treated. May I seek peace and righteousness in all that I do and say. God, help me to turn away from evil and interact peacefully with every person I come in contact with today. In Jesus' name, Amen.

> *Who is the man who desires life, and loves many days, that he*
> *may see good? Keep your tongue from evil, and your lips from speaking*
> *deceit. Depart from evil and do good; seek peace and pursue it.*
>
> PSALM 34:12–14

To love life means to desire a full life, and the only way to live a full life is to know the Author of life, Jesus Christ (see John 10:10). This kind of life has little to do with possessions, status, or fame; instead, it has a lot to do with character, faith, and a desire to honor the Lord. People who live this way seek the Lord and want nothing less than His will for their lives. Solomon had wealth, knowledge, fame, and power, yet he found himself hating life (Ecclesiastes 2:17–20). His experience exposes the emptiness of living for the things of the world.

Departing from evil means being willing to abandon sin once and for all, and to do good. God desires for us to be peacemakers, not troublemakers. Christians do not seek peace at any cost, for peace depends on purity (James 3:17), but Christians do make every effort not to make enemies. Today's passage says we must "pursue" peace, which means we have to work at it every day with the help of God.

I have learned that if you live solely to make others rejoice in God, you will face challenges and take risks, but your joy will be full. Life isn't about finding a way to keep from getting wounded; it's about finding a way to keep it from being wasted.

EVENING

Lord Jesus, help me to turn away from evil, do good, and pursue peace. May I always walk in Your grace. Plant me and use me as a godly resource in this world. I love You! Amen.

MORNING

Precious Jesus, there are times I feel so overwhelmed by the pressures of life. Your patience and love for me during those times are so real. Help me never forget the pain, heartache, and discontentment that are associated with the absence of Your peace in my life. I surrender my well-being and my life to You today. With a grateful heart, I praise You for who You are. In Jesus' name I pray. Amen.

The LORD bless you and keep you; the LORD make His face shine upon you, and be gracious to you; the LORD lift up His countenance upon you, and give you peace.
NUMBERS 6:24–26

As I write this devotion, I am facing the second year of my life without my earthly dad. I can honestly say that without the peace and presence of God, I would not have made it. But not only have I made it, I have done so with incredible peace and hope. The question is often asked, "How do people make it without God?" Well, they don't! They just survive . . . and hope the next day is better than the present day.

Although I still miss my father's physical presence, it is so encouraging to me to know that my heavenly Father desires to bless me. God enjoys blessing and encouraging His people. This prayer in Numbers can be thought of as the Lord's Prayer of the Old Testament (see Matthew 6:9–13). The priests were told how to pray for God's blessing on the people in the same way that Jesus instructed the disciples to pray for God's blessing in their lives.

The Lord's blessings are numerous in this prayer: He provides our food, shelter, clothing, and health. He promises us protection and that His face will always shine upon us. He gives us His grace, His attention, His pleasure, and His peace. Praise God for giving us His presence and His blessings every day!

EVENING

God, as I come to the close of another day, help me to recognize Your presence and sufficiency in my life. I am so content in knowing that Your grace and peace are enough. Thank You that I will have Your peace as I awake in the morning. May I never allow anything to come between Your Word and me, for Jesus' sake. Amen.

TIM ANDERSON, ATHENS, AL

Week 29, Friday

Dear Jesus, thank You for awakening me this morning and calling me to Yourself and Your Word. Spending time with You in prayer and in Your Word is so important to me as I begin my day. Every morning that I see Your face through Your Word, I receive Your peace. But every morning that I go my own way, I forfeit Your peace as a result of my own selfish plans. Forgive me and help me walk with You today. Amen.

Peace I leave with you, My peace I give to you; not as the world gives do I give to you. Let not your heart be troubled, neither let it be afraid.
JOHN 14:27

It's hard to imagine the heartache the disciples were feeling when they heard Jesus say these words. The Son of God, who had loved, taught, and lived with them, was about to leave them. He was less than twenty-four hours away from the Cross, yet He was comforting others. Jesus said He would give them His peace. This is the same peace that kept Him calm in the face of mockery, scorn, hatred, betrayal, and death. Likewise, it is the only peace that will get us through the difficulties of life.

We all know too well the pain associated with false peace and false hope. God says there is no peace for the wicked (Isaiah 48:22). The world bases its peace on its resources, while God's peace is based on our relationship with Him. To be right with God means to enjoy the peace of God.

Jesus told His disciples that He overcame two of their great spiritual enemies: the world and the devil. Neither Satan nor the world can trouble our hearts if we are yielded to the peace of God through the Holy Spirit. For me, the greatest peace imaginable is the peace of intimacy with God. It is the peace of the highest good. It is the peace that settles the mind, strengthens the will, and establishes the heart.

EVENING

Father, thank You for Your presence and peace in my life today. Please guard my mind as I sleep and give me a fresh view of Your grace and peace tomorrow. In Jesus' name. Amen.

Dear Jesus, it is such a blessing to know that I am fighting *from* victory and not *for* victory. Thank You for the blessing of knowing that today my victory doesn't depend on me; it has already been won through the death, burial, and resurrection of Your dear Son, Jesus Christ. Please guard my mind and thoughts today. Keep me sensitive to the things that I need to pray for. Warm my heart to spread Your Word with passion. I desperately desire to represent Your heart to the people You have entrusted me with on this earth. I love You! Amen.

"These things I have spoken to you, that in Me you may have peace. In the world you will have tribulation; but be of good cheer, I have overcome the world."
JOHN 16:33

———

This passage is the culmination of Jesus' Upper Room Discourse. It's important to notice that "in Jesus" there is peace, but "in the world" there is tribulation. Someone once defined peace as "possessing adequate resources." In Jesus, we have everything; in ourselves we have nothing. When Jesus tells us to "be of good cheer," He is literally saying, "Cheer up." We have cheer in Jesus' mercy, grace, forgiveness, power, and presence. Just like children finding security when they are with their parents, we can find strength and peace when we are with our Abba Father.

All of us are either *overcoming* or *being overcome*. A common view of the Christian life is that it involves deliverance *from* trouble, but Jesus came to deliver us *in* trouble, which is very different. Jesus says that we, as children of God, will still face troubles and that we should not be surprised when they come. But He does not give us an overcoming life; He gives us life as we overcome.

———

EVENING

Dear Jesus, thank You for giving me Your peace today. I am overwhelmed to know that You love me and desire an intimate relationship with me. The psalmist said You never sleep nor slumber, so please watch over me during my much-needed rest. Awaken me with a renewed spirit that is eager to share Your Word with Your people. Thank You for saving me and keeping me. Amen.

TIM ANDERSON, ATHENS, AL

Week 30, Monday

Lord, grant me the power to enjoy life today in Your peace. I want to begin this day surrendering every wayward thought to You. Fill my mind with thoughts that please You. In Jesus' name I pray. Amen.

Those who live according to the flesh set their minds on the things of the flesh, but those who live according to the Spirit, the things of the Spirit. For to be carnally minded is death, but to be spiritually minded is life and peace.
ROMANS 8:5, 6

A big part of professional sports is trash-talking! The goal of trash-talking is not actually focused on what one player is saying to another. The words are just tools. The players are engaging in mind games for the purpose of influence. They hope to get inside other players' heads so their opponents' performance will be adversely affected by these perfectly timed and newly planted thoughts.

In daily life, however, our thought lives are not a game; our thoughts dictate the way we live, and the results of low-level thinking can be deadly. Paul wrote in today's passage, "To be carnally minded is death."

There are basically two ways of living. One way is to take the low road, thinking and living like the unbelieving world. Such a life is dominated by selfish thought patterns rooted in a choice to live a sinful lifestyle. One writer correctly noted that to determine to think and live like the world is "spiritual suicide."

However, an opposite lifestyle offers an opposite result. It is the high road, which involves living with the mind focused on the Spirit of almighty God. Our lives and thought patterns are all about control. A person who lives "according to the Spirit" is the person whose life is controlled by the Spirit. The results of this high-road thinking are different from low-road thinking only because of the power of the One who holds the controls. He is the Lord God! Paul said, "To be spiritually minded is life and peace." When God holds your life in His hands, when you choose high-road thinking, the result is real life and lasting peace.

EVENING
Father, help me to surrender my life and mind to You so that I may enjoy Your peace. Amen.

Father, I pray to You in the name of Jesus. He is my peace. Help me to live this day with a grateful heart for the peace that I have with You through the sacrifice of Jesus on the Cross. Give me compassion and boldness so I will share this peace with the people I encounter throughout my day. May my life bless Your name! Amen.

> *Now in Christ Jesus you who once were far off have been brought near*
> *by the blood of Christ. For He Himself is our peace, who has made*
> *both one, and has broken down the middle wall of separation.*
> EPHESIANS 2:13, 14

When we think of *peace* in the context of the Christian life, we often focus on the idea of relief. We want relief from a hectic schedule. We want relief from an enormously painful situation. We want relief from a tumultuous relationship or a restless spirit or all of the noise in our lives.

For the follower of Christ, peace is much more than enjoying a calm day after a stormy night—although those restful moments are important. Rather, peace *with* God (not just the peace *of* God) is the real meaning of peace in the Christian life. Here's the amazing part about possessing peace with God: no one is born with it, but God has done everything necessary to make it happen. What has He done? He has given us Jesus. Jesus is all we need for real, lasting peace. Here's the picture. We were distant from God because of our sin—so distant that we were all called "enemies of God." Sin has stained us all and separated us from God and made it impossible for us to reconcile ourselves to God. But God changed all of that.

Jesus Christ is our peace. I hope you caught that as you read those two verses from Ephesians. When we experience God's salvation by grace through faith, we are transformed from enemies of God into His children. The hostility is gone, and we will always enjoy peace.

EVENING
Lord, thank You for Your peace. In Jesus' name, Amen.

TIM DOWDY, McDONOUGH, GA

Thank You, Father, for being my God! Empower me to live each moment of this day in absolute surrender to You. You own my life, and I am grateful. Fill me with Your Holy Spirit and use me for Your glory. Give me great passion for You and compassion for Your people. May my life and work be pleasing in Your eyes! In Jesus' name, Amen.

> *I, therefore, the prisoner of the Lord, beseech you to walk worthy*
> *of the calling with which you were called, with all lowliness and*
> *gentleness, with longsuffering, bearing with one another in love,*
> *endeavoring to keep the unity of the Spirit in the bond of peace.*
>
> EPHESIANS 4:1–3

We wouldn't ordinarily consider it a good thing to be a prisoner, but in truth, believers are prisoners every day. And that is a good thing. We belong to Jesus! He is our Savior and our Master, so we serve Him. Paul encouraged believers to live in a way that reflects the character and life of our Master. This kind of life includes enjoying the "bond of peace" with other believers. Though we cannot create this kind of peace, we can live in a way that promotes it.

What does it take to enjoy this kind of unity? Paul gave us a great list of required virtues in Ephesians 4:1–3. Ironically, the first characteristic on the list may be the hardest for all of us: humility. This kind of spirit has been shunned by the world, but it is to be embraced by the believer. The next virtue is a gentle spirit. We all should be giants in gentleness. Third, we are to extend patience to one another. Again, it's not easy, but it is necessary. Last on Paul's list is indeed the greatest: love. We must be consumed with love for God and for others if we are to share the bond of peace with fellow believers. In an age when everyone is choosing sides, let's choose to live like our Savior, be united in our spirits, and honor God together as we hold out the gospel to the world.

EVENING

Father, Your love amazes me. Now use Your love in us, Your children, to amaze the world! Amen.

MORNING

Lord, be blessed through every aspect of my life today. Give me the strength and grace to live in unity with other believers so that Your name may be honored through our lives and glorified in this world. In Jesus' name I pray. Amen.

Above all these things put on love, which is the bond of perfection. And let the peace of God rule in your hearts, to which also you were called in one body; and be thankful.
COLOSSIANS 3:14, 15

⁕

I am not sure how many times I sat in a classroom listening to a teacher assigning homework and realizing I did not know how to do the assignment. There is a difference between knowing what to do and knowing how to do it. When it comes to living in unity, Paul gives us the *what* and the *how* in today's passage. The *what* is to "let the peace of God rule in your hearts" (v. 15). The *how* is found in the preceding verse, where we are instructed to "put on love, which is the bond of perfection" (v. 14). God's love is the key to letting God's peace rule, and God's peace brings us together in unity.

What does that kind of love—God's love—look like? The answer is found in the great Love Chapter of 1 Corinthians 13. Perhaps you will find this description of love a bit different than any you have read before.

"Love suffers long and is kind; love does not envy; love does not parade itself, is not puffed up; does not behave rudely, does not seek its own, is not provoked, thinks no evil; does not rejoice in iniquity, but rejoices in the truth; bears all things, believes all things, hopes all things, endures all things. Love never fails" (1 Corinthians 13:4–7).

The *what* is "let the peace of Christ rule" and the *how* is to "put on love." When God's love reigns over us, God's peace rules in us.

⁕

EVENING

Father, thank You for this day. Thank You for loving me. I pray that You have been honored through the way I have loved others. Refresh my soul with Your love and fill my heart with Your peace. Help me rest in You. Amen.

TIM DOWDY, MCDONOUGH, GA

Week 30, Friday

Father, thank You for loving me. I pray that You will give me the grace and humility to live at peace with my brothers and sisters in Christ. Lord, set my heart right before You so I can share Your love with Your people. In Christ's name I pray. Amen.

We urge you, brethren, to recognize those who labor among you, and are over you in the Lord and admonish you, and to esteem them very highly in love for their work's sake. Be at peace among yourselves.

1 THESSALONIANS 5:12, 13

I'm not sure where I first heard this little rhyme, but it contains good, practical wisdom: "To live there above, with those we love, that will be heaven's glory. But to live here below, with those we know, now that's another story."

Relationships can be messy. Sometimes we find ourselves in relationships that have taken a wrong turn more often than we would like. In those moments of difficulty, the air gets thick and the tension palpable. It is in those times that relationships feel more like a burden than a blessing. The easiest thing to do is bail out, but if that is your answer to tense situations, your relationships will have short life spans. I hope you will listen to the encouragement of Scripture so your load will be lightened.

The New Testament repeatedly teaches believers to be at peace with one another because sticky moments are simply part of having relationships. How does Scripture help? Foremost, it provides godly wisdom. It also reminds us that we are not the first person to walk down a rocky road. But there is something more to these multiple encouragements for peace. The presence of these instructions assures us peace is possible. Jesus is the Prince of Peace. He brought us reconciliation with a holy God, and He can bring reconciliation in tense relationships with others. Embrace God's encouragement in this passage, and be willing to work toward peace in your relationships in His power.

EVENING

Lord, help me pursue peace. I pray for the compassion to forgive others and the strength to persevere through tough times so You may be glorified in all my relationships. Amen.

God, thank You for Your peace. I am eternally grateful for the peace I have with You through the Cross of Christ, and for the peace I enjoy in this life because of Your presence in me! Continue Your work of grace in me. Do whatever it takes to fashion me into Your image. Be glorified in me! Amen.

> *No chastening seems to be joyful for the present, but painful;*
> *nevertheless, afterward it yields the peaceable fruit of righteousness*
> *to those who have been trained by it . . . Make straight paths for your feet,*
> *so that what is lame may not be dislocated, but rather be healed. Pursue peace*
> *with all people, and holiness, without which no one will see the Lord.*
> HEBREWS 12:11, 13, 14

As a child, there were days when I wished my father had never read these words of Solomon: "He who spares his rod hates his son, but he who loves him disciplines him promptly" (Proverbs 13:24). Ouch! I also never really accepted the authenticity of my father's words when he said, "This is going to hurt me more than it hurts you."

Years later when I became a father, I realized it is more difficult to provide discipline than to receive discipline. Real discipline is rooted in genuine love. That is certainly true with God! Our heavenly Father disciplines us out of compassion for us. In fact, when God disciplines us, it is proof that we are His children.

We dwell on how much discipline *hurts*, but God knows how much it *helps*. In today's passage we are encouraged to endure the discipline of the Lord even though it may be difficult. The reward is a righteous life filled with God's peace. Nothing is sweeter. And through it all we are to "pursue peace with all people, and holiness" (v. 14). Aim to make that an accurate description of the way you live this day.

EVENING

Father, thank You for Your discipline, which continues to mature the fruit of righteousness in my heart. Thank You for the peace I have enjoyed today. May I live every day in Your peace and holiness. In Jesus' name, Amen.

TIM DOWDY, MCDONOUGH, GA

Week 31, Monday

Father in heaven, I praise Your name for being the God of peace. Your Son Jesus is the Prince of Peace. Please help me to be mindful of Your presence and to sow the fruit of righteousness wherever I go today. Guide me with the wisdom of Your Word so my life will reflect the peace that only You can bring into every life. Amen.

The wisdom that is from above is first pure, then peaceable, gentle, willing to yield, full of mercy and good fruits, without partiality and without hypocrisy. Now the fruit of righteousness is sown in peace by those who make peace.
JAMES 3:17, 18

There's a well-known rule in the natural world that helps us understand a spiritual truth: we will always reap what we sow. In other words, there are consequences to every choice we make. We reap wisdom either from the world or from the Word of God. The wisdom of the world only produces trouble, but the wisdom of God's Word produces blessings.

When a tree bears fruit, it shows signs of life and the blessings of God. The fruit contains seeds for more fruit, and those seeds are sown in the ground. James taught that "the fruit of righteousness is sown in peace." As we share God's fruit with others, they are able to eat and receive God's blessing, and as a result, bear fruit themselves.

Your life is all about sowing and reaping. Who you are is how you live, and how you live is what you sow. What you sow determines what you reap. If you live in God's wisdom, you sow the fruit of righteousness, which has seeds of meekness, purity, peace, gentleness, and mercy within. Sow this fruit sincerely and you will reap the peace of God.

EVENING

God, today You have led me by Your Word. Early this morning You reminded me to seek not the wisdom of this world but the wisdom of Your Word. Lord, Your Word is a light unto my path and a lamp unto my feet. It is always there to guide me in the way of peace. Surround me with the peace of Your presence, and may Your wisdom protect my heart and mind. In Jesus' name, Amen.

MORNING

Lord, I come to You with thanksgiving in my heart because I am part of Your family. Help me pursue the kind of life that honors You. Today will be full of choices; may I be mindful that I am a vessel for Your use. Help me to stay empty, clean, and available. Take my life, fill me up, and use me for Your glory today. Amen.

The solid foundation of God stands, having this seal: "The Lord knows those who are His," and, "Let everyone who names the name of Christ depart from iniquity" . . . Flee also youthful lusts; but pursue righteousness, faith, love, peace with those who call on the Lord out of a pure heart.

2 TIMOTHY 2:19, 22

In the first verse of today's passage, we can see several aspects of our salvation in Christ. Our salvation is solid because God's Word will stand forever (Isaiah 40:8). Our salvation is sealed because the Spirit seals us until the day of our deliverance (Ephesians 1:13, 14). Finally, our salvation is shared because we are heirs of God (Romans 8:14–17). Together, believers are the great house of God.

The phrase "depart from iniquity" in verse 19 refers to a time when God warned His people to get away from the rebellious people of Korah (Numbers 16:26). Sin in its purest form, rebellion against God, will divide your heart, your home, and the house of God. Paul admonished believers to flee sin, follow godliness, and fellowship with other believers. They should flee sin, just like God's people fled the rebellious people of Korah, and then pursue righteousness, faith, love, and peace. The word *pursue* means "to chase after in order to catch." Righteousness leads to peace. When you have caught peace, you should stay in fellowship with other believers. Nothing is more damaging to the great house of God than division.

The next time you come close to rebellion, remember Paul's admonition: flee sin, follow godliness, and fellowship with other believers.

EVENING

Heavenly Father, as I close this day I want to say thank You for filling me and using me today. Every day I face new challenges that test me to see if I will be a vessel of honor or dishonor. Thank You for the victory today. Help me to pursue the life that pleases You. In Jesus' holy name, Amen.

RUSTY WOMACK, TUCKER, GA

Week 31, Wednesday

Father in heaven, I praise Your name. Today, help me to have the mind of Christ and remember His example of a godly life. Fill me with the Holy Spirit so I may respond to criticism in a way that pleases You. In Jesus' name, Amen.

Be of the same mind toward one another. Do not set your mind on high things, but associate with the humble. Do not be wise in your own opinion. Repay no one evil for evil. Have regard for good things in the sight of all men. If it is possible, as much as depends on you, live peaceably with all men.
ROMANS 12:16–18

Is the Cross of your Christianity offensive, or is your Christianity offensive to the Cross? There is a difference between sharing in the offense of the Cross and being offensive as a Christian. As we seek to follow Christ, we are going to be criticized. We will have enemies. When Jesus ministered to the least, the last, and the lost, He was criticized. The apostles had opposition everywhere they traveled. Jesus told His followers they could even expect to have enemies in their own family (Matthew 10:36).

Paul taught that believers are to "be of the same mind toward one another," meaning that they ought to live their lives together. It means sharing the burdens and blessings of everyday life, not just exchanging friendly smiles and handshakes at church. If we are not able to get along with each other, how are we going to treat our enemies the right way? We need to be humble like Jesus, willing to share life with ordinary people.

Believers are called to live on a higher plane and not return evil for evil. This higher plane requires love, because naturally we want to fight back. This life of peace requires faith, believing God can right every wrong. Lastly, this life requires hope, knowing that God works all things together for good (Romans 8:28). Reach for the higher plane. Ask God to make your heart like Christ's—humble, loving, and peaceful.

EVENING

Lord, use the seeds of peace I have sown among those I came in contact with today. Bring any offenses to my mind, so I may seek forgiveness and be at peace with You and with everyone in my life. Amen.

Father God, I worship You this morning and give You praise because true peace comes from You. Help me to live in peace with You and with others. If I have any form of rebellion in my heart, reveal it to me. Show me how I can submit to You more. Guide me today. May my life reflect the power of Your glory. You are my eternal peace. Amen.

Let every soul be subject to the governing authorities. For there is no authority except from God, and the authorities that exist are appointed by God. Therefore whoever resists the authority resists the ordinance of God, and those who resist will bring judgment on themselves.

ROMANS 13:1, 2

Peace comes through submission. God has established three institutions where peace will always follow submission: in the home, the church, and the government. Paul wrote to believers at the high point of the Roman Empire. At the time, Rome was not actively persecuting believers for their faith in Christ; however, persecutions were not far off. It was soon to become difficult, if not impossible, to remain loyal to the emperor as a follower of Christ. Believers could not sprinkle incense on the altar and say, "Caesar is god."

Paul encouraged believers to submit to Rome's authority as much as possible because submission leads to peace. This biblical principle can be used in many arenas—at work (employee to employer), at home (spouse to spouse, children to parents), at school (student to teacher), and in faith (believer to Christ). God desires for us to lead a peaceful life. This is why He formed basic institutions in which we will find peace through submission. Whom do you need to submit to today?

EVENING

Lord, as the day draws to a close, I thank You for the authorities You've placed in my life and the opportunities I've had to learn that peace comes through submission. As I rest tonight, help me reflect on Your peace that is available to me when I submit to You. In Jesus' name, Amen.

Week 31, Friday

Father, help me to be mindful of Your presence today. Speak to my heart with wisdom and understanding. You are my strength, and I will lift You up so that others might come to know the saving grace that only You can give. May Your name be praised forever. Amen.

None of us lives to himself, and no one dies to himself. For if we live, we live to the Lord; and if we die, we die to the Lord. Therefore, whether we live or die, we are the Lord's . . . Let us not judge one another anymore, but rather resolve this, not to put a stumbling block or a cause to fall in our brother's way.
ROMANS 14:7, 8, 13

Disagreements among humans, and specifically God's people, are nothing new. The Bible records Israel's wars and family feuds and the early church's conflicts. The Corinthians argued about their leadership and even sued each other! Someone once said, "What amazes me about church is not how many people attend, but that people attend at all." That is so sad, but at times, we might see why others would say that.

Sometimes conflicts happen only because we are looking for something to criticize instead of looking for ways to bless people. Paul gave a clear instruction that would help believers settle disagreements: "Let us not judge one another anymore." When a person judges another, he or she is saying, "I am right and you are wrong." This leads to disagreement. What really matters in life is not who is right and who is wrong, but if we are right with God and right with others. Is there anyone you need to get right with? Have you been a stumbling block to anyone? May our response be obedience to Scripture. Live unto the Lord and commit to not being a stumbling block to anyone.

EVENING

Lord, it seems that disagreements are around every corner. Everybody wants to be right at any price. Unfortunately, the price we all pay is division with each other. Help me lay my pride down and instead take on Your humility that I may be at peace with You and others. May my words always be acceptable to You and peaceful toward others. In Jesus' name, Amen.

God, I praise You for another night's rest. Keep me mindful of Your presence today. In these moments of study and reflection before the day begins, teach me more about the peace I have in You and how I can be a peacemaker in the world. In Jesus' name, Amen.

> *Having been justified by faith, we have peace with God through our*
> *Lord Jesus Christ, through whom also we have access by faith into this*
> *grace in which we stand, and rejoice in hope of the glory of God.*
>
> ROMANS 5:1, 2

Jesus Christ pursued us so that we could have peace with God. The peace He brings is the foundation for the believer's life. Many people don't realize that they will still face the problems of life as God's children. What they should understand is that they will face life's problems with God, and His resources are more than sufficient to meet their needs.

God gives you three solutions to life's problems. First, you have peace with God because of the atoning work of Jesus Christ. Peace solves the problems of the past. Second, God gives you special access to Him through faith. This means you should approach the throne of God in your time of need in order to find grace and mercy. Faith solves the problems in the present. Third, God gives you hope in Christ, You can eagerly look forward to spending eternity in the presence of God, rejoicing "in hope of the glory of God." Hope takes care of your problems in the future.

Trust in God's resources, and let peace, faith, and hope reign in your heart.

EVENING

Lord, thank You for allowing me to walk with You in the light of Your presence. There is no one like You. Your love, Your grace, and Your peace are everlasting. Thank You for surrounding me with Your peace. Guard my heart and my mind from anything that would lead me away from You. I thank You for working in and through me. May I always be a vessel You can use for Your glory. In Jesus' name, Amen.

Lord, thank You for this new day. I praise You because Your mercies are new every morning and Your faithfulness is great. Thank You that You have a wonderful plan for me. I choose to walk by faith and not by sight today. Guide me, Jesus, as I seek You above all else. In Your name, Amen.

The thief does not come except to steal, and to kill, and to destroy. I have come that they may have life, and that they may have it more abundantly.
JOHN 10:10

⟨⟨⟨⟩⟩⟩

Are you living the abundant life? Is your heart filled and overflowing with the Lord's love and joy? Are your days exciting and meaningful? Is there a spring in your step, a song in your heart, and peace in your soul even in the midst of a storm? Sadly, many Christians cannot honestly answer yes to those questions.

But Jesus came to bring us life—abundant life! It is His gift to you and me. He wants us to experience the fullness of the Father's love and the Father's life. Now the devil, that thief, wants to steal it from us. But the devil is a defeated foe, and he can't steal anything from us unless we let him. Are you letting him steal God's abundant life from you?

What would you do if someone barged into your house with a furniture dolly and started to haul off your couch, your refrigerator, your TV, and the rest of your stuff? Would you sit idly by and let him do it? Wouldn't you stop him? Wouldn't you call the cops? Wouldn't you rise up and shout, "No!" Of course you would!

The time to stand up to the devil is now. He's a thief who comes to steal your love, joy, and peace. Stand up and shout, "No!" Jesus has abundant life for you, and it is time to claim that which is yours. Abundant life is not a pipe dream; it is the gift of a good and loving God, and it is yours to enjoy today. Claim it in Jesus' name!

⟨⟨⟨⟩⟩⟩

EVENING

Jesus, today I stood up to the devil and claimed what You came to give me, abundant life. It was wonderful! Help me walk in bold faith with You every day. In Jesus' name, Amen.

Father, although I am one of billions of people in the world, You know me intimately and are always willing to listen to me. The fact that I am special and precious to You is mind-boggling. I want to put You first today and let You shine like the sun through me. You, Lord, are worthy. In Christ's name, Amen.

> *Blessed is the man who walks not in the counsel of the ungodly, nor stands in the path of sinners, nor sits in the seat of the scornful; but his delight is in the law of the LORD, and in His law he meditates day and night. He shall be like a tree planted by the rivers of water, that brings forth its fruit in its season, whose leaf also shall not wither; and whatever he does shall prosper.*
>
> PSALM 1:1–3

If you are like most people, you want a life of stability, prosperity, and blessings. You want to get in on the good things of God, right? But exactly how is that accomplished? God tells us that the key is spending time in His Word. As you delight yourself in God's Word and meditate on His promises and His faithfulness, God does a work inside of you. He changes your attitude and your outlook on life. He fills your heart with hope, regardless of your circumstances. He gives you direction and the power to walk in His ways.

Perhaps you have not been spending much time with God these days. Don't get discouraged. The good news is that you can start today. God is faithful to meet with you every time you humbly open His Book and call upon His name. He wants to teach you the way in which you should go. He wants to bring fruitfulness and prosperity to your life. He is, indeed, a good God who loves you and desires to bless you. Give attention to His Word today, and do what He says. You will be glad you did!

Lord, I thank You for Your Word to guide me and change me. Help me make time every day to read and meditate on Your Word. Thank You that You are faithful to bless me as I do what You say. I choose to obey You, Jesus, because You are God and because You want what is best for me. Amen.

Week 32, Wednesday

Lord, it is a great privilege to know You and talk to You. Thank You for another day to walk with You, the King of the universe. I look forward to knowing You better and loving You more when this day is done. I praise You that You never leave me nor forsake me. Today is going to be a great day because You are the center of my life. In Jesus? name. Amen.

Why do you spend money for what is not bread, and your wages for what does not satisfy? Listen carefully to Me, and eat what is good, and let your soul delight itself in abundance. Incline your ear, and come to Me. Hear, and your soul shall live; and I will make an everlasting covenant with you—the sure mercies of David.
ISAIAH 55:2, 3

As a Pastor, I have talked to lots of broken people who have made bad choices in life. Like Esau, they have traded the priceless for pennies (in his case, it was his priceless birthright that he traded for a bowl of stew). While short-sighted choices are always pleasurable in the beginning (the stew sure tasted good going down), they always leave us shattered and forlorn in the end.

Have you been pursuing those things in life that cannot give real and lasting satisfaction? Are you selling for cheap your integrity and compromising your walk with God in order to gain momentary pleasures? God invites you and me to feast with Him, the King of kings and Lord of lords. He wants you to chose His will and His ways so that you can take hold of that which is life indeed? (1 Tim. 6:19). My friend, in Jesus are hidden all the treasures of wisdom and knowledge? (Col. 2:3). Let your soul delight itself in His abundance!

EVENING

Lord, what a treasure I have in You! What an unfathomable opportunity I have to live my life in Your immeasurable abundance. I praise You for being so good to me. I don't deserve it, but because of Your great grace, I can receive it. Thank You for all You do for me, Lord. Help me rightly value the things that really matter so that I never sell the priceless for pennies. May I always look to You to meet my needs. In Jesus' mighty name. Amen.

MORNING

Heavenly Father, I bless Your name. I thank You that You are the God who changes hearts. I want my heart to be like soft clay in Your hands. I want Your Word to dwell in my heart and change my thoughts, words, and deeds. I want people to see Jesus in me today. Have Your way, Lord. I yield all control to You. In Jesus' name, Amen.

Brood of vipers! How can you, being evil, speak good things? For out of the abundance of the heart the mouth speaks. A good man out of the good treasure of his heart brings forth good things, and an evil man out of the evil treasure brings forth evil things.
MATTHEW 12:34, 35

Have you ever had a problem with your tongue? Have you ever heard rotten words spew out of your mouth like water shooting out of a broken sewer pipe? Someone cuts you off in traffic, and you let him have it with your tongue. Your favorite sports team blows the game, and you go ape with your tongue. Your enemy gets a promotion, and you can't seem to stop the bitter, verbal jabs that trickle from your mouth. Be honest. Is your natural inclination to curse and criticize rather than to bless and encourage?

Most of us have trouble controlling our tongues. Although we try to bite our tongues and not let the evil come out, it often does anyway. The problem is not with your tongue; it is with your heart. Your tongue is just the bucket; your heart is the well. If you do not like what you see (and hear) in the bucket, direct your attention to the well. Let Christ reign in your heart, and your speech will be sure to follow suit.

EVENING

Lord, today I was much more aware of the words that came out of my mouth. Thank You that You will control my tongue as I live with my heart surrendered to Your Spirit. I want the well of my heart to be clean and pure. I want to bless, not curse, those I come in contact with each day. I am excited to see how You will change me as I let You be King in my heart. I love You, Jesus. Amen.

Week 32, Friday

Lord Jesus, there is nothing as wonderful as starting my day remembering that You love me. Wow! You know all about me . . . and You still love me. You have seen all my failures and sins, yet in spite of it all, You never let me go. You are a God I can know and love. Thank You that You are faithful and true. I am excited about this day because You are with me. Amen.

How precious is Your lovingkindness, O God! Therefore the children of men put their trust under the shadow of Your wings. They are abundantly satisfied with the fullness of Your house, and You give them drink from the river of Your pleasures.
PSALM 36:7, 8

Have you ever seen the TV program *Magic's Biggest Secrets Revealed*? It's a fascinating show that explains how some of the greatest illusions are performed. Once the secret is revealed, you find yourself saying, "Oh, so that's how it's done!" Typically, the secret is simple, yet hard to discover on your own.

Do you know the secret to living the abundant Christian life? It is all wrapped up in the precious love of God. The children's song contains the simple secret: "Jesus loves me! This I know, for the Bible tells me so." Honestly, how well do you believe and receive His love?

God wants you to be rooted and grounded in His love, because that is the foundation on which everything else is built. Jesus died for you while you were a sinner (Romans 5:8). God doesn't love and accept you based on your performance; He loves and accepts you based on His grace. Do something with me: right now, lift up your hands and truly receive His great and precious love for you. As you do, He will put His love in your heart so that you can love Him back and love your neighbor as you love yourself. Try it and see.

EVENING

Father, I know You love me, but I often struggle with that simple truth. I look at my life and all my failures and think, "How could You possibly love me?" But I choose to believe Your Word instead of my feelings. You tell me You love me, and the Cross of Christ proves it. I praise You, my Lord and my God. In Jesus' name, Amen.

MORNING

Lord, I praise You for Your great and awesome power. There is nothing too difficult for You. I lay all of my burdens at Your feet, knowing that You are able to masterfully handle the worst of my problems. You are able to work miracles and create beauty from ashes. I look with expectation toward the awesome things You will do today as I fix my eyes on You, Lord Jesus. Amen.

> *To Him who is able to do exceedingly abundantly above all that we*
> *ask or think, according to the power that works in us, to Him be glory*
> *in the church by Christ Jesus to all generations, forever and ever. Amen.*
> EPHESIANS 3:20, 21

Can you believe the verses above? They are WOW verses for sure! They tell us several really important things. First, God is able. Whatever difficulty you may be facing today, it is not impossible with God. Second, God is more than able. He can do over and above what is needed. When Jesus fed the multitudes with the young boy's five loaves and two fish, all the people (five thousand men plus women and children) ate and were satisfied. Afterwards, there were twelve full baskets of leftovers, presumably for that little boy to take home to his family. I'd say that was "exceeding abundantly," wouldn't you? Third, God is able to do beyond all we ask or think. If that is true, and it is, then you and I need to think big and pray big! Don't pray little, anemic, "barely-get-by" prayers. God is not the God of *barely*, He is the God of *abundance*. John Newton, the British clergyman who wrote many hymns in the 1700s, including "Amazing Grace," said it best: "You are coming to a King, large petitions with you bring, for His grace and power are such, none can ever ask too much."

God's power is available to work mightily within you today. He wants to shine through you like the sun so that all the glory will go to His Son and our Savior, Jesus Christ.

EVENING

God, You are a WOW God. Forgive me for approaching You in faithlessness with "barely-get-by" prayers. Teach me to pray big and believe big, for You are bigger than my mind could ever conceive. What a privilege it is to be Your child! In Jesus' name, Amen.

JEFF SCHREVE, TEXARKANA, TX

Week 33, Monday

Father, thank You for a new day filled with new mercies, grace sufficient for my every need, and love that endures forever. I ask You to bless my thoughts, actions, and reactions today. Help me to see others with a heart of compassion and to be willing to share Jesus' love with the people I meet. In Jesus' name I pray, Amen.

> *God, determining to show more abundantly to the heirs of promise the immutability of His counsel, confirmed it by an oath, that by two immutable things, in which it is impossible for God to lie, we might have strong consolation, who have fled for refuge to lay hold of the hope set before us.*
> HEBREWS 6:17, 18

I have three precious grandsons, and I always love it when they are around me. I want to pour only good things into their lives. When they want me, I am there, no questions asked. If they need something, I want to give them the most and best that I can. They love their Poppa, and they know their Poppa loves them. They never have to wonder how much I love them, because I show them every chance I get.

When God does something on our behalf, He doesn't just do the minimum required. He goes exceedingly, abundantly above and beyond what we can imagine. I have heard it said that just one sacrificial drop of Jesus' blood would have been enough to pay the full price for every sin ever committed. God made sure that we saw the extent of His love for us. He was determined to show more abundantly His covenant with us through His unchanging Word. He also confirmed that covenant by an oath that involved the sacrifice of His only Son, Jesus. Because of these "two immutable things," we can know without a doubt that God loves us with an everlasting love and, as we run to Him for refuge, we can confidently lay hold of the hope set before us.

EVENING

God, in a world that is constantly changing, I am thankful that You are unchanging. You are the same yesterday, today, and forever. No matter what trying circumstances come my way, I can always rely on the Rock of my salvation. You are always there, and Your love for me is so much bigger than any problem. You are my King forever. Amen.

God, I acknowledge You as my Lord and Savior. You are the Creator and Sustainer of everything. Thank You for loving me and for providing a way for me to have a personal relationship with You through Jesus. I am ready to obey You today. Make me sensitive to Your leadership. I surrender to Your will. My heart's desire is to bless You in everything I do. Amen.

Let the word of Christ dwell in you richly in all wisdom, teaching and admonishing one another in psalms and hymns and spiritual songs, singing with grace in your hearts to the Lord. And whatever you do in word or deed, do all in the name of the Lord Jesus, giving thanks to God the Father through Him.
COLOSSIANS 3:16, 17

In his letter to the church in Colosse, Paul encouraged believers to be sure their focus was where it should be—on knowing, praising, and honoring God through Christ. The community had been struggling with false teachings and disunity. Paul gave them a much-needed reminder to go back to the basics, like a good sports coach telling his players to practice the fundamentals of their game. It is tempting to chase every little rabbit trail that comes along in hopes of finding a shortcut to achieve a goal, but ultimately these shortcuts distract our minds from the main thing—worshiping God in Christ—and we become less effective in accomplishing what He's called us to do.

There is a treasure of wisdom in these two verses. Applying these truths to our lives will make all of us better disciples of Jesus. We can apply a multitude of adjectives and verbs to what Paul said, but the simplicity and beauty of his statement cannot be improved upon. Spend some time meditating on every word in these two verses, and you will begin to see the God-inspired wisdom that Paul has explained so powerfully for us. Does your life mirror these verses? Ask God to lead you in worship and to help you increasingly treasure the fundamentals of the Christian life.

EVENING
Father, thank You for Your holy, blessed, inerrant Word. It holds the answer to every problem I have ever faced or that will ever come my way. Help me to live out the truth that You've revealed to me today. In Jesus' name, Amen.

BILLY GOODWIN, BALL GROUND, GA

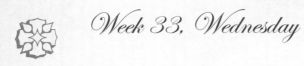 *Week 33, Wednesday*

Lord, I love You. Thank You for this new day with great opportunities to serve You. I pray for wisdom and discernment to make good decisions today. I don't want to allow the pressures of life to take priority over staying in fellowship with You throughout the day. Help me keep my heart and mind focused on You in every circumstance. Amen.

It is God who works in you both to will and to do for His good pleasure.
Do all things without complaining and disputing.
PHILIPPIANS 2:13, 14

It has been my incredible privilege and honor to be a part of NewSong, the contemporary Christian band, for the past twenty-nine years. Over that span of time, I have seen God move miraculously in thousands of lives. Even in the midst of those wonderful moments, there were times I walked onto the stage with some unresolved conflict in my life or something in my flesh that would tug for my heart's attention. I always tried to sing the best I could no matter what was going on in my life personally. When the time came for inviting people to make commitments to Christ, I would watch God do His amazing work and see so many people respond, but there would be no joy in my heart. I began to realize something about the way God works: He is going to accomplish His will no matter what my attitude is. I can choose to stay in fellowship with Him and rejoice in being a part of what He is doing, or I can allow petty things that have no eternal significance to rob me of the full joy of those precious times.

The more I walk with Jesus, the more I see that the problems and frustrations we all experience in life simply pale in comparison to the unspeakable joy we receive from being in the center of God's will for our life and realizing that He gets good pleasure in working through us to accomplish His will.

EVENING

Father, thank *You* for another wonderful day of life. Thank *You* for all the good things You allowed me to experience today. Thank *You* for Your peace that passes understanding and Your joy that is indescribable. I pray that You will give me a good night's rest and keep my family safe and healthy. In Jesus' name, Amen.

MORNING

Father, I confess You as my Lord and Savior today. You are King of my heart and life. My heart's desire is to please You in everything I do. Help me constantly listen to Your still, small voice and follow You wherever You lead me. In Jesus' name, Amen.

Rejoice the soul of Your servant, for to You, O Lord, I lift up my soul. For You, Lord, are good, and ready to forgive, and abundant in mercy to all those who call upon You.
PSALM 86:4, 5

In my sinful nature, it is not an easy thing to forgive someone for causing me pain or suffering. Usually my first reaction is to get even or at least to wish something as bad or worse would happen to whoever wronged me. As I've gotten older, I've developed a new perspective on dealing with the problems and stumbling blocks that inevitably appear in my path. Things that used to seem like huge problems that took over my life now seem like small inconveniences that I can trust God with. I can lean on His understanding and His strength.

Harboring resentment in your heart and refusing to forgive others harms you more than the actual act committed against you. As a matter of fact, whenever you decide to forgive and try to reconcile, it will always make you more like Christ, and often results in a healed relationship. Follow God's commands, and your life, as well as the lives of those around you, will be blessed. Consider God's readiness to forgive you when you call on Him, and ask Him to help you always be ready to offer the same kind of mercy to others.

EVENING

God, as I learn more about You and Your nature, I realize how much I have left to learn. You are so far beyond anything I can imagine, yet You still love me. Thank You for Your forgiveness and abundant mercy. Help me rest well tonight and wake up ready to follow You obediently tomorrow. In Jesus' name I pray, Amen.

Week 33, Friday

Father, thank You for another day of life. Help me to accept willingly the challenges that come my way today. I want to allow Your Holy Spirit to guide me as I deal with those challenges and as I interact with people around me. May they see Jesus in my life even in the little things I do. My heart's desire is to bless You today. In Jesus' name, Amen.

As the Father raises the dead and gives life to them, even so the Son gives life to whom He will. For the Father judges no one, but has committed all judgment to the Son.
JOHN 5:21, 22

My oldest grandson has a brother who is two years younger than him. It is so much fun to watch the little guy imitate everything his older brother does. He doesn't think about whether what he's doing will hurt him or get him into trouble—he just blindly follows his big brother. If his brother likes something, he likes it. If his brother wants something, he wants it, too. Our children do that with us as parents. They see how we act, and they want to be just like us. It is sobering to realize the influence we have on our children. We can pour good things as well as bad things into their lives. May God help us to pour only good things from our lives into the lives of those we love!

Jesus did only those things that His Father told Him to do. If you saw Jesus, you saw the Father. Jesus was totally human but totally God as well. Can you imagine being alive during Jesus' earthly ministry and realizing that you were looking at God in the flesh? Everything that God is and has belongs to His Son. Jesus gives life to those who believe on Him, and He passes judgment on those who reject Him. If we have trusted Jesus to be our Lord and Savior, then we should follow Him with absolute trust and willingness since He pours only His goodness into our lives.

EVENING
God, thank *You* for the privilege of calling You Father. Thank *You* for all of the good things *You* poured into my life today. Help me rest tonight in the peace of my relationship with *You* through Jesus. In His name I pray, Amen.

MORNING

Father, You are worthy of all praise and adoration. I yield my life to You today. I want to submit to Your will. Thank You for another day to enjoy Your blessings and to live life to the fullest. In Jesus' name, Amen.

> *If the Spirit of Him who raised Jesus from the dead dwells in you,*
> *He who raised Christ from the dead will also give life to your*
> *mortal bodies through His Spirit who dwells in you.*
> ROMANS 8:11

B eing a Christian is so much more than going to heaven when you die. If heaven wasn't real and there was no eternity after death, our life as Christians would still be so much better than anything the world has to offer. By allowing the truth of God's Word to guide us in our daily decisions and life choices, we can experience joy, peace, and contentment, not only in our own hearts but also in our relationships.

As today's scripture states, the same Spirit that raised Christ from the dead will also give life to our mortal bodies. While we are alive on this earth, we can experience real life through His Spirit who dwells in us as believers in Christ. If we allow His Spirit to guide us to the truth in God's Word, we begin to understand what our purpose is in this world.

Every time I allow God's Word to change my heart in any way, it makes me more like Christ. His ways are so much better than my ways. In addition to an abundant life on earth, I have the blessed hope of spending eternity in heaven with the One who created me and paid the price for my salvation. Thank You, Jesus!

EVENING

Father, I am so amazed and humbled by the life *You* have allowed me to live. Thank *You* for *Your* many blessings and the favor *You* have shown. I am so grateful that I not only have eternity in heaven with *You* to look forward to, but I also have a life worth living here on earth. I praise *You* and exalt *You* above everything in my life. In Jesus' name, Amen.

BILLY GOODWIN, BALL GROUND, GA

Week 34, Monday

Father, You know what type of day awaits me. Allow me to face today full of Your Spirit, trusting totally in Your grace. In all I do and say, I want to glorify You today. Amen.

Brethren, I do not count myself to have apprehended; but one thing I do, forgetting those things which are behind and reaching forward to those things which are ahead, I press toward the goal for the prize of the upward call of God in Christ Jesus.
PHILIPPIANS 3:13, 14

It happened during the 2004 Summer Olympic Games in Athens. American sharpshooter Matt Emmons was almost assured of a gold medal in the fifty-meter rifle competition. His margin was so great, no one felt there was any way he could lose. On Matt's final shot, he peered through the scope, aimed carefully, and pulled the trigger. Bull's eye! Strangely, however, the judges began shouting; somehow Matt had inadvertently shot the wrong target. He finished eighth, far from the gold medal he had anticipated. The lesson learned? You don't score points for hitting the wrong target.

The apostle Paul understood that the purpose of life is to become more like Christ (Romans 8:29). The apostle knew that Christlikeness is the only target worth aiming for. Paul's pursuit of living like Christ began with an honest evaluation of his life. When Paul said he hadn't "apprehended," he was simply saying, "I'm not as much like Jesus as I want to be." Paul cared enough about his faith journey to step aside from life's busyness to evaluate himself honestly. You see, you can't go where you want to go unless you first understand where you are. Next, the apostle refused to be distracted by his past. He was determined not to allow past failures, or even successes, to keep him from moving forward. When he said he was "forgetting those things which are behind," he affirmed his refusal to allow his past to influence his future negatively.

To Paul, nothing was more important than pursuing Christlikeness. Every other goal or ambition was secondary to it. He understood there is no abundant life apart from Christ. At what target are you aiming your life?

EVENING
God, as always, *You* have been completely faithful. Thank You for always being there for me. Tomorrow, please keep my eyes focused on the only target worth hitting—Christlikeness! Amen.

Father, my heart's desire today is to worship You, not just with my words but with my life. May it be a holy and acceptable living sacrifice to You. In Jesus' name, Amen.

Whoever finds me finds life, and obtains favor from the LORD;
but he who sins against me wrongs his own soul; all those who hate me love death.
PROVERBS 8:35, 36

Proverbs 8 is all about wisdom. Wisdom is the ability to live life with distinguished proficiency. It is living life with the skill to navigate through the tough stuff. Wisdom helps us make sound decisions and have appropriate boundaries that keep us safe, out of trouble and danger. It enables us to parent our children, conduct our finances, and strengthen our relationships. Wisdom teaches us to hate evil and to love what it good. Leaders can't lead without it, and true success comes as a result of it. God's Word says that wisdom is more beneficial than financial profits (Proverbs 3:14) and that it is the primary thing (4:7). Therefore, our most important acquisition in life is wisdom.

In our text today, God teaches that the difference between living with or without wisdom is a matter of life or death. It is as serious as it sounds. Those who find wisdom find life; those who sin against wisdom do so to their own detriment.

According to Scripture, wisdom actually has the capacity to lengthen our life (Proverbs 3:16; 4:10). Think of our feeble attempts to live longer and healthier. God says simply live with wisdom, and your days can be made longer. Not only does wisdom offer a prolonged life, but it also ensures a peaceful life (3:17). The truth is, so much of our lack of peace is caused by the poor choices we make. Wisdom is a necessary component to living a more enjoyable life—the abundant life. James said that God desires to give wisdom to all who ask for it; if you want wisdom, pray for it (James 1:5). Today, ask God for the skill to live life His way instead of your way.

Lord, You promised that if I would ask for wisdom, You would give it to me. Father, I ask You for wisdom in all areas of my life. Give me the skill to live a life that glorifies You. Amen.

TREVOR BARTON, LONDON, KY

Dear Lord, I confess that Jesus Christ is Lord. He has risen from the dead. I submit myself to You. Use me according to Your perfect will and purpose. Amen.

> *In the fear of the LORD there is strong confidence, and His children*
> *will have a place of refuge. The fear of the LORD is a fountain*
> *of life, to turn one away from the snares of death.*
>
> PROVERBS 14:26, 27

Fearing God isn't being afraid of God; it is a motivating respect for God's authority that results in obedience. In other words, a genuine fear of God always results in surrender to God. Surrender leads to obedience, which is the way of wisdom.

Scripture teaches that fearing God is healthy and beneficial in many ways. First of all, it brings restraint to our moral conduct. Without the fear of God, moral boundaries seem to disappear (Romans 3:10–18). It helps us love what God loves and hate what God hates (Proverbs 8:13).

Fearing God prompts us to obey God, even when it doesn't make sense. Because Noah feared God, he obeyed Him in the absence of logic or precedent (Hebrews 11:7). It motivates us to obey when we strongly prefer not to obey. Because Abraham feared God, he was willing to offer his only son, Isaac, to God (Genesis 22:12).

It also gives us the courage to stand apart from the crowd if necessary. Nehemiah's healthy fear of God kept him from having an unhealthy fear of people (Nehemiah 5:15). It prompts us to persevere when we feel like quitting. Joseph was mistreated, slandered, and hated, yet his fear of God kept him from giving up (Genesis 42:18).

Fearing God keeps us mindful of God's blessings and faithfulness in our lives (1 Samuel 12:24). And finally, it demands true, unadulterated worship. Seeing God as He is leaves us no choice except to worship Him (Psalm 22:23). His glory and splendor demand it! Fearing God isn't paralyzing; it is liberating. Learning to fear God is learning to live life abundantly.

EVENING

Father in heaven, Scripture teaches us that from the time the sun rises until the time it sets, You are worthy of praise. I worship You, my great God and King. In Jesus' name, Amen.

MORNING

God, my life is Yours. You created and redeemed me. All that I have comes from You and belongs to You. You deserve my very best today because You gave me Your best at Calvary. Amen.

> *He said to them, "Take heed and beware of covetousness, for one's life*
> *does not consist in the abundance of the things he possesses . . .*
> *Life is more than food, and the body is more than clothing."*
> LUKE 12:15, 23

In Luke 12, Jesus told a parable about a rich man experiencing his best days ever. He accumulated so much wealth he didn't have enough storage space. The rich man's solution: tear down his barns, build bigger ones that would hold more possessions, and then retire and make life one big party. This man thought accumulated wealth guaranteed a great, full life. His only problem was that he wasn't prepared for his impending death that very night. Jesus' story teaches that we can live life for the present or the future; for the visible or the invisible; for the short today or the long tomorrow; for time or eternity. Life is way too short to live for what is passing. We should live for what is lasting! Jesus' point was that we should invest our lives in what lasts. The rich fool lived for this life, not eternity. His possessions owned him, and he trusted them to bring him what only God could bring.

There are more than thirty thousand self-storage facilities in America providing over a billion square feet of storage for our "stuff." In the 1960s, the industry didn't exist; now Americans pay twelve billion dollars a year to store their excess. Yet people aren't happier. They are stressed and working long hours to get where the rich fool was—having perceived happiness from accumulated wealth. However, Jesus' message is different than that of culture: "Do not lay up treasure for yourself, but work to be rich in God's eyes. Don't worry about life, food, clothes, and other such things. Life is more than that. Spend your life seeking the kingdom first. Live for eternity, and you will enjoy a life of joy and value."

EVENING

Father, I take great comfort in knowing You are seated upon Your throne. You are in control of every situation in this world. I trust You with everything. In Jesus' name, Amen.

TREVOR BARTON, LONDON, KY

Dear God, every good and perfect gift comes from You. My heart is full of deep gratitude for Your graciousness toward me. I pray this in Jesus' name. Amen.

> *Give, and it will be given to you: good measure, pressed down, shaken together, and running over will be put into your bosom. For with the same measure that you use, it will be measured back to you.*
>
> LUKE 6:38

This verse teaches the truth that you reap what you sow. Jesus makes an awesome promise that should motivate us to have the heart of an authentic giver. We never miss anything we give away, because God will always replace it with something better. This isn't promoting some sort of prosperity gospel; it is simply stating that those who give won't miss it.

This message can be seen elsewhere in Scripture. Solomon taught that the generous will be blessed (Proverbs 22:9). He wrote, "Honor the LORD with your possessions, and with the firstfruits of all your increase; so your barns will be filled with plenty, and your vats will overflow with new wine (3:9, 10). He also said that the person who takes care of the poor lends to the Lord, and that the Lord will "pay back" what was given (19:17). Paul taught, "He who sows sparingly will also reap sparingly, and he who sows bountifully will also reap bountifully. So let each one give as he purposes in his heart, not grudgingly or of necessity; for God loves a cheerful giver (2 Corinthians 9:6, 7).

God has made it clear that to those who sow seed, He gives more seed. To those who water, He provides more water. And those who honor God with their possessions will never lack what is needed. What a great promise we have in Luke 6:38! However, don't forget that the promise is preceded by a verb—*give*. Everything begins with giving. Don't live life as a taker or hoarder, but as a Christ-honoring giver.

EVENING

Father, there is none like You. You are my peace and my strength. Your mercies are new every day. I know that without them, I would certainly be consumed. Thank You, God, for *Your* unchanging character. In the name of Jesus, my Lord and Savior, Amen.

MORNING

Father, I confess that I am nothing without You. You are the Creator; I'm merely the creature. You are the Redeemer; I am the redeemed. You are my everything. Amen.

Do not love the world or the things in the world. If anyone loves the world, the love of the Father is not in him. For all that is in the world—the lust of the flesh, the lust of the eyes, and the pride of life—is not of the Father but is of the world. And the world is passing away, and the lust of it; but he who does the will of God abides forever.

1 JOHN 2:15–17

When we love God, our love for the world fades. Conversely, when we love the world, it squeezes out the love we have for God. This is Satan's plan: to seduce us into loving the world, so we love God less. Satan's strategy to seduce us usually involves one of three things.

First, he tries to prompt us to succumb to the lust of the flesh—cravings for things we can't and shouldn't have. The lust of our flesh allows us to see only the pleasure, never the price tag. Second, he encourages us to follow the lust of the eyes. In many cases, the eyes are the front door through which temptation enters. Latent desires are aroused through the things seen by the eyes. Third, he wants us to get wrapped up in the pride of life. An inflated view of self leads to a deflated view of God. Life becomes all about loving and trusting in yourself, not loving and trusting in God. Bible commentator William Barclay said, "Pride is the ground in which all the other sins grow, and the parent from which all the other sins come."

Don't let your guard down and let Satan lure you into living foolishly. Don't waste your time loving the world, because it is not going to last. What can you do to make a positive, eternal impact with your life? It is simple: love God and live for His will.

EVENING

Dear Lord, protect me from the lust of the flesh, the lust of the eyes, and the pride of life. I desire to love You most and live for You alone. In Jesus' name I humbly pray, Amen.

TREVOR BARTON, LONDON, KY

Father, as I begin this new day, may I be mindful of *Your* presence in my life. Having that knowledge, may I walk before *You* in obedience, putting Jesus on display for others to see. Lord, thank *You* for loving and saving me! Amen.

Happy is the man who finds wisdom, and the man who gains understanding; for her proceeds are better than the profits of silver, and her gain than fine gold.
PROVERBS 3:13, 14

So many people think that if they just had enough money, they could solve all their problems and finally be happy. But throughout the Bible, we learn that there is no happiness apart from holiness.

The word translated *happy* in verse 13 can also be translated "Oh, the blessedness." Solomon's message is that a person who finds wisdom is blessed because wisdom is better than silver and gold. Jesus spoke about people who are blessed in His Sermon on the Mount (Matthew 5:3–10). Wise people humbly confess their sins, depend on Jesus for their righteousness, and bless others with mercy and peace. Their reward? God's mercy, justification, comfort, presence, purpose, and a place in His kingdom. What can compare with the riches of God's grace?

God gives the gift of His wisdom to draw us to Himself, to make us like Him, and to accomplish His work on earth through us. Have you received this gift from God? If you have, do you treasure it? Nothing in this life is more valuable than God's truth. No amount of silver or gold could ever purchase the presence, power, and peace of God that comes from being right with Him through Jesus Christ.

EVENING

Lord, thank *You* for allowing me to be blessed with another wonderful day of life. Thank *You* for loving me and helping me to cherish *Your* wisdom every day. Help me to seek *Your* wisdom always. I humbly pray in the name of *Your* Son, the Lord Jesus Christ. Amen.

Father, may I never forget my great need to receive direction and instruction from You every day. I need the wisdom of Your Word. I pray in the precious name of Jesus, my Lord and Savior. Amen.

Get wisdom! Get understanding! Do not forget, nor turn away from the words of my mouth. Do not forsake her, and she will preserve you; love her, and she will keep you.
PROVERBS 4:5, 6

Solomon was blessed to have a father like David who had learned lessons in many spheres of life throughout his days. But the greatest benefit of Solomon's upbringing with his father was learning about the things of the Lord. As David taught and trained his son, he could have drawn primarily from his war skills and his statesmanship. Instead, his trust in and love for God compelled him to be sure he passed on to his son what is most valuable in life: wisdom and understanding from God.

We teach our children about many things, but we must understand that teaching them about wisdom must be a top priority. Teaching them to be wise and to follow the Lord's will for their lives will bring the most important kinds of benefits. All parents want their children to experience the best that life has to offer. When we consider the benefits that wisdom and understanding bring, we will come to realize that we can offer them nothing more valuable!

If you are not a parent, remember that you are in a position of influence with every person you know. You can teach others through your godly conduct and counsel. Bless and take care of those around you, whether it is your children, other family members, friends, or co-workers, by humbly and lovingly sharing God's wisdom with them.

EVENING

Lord Jesus, thank You that You have a purpose and plan for my life. I praise You because the best of life is found in You. Amen.

Week 35, Wednesday

God, thank You for a new day. Thank You for making me healthy and strong enough to be part of this new day. May I be mindful of the value and blessings of Your wisdom in my life. Help me to walk in Your ways today. Give me understanding and guide me so I will be pleasing in Your sight. I pray in Jesus' holy name. Amen.

Wisdom is the principal thing; therefore get wisdom. And in all your getting, get understanding. Exalt her, and she will promote you; she will bring you honor, when you embrace her. She will place on your head an ornament of grace; a crown of glory she will deliver to you.

PROVERBS 4:7–9

I often think about the question, "Why would I ever want anything less than the very best for my life?" And yet every day I make decisions that are contrary to the best! They may not be decisions that are earth-shattering; but when all is said and done, they impact my life.

In those moments when I make poor decisions, I am forgetting exactly what this proverb teaches—that wisdom is better than anything else! There is no substitute for the best. We should begin every day by asking the Lord for wisdom. James 1:5 states, "If any of you lacks wisdom, let him ask of God, who gives to all liberally and without reproach, and it will be given to him." The Lord promises to give us wisdom. He wants us to become more like Him and to live as His wise servants.

When we gain understanding from the Lord and walk in His wisdom, we will please Him like we should. And in His grace, He will see to it that our lives are blessed and that honor comes our way.

EVENING

Lord, I get excited when I start to understand how much You love Your children. Help us to seek Your will for our lives. You have so much to give us in this life, and I can't even speculate what heaven will be like! Amen.

MORNING

Lord, I am grateful for this new day. As I walk in it, I pray for Your wisdom and understanding. Help me to be kind to others and to serve as a clear witness for You today. Help me to remember that every person's greatest need is to receive more of You. May my words and actions point others to the lovely Lord Jesus! Amen.

The fear of the LORD is the beginning of wisdom, and the knowledge of the Holy One is understanding. For by me your days will be multiplied, and years of life will be added to you.
PROVERBS 9:10, 11

Solomon revealed how our days can be multiplied and our years increased. Just glancing at the text, we see three key components of a long life: wisdom, knowledge, and understanding. While foolishness can lead to an early death, wisdom is the key to a long, blessed life.

According to Solomon, wisdom begins with the fear of the Lord. This beginning wisdom is what leads a person to conversion and ultimately to a life of consecration. Being consecrated, or being committed to Jesus, leads to a happier life based on an understanding of God's holiness.

Grasping the holiness of God prompts us to respect and honor Him. We understand His call to holiness and put our faith in His truth. Having the privilege of a personal relationship with Him prompts us to trust Him, obey Him, and become more like Him in holiness and wisdom.

If you hope that "your days will be multiplied," pursue a life of faithfulness to God. Praise Him for sharing His wisdom with us and graciously blessing us as we live according to it!

EVENING

Father, I am grateful that You bless faithfulness. Help me to desire to please You in all ways for all my days. I want to value what You value and despise what You despise. I ask for Your wisdom and understanding and that You will multiply my days. I pray this all in Jesus' precious name. Amen.

NORMAN HUNT, CANTON, GA

Father, thank You for this new day and for all the opportunities it will bring. Lord, I pray that You would guide me by Your Spirit and give me wisdom and understanding for every decision I will have to make today. Father, I love You, and I ask these things in Jesus' name. Amen.

Wisdom rests in the heart of him who has understanding,
but what is in the heart of fools is made known.
PROVERBS 14:33

⟶⟶⟵⟵

Jesus said, "A good man out of the good treasure of his heart brings forth good; and an evil man out of the evil treasure of his heart brings forth evil. For out of the abundance of the heart the mouth speaks" (Luke 6:45). What comes out of our mouths reveals what is in our hearts. Solomon said it another way in this proverb. Wise people have wisdom in their hearts—it's part of who they are. The same goes for those who lack wisdom; their heart is void of wisdom. Both the wise and the unwise expose the condition of their hearts through their speech.

They also expose it through their actions. In a discussion about identifying false prophets, Jesus told His disciples, "You will know them by their fruits" (Matthew 7:16). When we have God's wisdom in our hearts, we'll have the ability to make right choices. Those right choices are the fruit of hearts that have wisdom and understanding.

This concept is closely related to Paul's teaching in Romans 12:2, in which he told believers, "Be transformed by the renewing of your mind, that you may prove what is that good and acceptable and perfect will of God." Ask God to work in your heart and mind so you will become more like Him. Pray like Paul did, asking Him to "give you the spirit of wisdom and revelation in the knowledge of Him, the eyes of your understanding being enlightened" (Ephesians 1:17, 18). Changes that begin within will become evident in your words and actions!

⟶⟶⟵⟵

EVENING

God, thank You for blessing me with Your Holy Spirit. I pray that You would search my heart, Lord, that I may confess anything that would hinder me from walking in Your wisdom and understanding. Lord, change in me what needs to be changed for Christ's sake and my good. Amen.

Father in heaven, I pray for a clean heart that I might walk upright in Your presence today. Guide me with Your perfect wisdom throughout this day and fill me with Your Spirit. In Jesus' precious name, Amen.

> *How much better to get wisdom than gold! And to get understanding is to be chosen rather than silver. The highway of the upright is to depart from evil; he who keeps his way preserves his soul.*
> PROVERBS 16:16, 17

Solomon's statements in verse 16 go against the grain of our materialistic culture. The TV commercials that air day and night encourage everyone to buy, buy, buy. Do you ever find yourself valuing things you can buy with money more than you value the things of God? If we are not careful, we may forget Jesus' admonition: "Do not lay up for yourself treasures on earth . . . but lay up for yourselves treasures in heaven" (Matthew 6:19). Living in God's wisdom and being rich in Him forever is far better than having the empty, temporary wealth of the world!

Solomon said that turning away from evil is the way wise people live—it is "the highway of the upright." The highway to heaven begins at Calvary. Jesus said, "Narrow is the gate and difficult is the way which leads to life, and there are few who find it" (Matthew 7:14). Stay on the path of life! Guard your heart from temptations and worldly distractions. Pray David's prayer in Psalm 139:24: "See if there is any wicked way in me, and lead me in the way everlasting." Seek God's wisdom that brings direction, purpose, and peace for today and the promise of a glorious future with your Father in heaven.

EVENING

My God, thank You for this day. As I rest, prepare my heart and mind for the journey before me. Give me wisdom and help me not to turn aside from the path You have set for me. I pray this in the name of Jesus, my Savior. Amen.

NORMAN HUNT, CANTON, GA

Week 36, Monday

Precious Father, I come before You confessing that my greatest need is to receive more wisdom and understanding. While I may get knowledge from a book, wisdom only comes from Your heart. For all the decisions, discussions, and deliberations that will be part of this day, give me the wisdom to know and to do what is right. Remind me to keep asking for wisdom so I will do what pleases You. In the wonderful name of Jesus I pray, Amen.

The wise in heart will be called prudent, and sweetness of
the lips increases learning. Understanding is a wellspring of life
to him who has it. But the correction of fools is folly.
PROVERBS 16:21, 22

Imagine God giving you a blank check and allowing you to fill it in for anything you want. That actually happened to Solomon. He was given carte blanche by the One for whom nothing is impossible. God did something for Solomon that, as far as the Bible reveals, He had never done before and has never done again. What did Solomon ask for? He asked for wisdom, which is not just a matter of the head but also a matter of the heart.

An anonymous thinker wrote these words: "Tell me your dreams, and I will read the riddle of your life. Tell me your prayers, and I will write the history of your soul. Tell me your askings, and I will tell you your gettings. Tell me what you seek, and I will tell you what you are. I do not wish to know your possessions . . . only your wants. I do not care to know what you have . . . only what you have not and desire to have . . . the ideal you set before you, the things you approve as excellent, what you seek after and have given your heart to, these are the measure of a man."[14]

EVENING
God of all wisdom, at the close of this day, I pray that I displayed wisdom in both word and deed. If at any time I rejected Your wisdom for my own counsel, I ask for forgiveness. Give me the wisdom to be all that You want me to be. I pray in Your name. Amen.

Dear Father, I know that words are very important to You, because You have chosen to reveal Yourself primarily through the power of the written Word and the spoken word. Today I will use many words with many people. Give me the wisdom to speak at the right time and in the right way. I pray in the name of Jesus Christ my Lord. Amen.

> *He who has knowledge spares his words, and a man of*
> *understanding is of a calm spirit. Even a fool is counted wise*
> *when he holds his peace; when he shuts his lips, he is considered perceptive.*
> PROVERBS 17:27, 28

One of the most groundbreaking, far-reaching judicial opinions ever handed down by the Supreme Court was the *Miranda* decision, which determined that every criminal suspect has a constitutional right to be advised of the availability of counsel. Under the *Miranda* ruling, police officers are required to tell suspects: "You have the right to remain silent. Anything you say can and will be used against you."

We should consider exercising that right to remain silent more often in everyday circumstances. Many times it is wisest to say nothing at all. Someone has said, "A wise man is one who thinks twice before saying nothing." People who are always putting in their two-cent's worth often only say things that are worth about two cents! Someone else has said, "He who thinks by the inches and speaks by the yard should be kicked by the foot."

Your words matter to God. Jesus said, "For every idle word men speak, they will give account of it in the day of judgment" (Matthew 12:36). Your words impact others. Solomon said, "The hypocrite with his mouth destroys his neighbor" (Proverbs 11:9). Embrace the wisdom of thinking calmly before you speak. Be self-controlled and careful with your words. Depend on the Spirit to know how to use your words, or silence, to bring honor and glory to the Father throughout the day.

EVENING

Dear God, You know all the words I spoke today. Forgive me for speaking when I shouldn't have and for not speaking when I should have. Thank You that Your words never fail. Amen.

DR. JAMES MERRITT, DULUTH, GA

Dear Lord, as I meet a new day, I realize that someone may wrong me today. They may say something to me that is inappropriate or do something to me that is undeserved. If that happens, help me not to react in my flesh, but to respond in Your Spirit. May I be so full of Your Holy Spirit that, if I am jostled, it will be Your Holy Spirit that will come out of me and nothing else. I pray in Jesus' name. Amen.

He who gets wisdom loves his own soul; he who keeps
understanding will find good . . . The discretion of a man
makes him slow to anger, and his glory is to overlook a transgression.
PROVERBS 19:8, 11

You undoubtedly already know this, but forgive me while I state the obvious: you are going to be wronged in this life by other people. When it happens the question is not, "Are you big enough to do something about it?" The question is, "Are you big enough to let it go?"

I heard about two brothers who got into an awful fight. After their mother broke it up, she asked how the fight got started. The older brother said, "It all started when he hit me back!"

We are all born with a tendency to "hit back." Although there is a time and a place to defend ourselves, we need to ask two questions when we feel our temperature rising. First, "Is this really worth my anger?" If the answer is yes, then ask, "Is this the best way, place, and time to express it?"

Anger in and of itself is not wrong. There is a place for righteous indignation. Be quick to be angry when injustice happens to others. But be even quicker to forgive and to forget when it happens to you. That is not only the wise thing to do, but also exactly the way Jesus lived.

EVENING

Dear God, I realize that anger is not to be a master, but a servant. Help me remember that either I control my temper or my temper controls me. If at any point today I let my emotions and my flesh get the best of me, I ask for forgiveness. Thank You that You prefer mercy over wrath. In Jesus' name, Amen.

God, thank You for giving me Your wisdom. I realize I will never have all the wisdom I need without You. Deliver me from a know-it-all spirit. Help me to seek and find godly counselors, and lead me through their godly advice. I pray this in the name of the Wisest Counselor of all. Amen.

A wise man is strong, yes, a man of knowledge increases strength; for by wise counsel you will wage your own war, and in a multitude of counselors there is safety.
PROVERBS 24:5, 6

One of the most valuable lessons I learned early in my first pastorate was that good godly advice from good godly people is twenty-four-karat gold. Though I have made many mistakes in my ministry, I probably would have made many more if I had not sought out and listened to godly counsel.

Tommy Bolt was one of the greatest golfers of all time, but he had one major flaw—a volcanic temper. You may know that professional golfers play with a caddie, who is there to offer advice as well as to carry clubs. One time Bolt was having a bad round in a tournament and told his caddie only to say, "Yes, Mr. Bolt" or "No, Mr. Bolt," and keep his advice to himself.

Bolt hit his first tee shot and it appeared to land behind a tree. When they reached the spot, Bolt asked his caddie, "Do you think I should hit a five-iron?" Obeying orders, the caddie replied, "No, Mr. Bolt." Bolt hit the five-iron anyway and made an unbelievable shot that landed on the green a few feet from the hole.

He turned to his caddie and proudly said, "What did you think about that shot?" As the caddie picked up the bag and headed toward the green he said, "It wasn't your ball, Mr. Bolt."[15] Wise people know that it pays to seek the advice of others!

EVENING
Father, I want to thank You that I have at my fingertips and in my heart the greatest counsel of all—the counsel of the Word of God and the counsel of the Father, the Son, and the Holy Spirit. May I always hear it and heed it, knowing it will lead me to do what is best and wise. In Jesus' name, Amen.

DR. JAMES MERRITT, DULUTH, GA

Father, there are times when I wonder why unbelievers don't believe in You. Sometimes it seems like the wicked prosper while the righteous struggle. Help me remember that it is how we finish life and what awaits us when it's over that counts. I recognize that I am rich in the things that matter. Today, I choose to be grateful for Your many blessings. In Jesus' name, Amen.

My son, if your heart is wise, my heart will rejoice—indeed, I myself; yes, my inmost being will rejoice when your lips speak right things. Do not let your heart envy sinners, but be zealous for the fear of the LORD all the day.
PROVERBS 23:15–17

It is the tale of two athletes. Our church was sponsoring what was called a Starlight Crusade. I was bringing in two of the most famous athletes in America. One was a professional football player who had won multiple Super Bowls, the other a professional basketball player. To be honest, I was more excited about meeting the quarterback than the basketball player who had never won one championship.

The quarterback came to my home before the crusade, and all he wanted to talk about was himself, his greatness, and his victories. Frankly, my envy soon turned to boredom, and then disgust. That night he gave a very weak testimony and left.

On the other hand, the basketball player sat down with me over dinner, and when I tried to talk about basketball, all he wanted to talk about was Jesus. The difference was striking. One man focused on himself; the other man focused on God. One man focused on his riches and reputation; the other man focused on his Redeemer. That night "Pistol Pete" Maravich gave one of the most edifying testimonies I have ever heard. As we said good-bye, his last words were, "Pastor, there is nobody like Jesus." That night I realized that there is nothing wrong with admiration. We just need to make sure we give it to the right person.

EVENING
Dear God, forgive me for envying the Hollywood crowd, the Wall Street moguls, and the Washington influencers. Help me to remember that the single greatest possession I will ever have is eternal life through Jesus Christ, my Lord. Because of that, I don't ever have to envy anyone. In Jesus' name, Amen.

MORNING

Dear God, help me remember that at the end of the day what matters is not our methods, our money, our might, or our manpower. All of these things are useless apart from Your mighty hand. In everything You want me to do today, I am responsible to do my best, but ultimately I am dependent upon You to give me victory. I pray this in the name of the One who always gives victory. Amen.

> *There is no wisdom or understanding or counsel against the* LORD.
> *The horse is prepared for the day of battle, but deliverance is of the* LORD.
> PROVERBS 21:30, 31

It is a day I will never forget if I live to be a hundred. We were having a one-day offering in our church, and we desperately needed to collect at least three hundred thousand dollars. We had assembled a team of people, made appeals, and written letters. In short, we had done all we could.

We asked our people to give their offerings at the end of each service. As I was going into the second service, one of the members of our Finance Ministry Team literally ran me down and breathlessly said, "I have to talk to you!" His hands were shaking as he showed me a check for one hundred thousand dollars. He had brought me the check because the donor was not a member of our church. When I saw the name on it, my jaw almost hit the floor. I knew that this man had only recently started coming to our church and was not even a believer! He had started attending because he had seen our services on television after not attending any church for over thirty years!

God used an unbeliever to give us our largest gift and put us over the top of our goal. I was reminded in the starkest of terms that we can do all the preparation and praying we want, but ultimately, victory really does belong in the hands of God. He can use even an unbeliever to show that He is still in control!

EVENING

Father, may I always remember that You don't depend on me for anything. I depend on You for everything. No one can stand against You, but when You stand for me, nothing can stand against me either. I rejoice in that! Amen.

DR. JAMES MERRITT, DULUTH, GA

Week 37, Monday

Father, I ask in faith for You to pour Your wisdom into my life. I must have it as I begin this new week and this new day. Thank You for the gracious gift of Your wisdom. You are such a great and generous Father. Amen.

If any of you lacks wisdom, let him ask of God, who gives to all liberally and without reproach, and it will be given to him. But let him ask in faith, with no doubting, for he who doubts is like a wave of the sea driven and tossed by the wind.
JAMES 1:5, 6

Do you need wisdom? If you are breathing, then you do! We all face major decisions and seemingly unsolvable problems. Perhaps this describes you: your need is huge, your time is short, and your options are zero. If so, God gives an awesome invitation: "If you need wisdom, just ask Me and I will pour it into your life!"

Wisdom has been described as the best choice with the best result in every situation. This is life at its best, and this is the life God desires for you! God doesn't want you living in confusion (1 Corinthians 14:33). He desires for you to have clarity in your life. This wisdom is a gift right from heaven and His heart. "Every good gift and every perfect gift is from above, and comes down from the Father" (James 1:17).

Do you want God's wisdom? Then "ask of God." We must admit our need and acknowledge our source. Confess to God: "I am inadequate and desperate. I must have Your wisdom to make the right choices in life. You have what I need, and I ask You to give it as You have promised." Remember, we must "ask in faith, with no doubting." God says, "Without faith it is impossible to please Him, for he who comes to God must believe that He is, and that He is a rewarder of those who diligently seek Him" (Hebrews 11:6). Instead of wringing our hands, we need only to bend our knees and request His wisdom. When you do, get ready for a heavenly outpouring from the Father!

EVENING
Father, thank You for Your Son and my Savior, the precious Lord Jesus, "in whom are hidden all the treasures of wisdom and knowledge" (Colossians 2:3). I am speechless. Amen.

God, I know the wise choice for me this new day is to say, "Not my will, but Your will." I submit my life to Your lordship and to the authority of Your Word. Help me to walk in wisdom. Keep me far from foolishness. I am Yours completely. Amen.

The wise in heart will receive commands, but a prating fool will fall. He who walks with integrity walks securely, but he who perverts his ways will become known.
PROVERBS 10:8, 9

The wise and the foolish—which one are you? Which one will you choose to be? The Book of Proverbs presents both sides and clearly calls us to receive one and resist the other. We are to desire wisdom and to distance ourselves from foolishness. "Wisdom is the principal thing; therefore get wisdom" (Proverbs 4:7). Wisdom is from God, and it is all about the ability to make right choices. It's living life skillfully and successfully. Wisdom protects. Wisdom brings peace. Wisdom is immensely practical. Wisdom is selecting and staying on the right path.

If wisdom is living life skillfully, then foolishness is living life recklessly. Choosing foolishness has resulted in wrecked lives, mangled families, and crippled futures. The tsunami of devastation that foolishness brings into a life is incalculable. Recognize it so you can avoid it!

In today's passage Solomon said, "The wise in heart will receive commands." Foolishness is the stubborn refusal to do what wisdom dictates. The fool says, "My way is better than God's way." God says, "There is a way that seems right to a man, but its end is the way of death" (Proverbs 14:12). God knows best, and the best choice is always wisdom. There's no future in foolishness; the "fool will fall." Jesus said choosing a foolish life is like building your life on the sand, which results in destruction (Matthew 7:26, 27). Instead we're told to "get wisdom! Get understanding . . . for she is your life" (Proverbs 4:5, 13). Choose to walk in wisdom today!

EVENING
God, how faithful You are to me. You have ordered my steps and stops throughout this day. I am so grateful for Your constant presence. I am overwhelmed by Your wisdom made available to me today. By Your grace and power I will continue to cling to Your wisdom and abhor that which is foolish. Amen.

JEFF CROOK, FLOWERY BRANCH, GA

Week 37, Wednesday

Lord, I begin this day like a sponge. I want to absorb all that You desire to teach me. I desire not only to hear Your Word, but also to do Your Word. Make my heart tender and receptive to You. I am Your disciple. I love You, Master. Amen.

A wise man will hear and increase learning,
and a man of understanding will attain wise counsel.
PROVERBS 1:5

Wisdom is a choice. I choose to receive from God His gift of wisdom. It's also about continuing to choose. Wisdom is expansive. We are to grow in wisdom. It's not a one-time deal but an ongoing pursuit.

Today's passage is about having a teachable spirit so that you might "increase learning" and "attain wise counsel." Are you teachable? This is one trait you will not find in a fool. "The way of a fool is right in his own eyes, but he who heeds counsel is wise" (Proverbs 12:15). Fools will not listen. They become angry when someone tries to teach them or to point out a blind spot in their life. There's a Yiddish proverb that goes like this: "If one man calls you a donkey, pay him no mind. If two men call you a donkey, go buy a saddle." When we refuse to listen, we make ourselves foolish. Wisdom is expressed and expanded when we listen and have teachable spirits.

I have five simple wisdom keys to share with you. First, we should listen to those who disagree with us. Second, we should listen to those who love us. Third, we should listen to those who have achieved the spiritual success we desire for our own lives. Fourth, we should listen to those who have godly wisdom and insight into God's Word. Fifth, and most importantly, we should daily depend on God's Spirit and humbly submit to the authority of His perfect Word. Jesus said of the Spirit, "He will teach you all things, and bring to your remembrance all things that I said to you" (John 14:26). Just how teachable are you? Are you *wise* or *otherwise*?

EVENING

Lord, I know You love me. Your instruction and guidance are gifts of love. Thank You for the people in my life who are wise counselors, another expression of Your great love. I am so secure in You, my Lord and my God. Amen.

MORNING

Almighty God, I praise Your name. I praise Your greatness. Your name is great. Your power is great. Your ways are great. You are greatly to be praised! May Your name be glorified through my life today. May Your power be manifested in my life today. Amen.

The fear of the LORD is the beginning of wisdom; a good understanding have all those who do His commandments. His praise endures forever.

PSALM 111:10

D o you remember the "No Fear" brand of the 1990s? Those words were commonly seen on clothing and even made their way to the label of an energy drink. It's a catchy phrase, but not what God's Word teaches.

No fear means no wisdom. However, to know fear is to know wisdom. Today's verse actually says fear is the *beginning* of wisdom. Fear of the Lord is the very basis for receiving spiritual wisdom and understanding. Don't mistake this fear with the anxiety, dread, or terror associated with pain or danger. It's reverential fear, such as a child has for his parents; it's a great respect and a deep desire to please. For believers, it's full recognition that God is Creator, Lord, Master, and Father. Fear of the Lord has been described as "loving God on our knees."

There are many benefits of fearing God. One is that we gain great confidence (we might say a life of "no fear"). "In the fear of the LORD is strong confidence . . . a place of refuge" (Proverbs 14:26). Oswald Chambers once said, "The remarkable thing about fearing God is that, when you fear God, you fear nothing else; whereas, if you do not fear God, you fear everything else." Purity and power accompanies fear. "By fear of the LORD one departs from evil" (16:6). It also brings full lives of God's favor and blessing. "The fear of the LORD prolongs days" (10:27). A God-fearing life is a God-blessed life!

EVENING

Sovereign God, thank You for daily loading me with Your benefits. It is so true that "the fear of the LORD is a fountain of life" (Proverbs 14:27). I am so overwhelmed by Your overflowing blessings. I know what I deserve, and I am humbled by Your grace. It is by Your grace and power that I will continue to walk in the fear of You, almighty God. In Jesus' strong name, Amen.

JEFF CROOK, FLOWERY BRANCH, GA

Father, as I begin a new day, "Let the words of my mouth and the meditation of my heart be acceptable in Your sight, O LORD, my strength and my Redeemer" (Psalm 19:14). Amen.

If a wise man contends with a foolish man, whether the fool rages or laughs,
there is no peace . . . A fool vents all his feelings, but a wise man holds them back.
PROVERBS 29:9, 11

Walking in wisdom means knowing when to speak and when to remain silent (Ecclesiastes 3:7). The Book of Proverbs is filled with warnings concerning our use of words: "He who guards his mouth preserves his life, but he who opens wide his lips shall have destruction" (Proverbs 13:3). Proverbs 10:19 says, "In the multitude of words sin is not lacking." In other words, be careful with your words because you may have to eat them.

There is a story about a vacuum cleaner salesman who was assigned to a rural area. On his first day, he nervously knocked on the door of a country farmhouse. When a woman answered the door, the salesman aggressively pushed his way in and started his sales pitch. He said, "Ma'am, before you say anything, I want to show you something incredible!" The lady of the house was taken aback as she watched him reach into his bag, pull out a bucket of dirt, and dump it on her wooden floor. "If my product won't pick up all that dirt," he boasted, "I'll eat it!" She looked at him and said, "Then you better get busy, 'cause we ain't got no electricity in this here house."

Fools often regret their words; they can cause great damage with what they say. "Death and life are in the power of the tongue" (Proverbs 18:21). Remember, we seldom regret our silence. The saying goes, "I am the master of my unspoken words and the slave to those which should have remained unsaid." Well said.

EVENING
Father, thank You for the words You have spoken into my life today—words of love, acceptance, assurance, and blessing. I desire to be in no other place but Your presence, for You have the words of eternal life (John 6:68). There is none like You. Thank You, Lord. I love You, Lord. You are my Lord. In Your name I pray, Amen.

MORNING

Jesus, thank You for saving my soul. Oh, how wonderful it is to have a real relationship with You. I also want to thank You for those who cared enough to share the gospel with me. I am so grateful for their obedience to You. I ask You to use me today as Your instrument to win a soul for Your glory. In the power of Your name I pray. Amen.

> *The fruit of the righteous is a tree of life, and he who wins souls is wise.*
> PROVERBS 11:30

A mong the greatest moments of my life were the births of my two children. It is a surreal time, an unforgettable experience, to be present when your child is born into this world. New life is so captivating and thrilling!

Is the wonder of new life what the wise Solomon had in mind when he said, "The fruit of the righteous is a tree of life, and he who wins souls is wise"? What a thrill it is to be present when someone is born again (John 3:3) and given new life in Christ (2 Corinthians 5:17). There's nothing like it! Have you personally experienced the joy of leading someone to life in Christ? God so desires for you to have this experience and will use you as His instrument to do it. Ask Him to use you to begin a conversation with someone today. Share your testimony and, in the power of God's Spirit, invite that person to trust Jesus and receive new life in Him.

This is a life of wisdom in the truest sense, investing your energy and time to advance God's kingdom. After all, what is more important than winning a soul? Jesus said, "For what will it profit a man if he gains the whole world, and loses his own soul?" (Mark 8:36). The wise will be rewarded in eternity with the soul winner's crown (1 Thessalonians 2:19). Will this be your reward?

EVENING

Jesus, I praise You once again for being my personal Savior. Ignite within me a strong passion to see others come to You. May I be consumed by this compelling passion. May I use the wisdom You impart to my life as a means to win souls. With my whole heart I make this prayer in the name of Jesus. Amen.

JEFF CROOK, FLOWERY BRANCH, GA

Lord, as a Christian, I have talked a lot about love, but You are the One who has shown me how to do it. I am continually amazed at how You have shown Your love for me. Lord, I pray that someone might look at my life today and say, "He must be a follower of Jesus because of the way he loves other believers." Keep me focused on sharing Your love with a world that needs to know You. In Jesus' name, Amen.

> *A new commandment I give to you, that you love one another;*
> *as I have loved you, that you also love one another. By this all*
> *will know that you are My disciples, if you have love for one another.*
>
> JOHN 13:34, 35

Jesus' disciples had been taught to love one another before (Matthew 22:39). But Jesus gave them what He called "a new commandment" to love one another because He was setting a new standard: "Love as I have loved you." He not only gave them instruction, but He also gave them a clear model to follow.

When we follow this commandment and reach for Jesus' standard of love, it can make a powerful impact on unbelievers. They are not impressed by our knowledge, our programs, or our discipline. But they know we are followers of Christ when they see the way we love one another. In a world where there is a tremendous amount of talk about love, people don't get to see a lot of the real thing! We have tried to make it more complicated than it is. We must keep our eyes on the Savior and love others as He loved us. We won't have to look very far to find opportunities.

EVENING

Father, thank You for all You have done for me. It is such a privilege to touch the lives of other people for Your honor and glory. Forgive me for the opportunities I have missed, and give me a vision for how I can share Your love with those around me tomorrow. I pray that You would draw me closer to You so I might serve You in a greater way tomorrow. I pray this in the name of Jesus. Amen.

Week 38, Tuesday

Lord, I bless Your name this morning. I praise You for another day that I can use for Your glory. I pray that the time I spend in Your Word today will be the foundation for everything that I do. I pray that my words and my actions will bring glory to You and that I will spend my time serving others rather than doing the things that are only pleasing to myself. Make me a servant for Your glory. In Jesus' name, Amen.

> *You, brethren, have been called to liberty; only do not use liberty as an opportunity for the flesh, but through love serve one another.*
> GALATIANS 5:13

We love to talk about our Christian liberty! We have the right to be free. But somehow it becomes a problem when we are reminded that we are free in order that we might serve. We think serving others is not quite as much fun as using our liberty. Yet the Bible teaches that we are only liberated when we are willing to serve. We are free to invest in the lives of others as we serve them in the name of the Lord Jesus.

The people around us who are really free are those who are seeking to serve others for the glory of the Lord. That is difficult for someone like me—I have a tendency to keep score. There are times I find myself taking advantage of my liberty while putting unnecessary requirements on others. I want accountability for those around me and grace for myself!

My liberty is not a free pass to do what I want. Instead, it should remind me that the grace of God demands my very best today. We don't need to protect ourselves; we need to be bolder in serving others.

EVENING

Lord, I praise You for the liberty that can only be found in a relationship with You. Help me to stay focused on You and give grace to others. Forgive me for the times when I have been so legalistic, trying to hold others accountable to my ideas. Forgive me for causing them to stumble. Thank You for being so patient with me. May my life be a picture of Your grace and Your glory! Amen.

DR. MICHAEL HAMLET, SPARTANBURG, SC

Week 38, Wednesday

Father, this morning I am reminded of Your grace and how You loved me so much that You sent Your Son to die on the Cross for my sin. Your grace is so amazing, and I never cease to be astounded at how You were willing to pay such a price for me. I give this day to You, and I ask that You use it for Your glory alone. When people see my inadequacy, may they be reminded of Your awesome power. Amen.

> *Brethren, if a man is overtaken in any trespass, you who are spiritual restore such a one in a spirit of gentleness, considering yourself lest you also be tempted. Bear one another's burdens, and so fulfill the law of Christ.*
> GALATIANS 6:1, 2

Today's passage is not the picture of super-spiritual people hovering over someone who has fallen and deciding his or her fate. These verses depict people who realize that only by the grace of God have they not been caught in the same type of problem. When we see those overtaken by sin, our attitude should be, "It could easily have been me."

Christ summed up God's commands for His people by saying that we are to love God with all our hearts, souls, and minds, and to love our neighbor as ourselves (Matthew 22:37–39). Our task is not to pass judgment on fellow believers or cast stones at them, but to put our arms around them and restore them. In this way we are able to show the love of the Lord. We should be gentle toward them and grateful to God that we are not in the same situation. God has not made us their judge. He does not need our help in that area. When we bear others' burdens, we give them the love of the Lord and encourage them to live a life in line with His direction.

EVENING

God, thank You for what You have done in my life. Use every experience to remind me of Your love and patience. I am so grateful that You put people in my life to hold me accountable and love me with Your love. Help me to do the same for others. May I bear the burdens of others, and as a result, see them restored in their walk with You. In Jesus' name, Amen.

Lord, I come to You this morning with great confidence, knowing that there is nothing that I will face today that is too large for You to handle or too small for You to notice. You have not given me a spirit of fear, but of power, love, and a sound mind. I pray that You will make this a productive day as I seek to serve You effectively. In every situation, give me the wisdom to come to You first rather than waiting until I cannot figure it out myself. Your way is always better. Amen.

> *Since you have purified your souls in obeying the truth through the Spirit in sincere love of the brethren, love one another fervently with a pure heart.*
>
> I PETER 1:22

The purification that Peter speaks of here is a work that God does in us, not a work we do on our own. It is a result of our obedience to the truth of the Word of God as we walk in the Spirit. We are then able to love fellow believers.

Here is the secret to getting along with our brothers and sisters in Christ: putting God and His truth first. Then, we are able to love fervently with a pure heart. It is impossible to love someone fervently without a pure heart. This love is not just for show. A pure heart gives us the ability to love when we do not feel like it. We run into all types of people, some easier to love than others, but when we are submitted to God, we are able to see everyone through the eyes of the Lord. When we learn to love people in spite of all their weaknesses and our own weaknesses, then life can take on a whole new level of excitement. God gives us the ability to do things that are truly miraculous!

EVENING

Lord, how exciting it is to see things take place that can only be explained by Your power and love. I acknowledge that I have no ability to have a pure heart outside of my relationship with You. It is obvious that I have so little to do with the good that is happening in my life. All the glory and honor belong to You! I am excited to see what You will do tomorrow. I love You, Lord. Amen.

DR. MICHAEL HAMLET, SPARTANBURG, SC

Lord, I pray that You will make me sensitive to the needs of the people I will interact with today. Give me the opportunity to demonstrate the love that You have for them. May the words of my mouth and the meditation of my heart be acceptable to You. Help me to have a heart for You, and as a result, to have a heart for those who need to know You. Amen.

Be hospitable to one another without grumbling.
1 PETER 4:9

I n the time of the New Testament, there was not a hotel on every corner. When people traveled through your area, you were expected to provide hospitality, which could mean offering food and shelter for several days. In most cases you would not expect to be paid for your trouble. Sometimes people who were in this position would grumble behind the backs of their guests. The Bible says we are to be hospitable without grumbling. Christians are to be different. We are to look for ways to minister in the lives of people. Peter encouraged these Christians to serve their visitors cheerfully as a way of showing the love of the Lord.

In a society that is so selfish, a spirit of hospitality becomes very obvious to others. We must remember that we are not just serving people; we are serving the Lord, especially when we do it without grumbling. If we really care about serving the Lord, then we will look for ways to serve those whom He loves. Being hospitable requires great personal sacrifice, which gives us a chance to be generous and hospitable as unto the Lord. Today, look for people to serve in Jesus' name!

EVENING

Father, in hectic times it is hard for me to stop what I am doing and concentrate on the needs of the people around me. There is so much to be done that sometimes the details fall through the cracks. Give me a greater desire to meet the needs of people and show them the love of Christ. It is easy for me to justify neglecting this area because I am so "busy." Help me to focus on the needs of people rather than on the next item on the agenda. In Jesus' name, Amen.

MORNING

God, as I approach the weekend, I pray that You will be in the midst of our services on Sunday. I pray that You will begin even now to work in the hearts of those who will be there. Help us remember that we are to be in the business of seeing lives changed. Give our staff and lay people a great attention to detail. We know that the little things can make a tremendous difference in people's lives. May Your name be lifted up as we worship. Amen.

Continuing daily with one accord in the temple, and breaking bread from house to house, they ate their food with gladness and simplicity of heart.
ACTS 2:46

The followers of Jesus developed a lifestyle that included worship, discipleship, fellowship, and prayer. Their lives were consistent with their commitments to the Lord and to their relationships with other believers. There are those who say they can have a relationship with the Lord without having fellowship with other believers, but that is not biblical. You cannot love Him and serve Him if you do not love His church.

In the days referred to in Acts 2, there was great unity among the believers. This was a result of their worship to God and their fellowship with other believers. We find division in the body of Christ today, and that division is often a result of our choice to focus on ourselves and our own desires. We must constantly remember that Jesus Christ is Lord, and when He is on the throne of our hearts, it becomes easier to walk in one accord with other believers. As you direct your heart's worship to God today, your capacity to love and serve the body of Christ will supernaturally increase!

EVENING

Lord, I thank You for what You are doing in Your church. What a joy it is to be a part of the living body of Christ! I am so grateful to have the opportunity to serve You alongside many wonderful believers. We live in the midst of uncertain times, but we can put our trust in You as we stimulate one another to love, faith, and good works. You are the King of kings and Lord of lords, and I pray that You will use us to make a difference in people's lives for Your glory. In Jesus' name, Amen.

DR. MICHAEL HAMLET, SPARTANBURG, SC

Week 39, Monday

Father, thank You for this day and for the unique person You made me to be. Open my eyes in a fresh way today to celebrate who I am in You. Help me identify and value the differences in others. Give me an open mind to read Your Word and understand what You want to say to me right now. I look forward to experiencing joy and excitement as I see Your purpose for me and for others today. Amen.

To one is given the word of wisdom through the Spirit, to another the word of knowledge through the same Spirit . . . The body is not one member but many.
1 Corinthians 12:8, 14

T he church is a group of people who have surrendered to Jesus Christ as Lord. God designed these people to be different yet united together as one. Each person is unique and important.

Take some time to read 1 Corinthians 12:8–14 at least a few times, and then circle or write down repeated words and themes. Which words and themes stand out to you, and why?

It's obvious that we are not all the same, and this is not a mistake. So why do we tend to think everyone needs to be like us or see things the way we do or respond the way we would? Imagine what the world would be like if everyone was just like us. If you think that would be a good thing, then get another opinion! In Christ, we should not just be tolerant of our differences, but celebrate them, because they paint a bigger picture and include a much more vibrant story than we could ever paint or be a part of on our own. Together, we are God's diverse and unified church that is alive and active!

Sometimes our view of ourselves or others is too high or too low. How do you need to change your view of yourself in order to be the person God made you to be? How do you need to change your view of others in order to celebrate your differences and unite with them to accomplish God's bigger vision for the world?

EVENING

God, thank You for the diversity within Your church. Your body is made up of many unique people. Open my eyes to see and appreciate how You accomplish Your will through all of us together. Amen.

MORNING

Father, thank You for a new day—a fresh start. Yesterday is gone and today is here. Keep me focused on who You are and Your desire to lead me and guide me today. I pray I will see new opportunities to bring You honor in everything I do. Thank You. Amen.

> *No one, when he has lit a lamp, covers it with a vessel or puts it under a bed,*
> *but sets it on a lampstand, that those who enter may see the light.*
> LUKE 8:16

I have a few flashlights around my house. We use them in dim areas, when there is a blackout, and when we walk around the house in the middle of the night because we heard a noise (as if carrying around a flashlight is sneaky!). I keep these flashlights in a drawer in our kitchen for the times we need them.

Imagine that I needed a flashlight for a specific reason and went to the drawer, turned on the flashlight, and then left it in the drawer. That would seem crazy. I would walk away, fumble around in the dark, and then trip and fall or never find what I was looking for—all because I left the flashlight in the drawer.

That is what we are like when we possess God's light and keep ourselves hidden from those who would benefit from it. God has given us His light—His truth, His revelation, His Spirit. This light is meant to be useful in helping others find their way to Him, but we often cover it up or hide out where no one can benefit from it. Why do we do this? Why do you do this? What is the first reason that comes to your mind? Is it fear? Is it not realizing that you were created to be a light for others? Ask God to reveal this to you, and surrender whatever it is that is keeping you from being the light that you are meant to be for the good of others.

EVENING

Jesus, thank You that You made me right with God. It's not my own righteousness but Your righteousness that gives me the light to help others find their way to You. Help me to rest in the truth that Your light is in me. Amen.

PETE HIXSON, MABELTON, GA

Week 39, Wednesday

Father, thank You for this day. Thank You for Your love for me and for the fact that I can only love You because You first loved me. Help me to rest in You and in Your love for me. I also thank You for people You have placed in my life. Thank You that You didn't intend for me to do life alone, and this is not just for my benefit, but for the benefit of those around me and the entire world. Amen.

For in this the saying is true: "One sows and another reaps."
JOHN 4:37

Have you ever heard or said the phrase, "You complete me"? What is it that is "completed"? For a marriage, it is two people becoming one, making up differences for each other and complementing each other. For a football team, a quarterback works with a receiver in order to complete a pass and score a touchdown.

God desires for His children to work together for the good of each other and for the good of those who will benefit as a result of our working together. The point is never to overemphasize one role over another or to see one person as more important than the other. God's plan is to redeem the world back into a relationship with Himself, and He has purposefully designed us to work together in order to accomplish this.

Maybe you feel you are always "sowing" and never "reaping," and you don't see yourself as being helpful or useful. Take God's words to heart today and remember that He is in control. Regardless of the role you play, His desire and plan is greater, and it's only in His strength that His will can be accomplished.

Who in your life might you need to recognize as a person God wants to use to complement you, or vice versa, in order to fulfill a greater purpose?

EVENING
God, thank You for another day. Help me not to be so quick to take this day for granted, but to pause and thank You for all You have done. I worship You for Your grace that carried me through all the good and the bad of today. I trust You with it. In Jesus' name, Amen.

Father, thank You for who You are and who You have always been. I choose to worship You today. Show me areas in which I am trusting in myself instead of You. Help me shift that trust back over to You, or help me fully trust You with something I have never trusted You with before. Thank You for making me right with You. In the mighty name of Jesus I pray. Amen.

> *In the way of righteousness is life, and in its pathway there is no death.*
> PROVERBS 12:28

This scripture talks about the option of walking in the pathway of life and righteousness and about where this pathway leads. It seems pretty clear and simple; most of us would say that we would definitely choose life over death. But why don't we choose this path more often in everyday circumstances? Most of us can think about an experience when we have brought "death" to something—a relationship, a reputation, an emotion, or anything that has come to an end because of a wrong decision.

Now think about the word "righteousness" in this scripture. This word literally means "to be made right." What comes to your mind when you think about the meaning of this word? How does its meaning affect you? How do you wish it could affect you? Jesus is the One who makes us right with God. It's never our own righteousness or good works or trying our very best that makes us right with God. It's only in surrendering to Jesus and receiving the life that He offers that we can be made right with God. This is the kind of righteousness that you and I need, and this is the path that leads to life, not death.

Jesus said about Himself, "I am the way, the truth, and the life. No one comes to the Father except through Me" (John 14:6). Have you tried to be made right with God any other way? Or even as a Christian, do you see yourself as right with God because of anything other than your relationship with Jesus? If so, confess that. Turn to Jesus alone for your righteousness and walk in His path for your life.

EVENING

Jesus, thank You for making me right with God. Help me to trust in nothing and no one else for this "rightness"—only in You! Amen.

Week 39, Friday

Dear Lord, thank You for this new day. Thank You for another day to learn, listen, and be alive. Thank You that life in You is better than any other life outside of You. I ask You to help me rest in Your peace that will guard my heart and mind and to keep me focused on You—not the troubles, questions, or even good things that this world offers me today. May I find my peace in You. Thank You, Lord. Amen.

> *Righteousness guards him whose way is blameless,*
> *but wickedness overthrows the sinner.*
> PROVERBS 13:6

I have two beautiful daughters, and I love them very much. If you are a parent, you know what I mean, and you also understand that I would do anything to protect them. If I can do anything to keep them out of harm's way, I do it. There are times that I can physically prevent them from getting hurt or tell them how to avoid danger. However, even if I tell them the right thing to do, they can still make the choice to disobey me, walk right into a harmful situation, and end up getting hurt. That is not my desire for them, and again, as an earthly father of two young girls, I often can prevent this.

In this scripture we see another set of options, just like the proverb from yesterday. And here is this same word again: "righteousness." This time we see that it is this "rightness" with God (found only in Jesus) that guards us, protects us, and keeps our way "blameless." But there are times, even as a child of God, when we ignore God's leading and go in our own way. When we do, we can end up getting hurt and hurting others.

Again, this is why we need Jesus. This is why we need to lean continually on our relationship with Him and not rely on our own strength. Because Jesus is the One who makes us right with God; He is the One who keeps us blameless.

Ask God to reveal to you one new way you can lean on your relationship with Jesus today instead of leaning on your own strength.

EVENING
Father, thank You for this day. You are all I need. Help me to rest in Your strength, not my own. Amen.

Dear God, thank You for Your love for me today. Scripture says that You reveal Yourself as love and that You have proven that love by giving Jesus, Your only Son, so that the world can be completely forgiven and redeemed back into a relationship with You. I ask You to deepen my understanding of and appreciation for this truth today. Thank You in advance for what You are going to do today! Amen.

Just as Abraham "believed God, and it was accounted to him for righteousness."
GALATIANS 3:6

D o you remember being a child? What is it that comes to your mind when you think of being a child? It was simple then, wasn't it? We had a simple view of the world. We had hope that seemed automatic, like we didn't even think about it. If you had a trusting relationship with your dad, he would say something and you would accept it as truth. Why does that change? Whatever the reasons, things are different now, aren't they?

In this scripture, we see a childlike acceptance of what God offers. We also see what was given as a result of this acceptance. It's the same word once again: "righteousness." How was it attained? Was it through working hard or proving something or even being faithful to a task? No. It was through believing God. It is the kind of belief that involves trusting God and resting entirely in what He has done.

God made promises to Abraham, and Abraham simply but fully trusted and rested in everything God said. As a result, Abraham was made right with God. It happened through nothing more on Abraham's part than this trusting belief that a child would have in a trustworthy father.

Maybe you have been reading these devotionals and Bible verses or going to church, but you have never simply but fully trusted and "believed God" for what He offers you— forgiveness and redemption through Jesus. Believe Him today and share His work in your life with someone.

EVENING
Dear God, I will simply believe You, like a child believes a father. I believe You sent Jesus to die, to be buried, and to rise again from the dead for me. I fully trust in Jesus today. Thank You, God! Amen.

PETE HIXSON, MABELTON, GA

Lord, I thank You for a new week and a new day. As I begin, I pray that You will speak to my heart in new ways. Reveal to me the areas of my life that are out of sync with You. Give me the courage to be quiet and listen, and then to obey what You reveal to me. I know there are areas of my life that need a course correction. Change me, oh God, from the inside out. In Jesus' name I pray. Amen.

Little children, let no one deceive you. He who practices
righteousness is righteous, just as He is righteous.

1 JOHN 3:7

Have you ever been deceived? Have you ever discovered that you didn't have all the facts in a situation or that you were missing the big-picture perspective?

The word *deceive* means "to lead astray or to seduce." We can deceive ourselves by entertaining fantasies, ignoring truth, or bypassing common sense. We can also be deceived by others—people who flatter us or twist words to their own advantage. Either way, deception leads to betrayal and hurt. The road to healing and wholeness is often a long road.

So how do we protect ourselves from deceit? The Bible tells us to pursue righteousness. A righteous person is one who conforms to the character of God. By pursuing Christ and emulating His character, we become righteous. He is the standard. We are the students. This pursuit of Christ and His standard for truth builds safeguards against deception. As you begin this week, consider this: are you actively pursuing Christ and His righteousness and truth? What are the characteristics of Christ that need to be emulated in your life?

EVENING

Lord, I want to live in a right relationship with You. Open my eyes to see the areas of my life where I have deceived myself. Open my eyes to see the conversations, relationships, and practices in which I have been deceived. Help me to respond to truth with obedience. Give me the strength to forgive others because You have forgiven me. Help me to keep my eyes fixed on You and live in complete surrender to Your will and Your way. I long to be like You in both my thoughts and my actions. Amen.

MORNING

Good morning, Jesus. I'm so thankful that You are God and I am not. This week, I'm on a journey to be changed by You. I pray that today I will conform to Your image more than ever before. May Your life, not others' lives, be my standard. Continue to show me areas of my life that are out of line with Your character. Grow me in my love for You and for Your people. In Jesus' name, Amen.

What shall we say then? Is there unrighteousness with God? Certainly not!
For He says to Moses, "I will have mercy on whomever I will have mercy,
and I will have compassion on whomever I will have compassion." So then it
is not of him who wills, nor of him who runs, but of God who shows mercy.
ROMANS 9:14–16

God does not show partiality (Romans 2:11). But oftentimes we do! We play comparison games and judge our holiness in light of others' faults. We inflate our own worthiness by comparing ourselves to others who are not as far along as we think we are. But God's standard is not other people; God's standard is His Son. Isaiah reminds us that God's ways are higher than our ways, and His thoughts higher than our thoughts (Isaiah 55:9). So the standard starts with God and ends with God. He is God; we are not!

To live in righteousness as God defines it is to live like Jesus. His life is the only consistent standard that transcends culture and time. Everything else is a substitute. Likewise, the Word of God is consistent and is the only measurement by which to receive and heed instruction. Deception looms when we try to excuse our behavior or redirect our beliefs based on measures outside the Person of Jesus and the Word of God.

EVENING

God, I admit I can't do this on my own. I get it all backwards by comparing myself to others instead of looking to You as my standard. I have to change. Tonight, I'm coming clean with You, asking for Your help. I've grown weary of trying and failing. Give me more of Yourself as I strive to leave this old pattern of selfishness. Help me to live a life of true righteousness that reflects Your glory to others. In Jesus' name, Amen.

Week 40, Wednesday

God, thanks for a new day. Quicken my heart and my mind to things of You today. Guide my thoughts and direct my paths. Teach me Your ways. Open my eyes to opportunities to live Your truth for Your glory alone. Do not let me get ahead of You with unbridled zeal, nor allow me to drag behind You with a stubborn unwillingness to obey immediately. This is Your day, and I am Your servant. Use me for Your glory. Amen.

If there is any consolation in Christ, if any comfort of love, if any fellowship of the Spirit, if any affection and mercy, fulfill my joy by being like-minded, having the same love, being of one accord, of one mind. Let nothing be done through selfish ambition or conceit, but in lowliness of mind let each esteem others better than himself.

PHILIPPIANS 2:1–3

These are some of the most challenging verses in all of Scripture. To consider others better than ourselves goes against every natural desire within us. We tend to think the opposite way. We often treat others as if we are more important and our time is more valuable. Our expectations and demands of life say so. To crucify this kind of selfishness, we simply shift our focus. We look for ways to serve others and to be a blessing, no matter the role or status of those we encounter. And we do so even with people who seem to ignore our needs.

As Christ-followers we all have unique personalities, yet we are to live with unity of purpose. Unity defies selfishness. Selfishness gets in the way of God's glory and the spread of the gospel. So in pursuit of righteousness, we must crucify selfishness and esteem others as better than ourselves.

EVENING

Father, I'm not good at this. I'm better at being selfish than I am at being a servant. Help! I want to reflect Your glory to others. I want them to see Jesus in me, not the selfishness I tend to put on display. Break my heart over this sin of selfishness. Mold me into the person who seeks to serve, not to be served. May I live with unity of purpose within my church, my family, and my relationships. I'm laying it all on the altar for You. I am Yours. Use me for Your glory. In Christ's name, Amen.

MORNING

God, thank You for a new day that I get to live with You! Thank You for being patient with my stubbornness and consistent in spite of my inconsistency. Guide me in Your truth and walk with me this day. Make me aware of opportunities to put into practice what I'm learning from You through these daily devotions. Thank You for loving me. In Jesus' name, Amen.

If we are beside ourselves, it is for God; or if we are of sound mind, it is for you. For the love of Christ compels us, because we judge thus: that if One died for all, then all died; and He died for all, that those who live should live no longer for themselves, but for Him who died for them and rose again.

2 CORINTHIANS 5:13–15

Yesterday, we looked at the call to regard others as better than ourselves. Today, we are challenged to live no longer for ourselves. Ouch! Where are my rights? What about my wants and desires? They are all laid at the Cross. We are called to rally around the gospel, full force. Our life message and life passion must be about Jesus and His message of freedom through forgiveness. In our culture, people who live with such intensity are considered unstable, weird, or freakish. But that's the life God has called us to live in wreckless abandon to Him, for Him, and with Him!

As we pursue righteousness, may our lives sing that old hymn: "All to Jesus I surrender, all to Him I freely give . . . I surrender all."

EVENING

Lord, choosing to surrender and sacrifice seems too hard. I'm not there yet, but I want to be. I confess that I need You. I can't do this on my own. To do it out of duty seems too religious. I want to be devoted to You out of the overflow of my love for You. So increase my faith in You, my ability to focus on You, and my personal desire for Your glory instead of my own. As I wrap up this day, I'm longing for You to work supernaturally in my life. Bring to my memory these verses so that I can live them when faced with competing challenges. I pray that You will find me faithful instead of foolish. I love You, Lord. Amen.

Week 40, Friday

Lord, I can't live in a right relationship with others without having a right relationship with You. Often, I'm more concerned with my agenda than Yours. Convict me and point out the adjustments I must make to be wholly Yours. Grow me and change me from the inside out to be fully devoted to You. I love You, Lord Jesus. Grant me the grace to live like it. In Christ's name, Amen.

I do not pray for these alone, but also for those who will believe in Me through their word; that they all may be one, as You, Father, are in Me, and I in You; that they also may be one in Us, that the world may believe that You sent Me.

JOHN 17:20, 21

During His final days on earth, Jesus prayed for and thought about you and me. He prayed that we would have a spirit of unity, so that the love we have for one another through Christ would draw a watching world to Him.

When Jesus prayed that we would be one, did He mean that we would agree on every detail? Did He mean that we are all supposed to be carbon copies of one another? No! Jesus prayed for unity, not uniformity. Jesus asks that we be one, just as the Father and Jesus are one. The phrase "may be one" literally means "one thing." Jesus asked not for the elimination of individual lives, but for oneness of a unified body, with its various members developing as a part of the whole. Why? So that the world will believe God sent Jesus and understand God's love initiative for all people. Therefore to fulfill Jesus' prayer, we must grow to become more like Him, unified in His love and focused on His purposes.

EVENING

Lord, I'm humbled to know that You prayed for me long before I was born. Thank You for caring for me and for giving me a reason to live: to point people to You. Give me strength to live out the unity of the gospel. Help me to put aside petty arguments and to focus on kingdom matters. Forgive me for the times I've made minor issues major battles. Help me to be a part of the solution, not a part of the problem. I am Your servant. Amen.

MORNING

God, I thank You for the people You've placed in my life: family, friends, co-workers, neighbors. Admittedly, sometimes they are hard to love. Even so, help me to love them well. Thank You for how You are growing me and challenging me in my relationships. Bring me opportunities today to make a difference in someone's life by Your power. In Jesus' name, Amen.

> *As iron sharpens iron, so a man sharpens the countenance of his friend.*
> PROVERBS 27:17

This verse is often quoted, but how often is it lived? Everyone needs to be mentored and, at the same time, to be mentoring someone else. True friends add value to one another; it's give and take. It's listening and learning. Growing relationships are not all one-way communication. We aren't smart enough to do all the talking. That's why the best relationships are those in which each person adds value to the other.

Honest conversations, in which it is safe to challenge and be challenged, are rare. That should not be so. It is that sharpening of the iron against iron that strengthens both. It works with metal, and it works with relationships. Pursue relationships in which you can both give and receive honest and loving feedback. These are the kind of friendships that grow us in our pursuit of righteousness.

I'm thankful for the men and women who have influenced my life and challenged me to step up and step out. What about you? Take time to thank God for those who have invested in you and coached you up! A friend who has made an impact in your life for the better is a rare treasure. Have you paid it forward? Are you investing in others? Who are you calling to godliness, holiness, righteousness, and purity? Sharpen the iron and be a blessing!

EVENING

God, I see how You've been at work in me and around me. Thank You for the friends who love me and challenge me. Thank You for those who push my buttons and give me opportunities to grow! Lord, I pray that You would help me to see others as You see them. Use me as a blessing and encouragement to them, whether they return the investment or not. Thank You for those who have sharpened me in personal holiness. Bless them this night I pray. In Jesus' name, Amen.

DR. RICHARD MARK LEE, SUGAR HILL, GA

Week 41, Monday

Good morning, Lord. Today I enter Your courts **boldly** in the mighty name of Jesus, knowing You hear me and long to answer me. You do not slumber; You do not sleep; You wait on me to call upon Your name and claim Your promises. Lord, grant me the courage to live in obedience to Your will that I might see these prayers answered in Your timing and through Your power. In Jesus' name, Amen.

> *Now this is the confidence that we have in Him, that if we ask anything*
> *according to His will, He hears us. And if we know that He hears us, whatever*
> *we ask, we know that we have the petitions that we have asked of Him.*
> 1 JOHN 5:14, 15

As a Christ-follower, you have the guaranteed assurance that you can **boldly** approach God in prayer and that He will not only hear but also answer. We can approach **boldly**, not with knocking knees and trepidation. Our **boldness** should not be based on our goodness or human efforts, but rather on His promise. Yes, a promise! A promise that He will answer requests that align with His will.

We act and react according to His will when we obey Him. I have learned the hard way that obedience is the only way to live in God's will. If I am to approach God **boldly** and **confidently**, then I must be living obediently. Jesus said in John 14:15, "If you love Me, keep My commandments." That verse isn't a scolding disclaimer—it's a promise. A gentle, loving promise that if you truly love Jesus, you will obey Him. So let me ask you a simple question: if your prayer life is an indicator of your level of obedience to Christ, do you have some soul searching and housekeeping to do today? Before we can approach with **bold assurance**, we must first prepare our hearts with fierce preparation.

EVENING

Good evening, Lord. Thank You for Your courage and assurance throughout this day. Lord, I realize that Your will isn't like running water. It rarely follows the path of least resistance, and I may also have to overcome obstacles as I walk in obedience with You. Allow me discernment that I might walk in perfect timing with Your will for my life. Amen.

MORNING

Good morning, Lord. Allow me to live in obedience to Your will that I might be a testimony of Your grace today. I know You can do anything and that You can do anything through me. May I act and react in such a way that You will smile upon my day and richly bless my efforts. Amen.

Most assuredly, I say to you, he who believes in Me, the works that I do he will do also; and greater works than these he will do, because I go to My Father. And whatever you ask in My name, that I will do, that the Father may be glorified in the Son. If you ask anything in My name, I will do it.
JOHN 14:12–14

If you ask anything in My name, I will do it. Wow! That's a big promise with huge implications. Jesus promised great power on earth—not more power than Jesus, but the necessary power to accomplish His work in and through you. Think about it: Peter saw more people come to faith at Pentecost than Jesus did in His three years of ministry. And thanks to modern technology, you can "preach" to thousands daily. Those are "greater works"!

You have also been given great authority in heaven. Through Jesus, you have the authority of God. You can be a big-time name dropper and pray in His name with the assurance He will hear and answer when you live and pray according to His will. So go ahead and ask for it! The secret is in the asking. Your ability to continue the work of God in and through you requires power from heaven, but it also requires action from you! St. Augustine, the great theologian who championed salvation by faith and divine grace, once said, "Pray as though everything depended on God. Work as though everything depended on you." May your prayers be in accordance with God's will, and may your actions follow your prayers. When these come into alignment, God's power is right around the corner.

EVENING

Good evening, Lord. Please grant me the courage to pray and act in Your will that I might see Your power in my life this week. You are my strength and my hope. Allow me to see Your power and the clarity of Your will. In Jesus' name, Amen.

CHUCK ALLEN, DULUTH, GA

Week 41, Wednesday

Good morning, Lord. Please calm my spirit and remove any anxiousness there. Lord, I need You today. I need You and You alone. Breathe into my heart a spirit of thankfulness and joy that will dispel doubt and despair. Lord, I long to be a champion for You today. There is nothing I cannot overcome in Your strength as I walk in Your will. Amen.

Be anxious for nothing, but in everything by prayer and supplication, with thanksgiving, let your requests be made known to God; and the peace of God, which surpasses all understanding, will guard your hearts and minds through Christ Jesus.
PHILIPPIANS 4:6, 7

I read recently that worry and stress can cause heart disease, cancer, migraines, and even diabetes. Worry causes sickness, but it also causes spiritual chaos. Worry changes the way we treat God, others, and ourselves. We get short-tempered and terse, and we tend to direct our frustration at those we love the most. We all worry, don't we? But worry is a bit like a rocking chair—it's something we can do, but it doesn't get us anywhere.

So what does God's Word say about worry? Matthew 6:25 says, "Do not worry." And Jesus told us in Matthew 6:34, "Do not worry about tomorrow." The God of all creation wants you to bring all your worries to Him and leave them for Him to handle. In today's passage, God tells us to be thankful and bring all our requests (and worries) to Him. And don't just take them to Him—leave them there! Trust Him with them! Now that's a deal you just can't beat! Go ahead, say a hearty "Amen!" to that and leave your worry with Him today.

EVENING

Good evening, Lord. Thank You for being God. Thank You for hearing me and answering me. Thank You for taking my worry, my fret, and my anxiety away because I can always count on You. You are my peace, and in You I find my joy. Lord, I have so much to do and so much to be concerned with. Please grant me the ability to prioritize what is most important in Your eyes as I seek Your perfect will for my life. In Jesus' name I pray. Amen.

MORNING

Good morning, Lord. As You taught me, I am calling on You for deliverance. Lord, I praise and honor You today. You alone are God. You alone are worthy to be called upon and praised. You hear the desire of the afflicted and encourage them. Encourage me today, Lord, to live for You and to seek Your face and Your will throughout this day. In Jesus' name, Amen.

> *Call to Me, and I will answer you, and show you great*
> *and mighty things, which you do not know.*
> JEREMIAH 33:3

Prayer unlocks great promises of God—promises like the one in today's scripture: "Call to Me, and I will answer you," which can also be translated, "Cry to Me!" James tells us, "The effective, fervent prayer of a righteous man avails much" (James 5:16). Hannah prayed and God gave her a son (1 Samuel 1:9–20). God answered Elijah's prayer for no rain and then for rain (James 5:17, 18). Elisha prayed for life to return to a dead child (2 Kings 4:18–36). Samson prayed for strength to return (Judges 16:28–30). Paul and Silas prayed in prison (Acts 16:25). In each of these prayers, God answered, and He still answers our prayers!

Prayer has power that we cannot imagine. The "great and mighty things" referred to in today's verse can be translated "that which has been previously hidden and that God has committed to deliver to His people." If you are like me, I need some of that power source. When Jeremiah wrote this he was a prisoner. He was in need of great power, something beyond the human norm to happen in his life. With all the technology available to us, we often want to be able to immediately understand everything that is in front of us. However, God says we are to call out to Him, and He will show us a power source that we cannot understand and we do not know. Call out to Him today and expect great and mighty things!

EVENING

Good evening, Lord. I need Your power. Thank You for making it available to me as one of Your children. Thank You for its availability and its capability. Lord, allow me to trust You to do mighty things in and through me. Amen.

CHUCK ALLEN, DULUTH, GA

Week 41, Friday

Good morning, Lord. Everywhere I turn there are people in need. Give me a broken heart to pray earnestly for hurting people today and to minister to them. By faith I acknowledge that all healing comes from Your hands. Amen.

Is anyone among you sick? Let him call for the elders of the church, and let them pray over him, anointing him with oil in the name of the Lord. And the prayer of faith will save the sick, and the Lord will raise him up. And if he has committed sins, he will be forgiven.
JAMES 5:14, 15

I'll never forget the day my thirteen-year-old daughter asked, "Daddy, when is Mommy going to die?" In the midst of my wife's battle with cancer, all my theological training counted for nothing at that moment. We had prayed, anointed her with oil, fasted, and wept. I said, "Honey, God is going to heal Mommy. He may choose to heal her immediately, and we pray for that. He might choose to heal her through doctors, surgeries, and medicines as she keeps fighting. Or God might choose to heal her in heaven. Any way you look at it, God is going to heal Mommy." Eleven months later God healed my wife in Glory as she stepped onto streets of gold.

In today's passage, James instructs us to pray for healing. He tells us to call on the body of believers and church leaders to pray for us and anoint us with oil. Remember that the oil isn't special—the prayers of faith are special. Because of God's answer to prayer, my wife is now happy and healthy and healed in heaven. The most valuable lesson I learned through my wife's illness and passing is that God can and will use anything and everything to accomplish His will in His timing. Have faith, pray for healing, and wait on God to carry out His perfect will.

EVENING
Good evening, Lord. I may not need Your healing powers in my life today, but at some time I will. When I do, grant me the faith to call upon You for healing, to call upon my church leaders for prayer, and to believe that the anointment of oil is a picture of Your Spirit at work. Lord, I trust in You. In Jesus' name, Amen.

God, You are my comforter, my rock, my strength, and my shield. When I am lonely, remind me of Your presence. When I am desperate, remind me of Your provision. When I am anxious, remind me of Your peace. Allow me to walk in the certainty of that truth in uncertain times. Amen.

> *Hear my prayer, O Lord, and let my cry come to You.*
> *Do not hide Your face from me in the day of my trouble;*
> *incline Your ear to me; in the day that I call, answer me speedily.*
> PSALM 102:1, 2

I remember walking into my bedroom after preaching at my wife's funeral and falling to the floor, crushed by the weight of loneliness. Lying there, the Lord spoke this to my spirit: "Peace be still!" After more than seven years of serving as a caregiver to my high school sweetheart and bride of twenty-five years, I was suddenly and overwhelmingly alone. As I cried out to God in my hour of need, the reply I heard was, "Peace be still!"

Five years later I was with a group of high school students traveling across the Sea of Galilee when I asked the boat's captain to stop. Suddenly overcome by emotion, I was reminded that on those same waters, Jesus had indeed brought comfort to the disciples in their hour of need and that He had calmed the storms of life.

Despair isn't something to be ashamed of—we all face times of loneliness, despair, or depression. But how do we change that pattern of despair? First, we change our way of thinking. Believe God is capable to see you through. Our God is able! Second, understand God's sovereignty. It's like the saying goes: "There's only one God, and you're not Him." Trust that He knows what is best for you. Third, remember that God loves you enough to send His own Son to calm the storms in your life. Cry out to Him and ask for the peace that only He can bring!

EVENING

Good evening, Lord. Allow me to rest in the unfailing love and power found only in Your arms. God, You are my ever-present help in times of trouble. Thank You for always being here and never leaving me alone. Your voice is my comfort; allow me to hear from You as I find hope in Your presence. Amen.

CHUCK ALLEN, DULUTH, GA

Precious Lord Jesus Christ, I surrender my life to You. I ask that when this week is complete, I will be able to see Your signature all over my life. There is nothing like knowing that You are with me and that Your power is upon my life. Lead me. Empower me. Show me Your will in all things. May this be the week that I learn about the power of prayer. Whatever life throws my way, may I honor You. You alone deserve to be praised. Amen.

Confess your trespasses to one another, and pray for one another, that you may be healed. The effective, fervent prayer of a righteous man avails much.
JAMES 5:16

True fellowship among God's people involves sharing struggles, victories, defeats, hurts, and even sins with one another. No one can forgive sin other than God, but when we share our spiritual struggles with others, we move to a new level of responsibility and accountability to them. When we see others as members of our spiritual family, we carry their burdens and pray for them. The result may be not only spiritual healing but also physical healing. This is when we begin to experience the power of prayer in our lives.

Effective prayer occurs when you talk to God and listen to what He is saying to you. When we pray effectively and passionately about specific things in life with hearts that are clean before God and others, our prayers will begin to accomplish much. Nothing will ignite your prayer life more than seeing prayers answered. Pursue the God-glorifying experience of seeing God work through prayer!

EVENING

Dear Father, You have been faithful to me. I have seen You move in my life. If You desire for me to pray in the middle of the night, wake me up, call me to Yourself. I am available. I want to learn what it means to experience the power of prayer. Lord, I give You my life tonight. Amen.

Good morning, Lord. Here am I. Your servant is listening. I desire to hear from You and receive a special word from You for this day. When I open Your Word, speak to my heart. May Your Word speak in a roar and become like fire in my heart. Open the eyes of my heart, Lord. I want see You. I want to hear You. I want to live for You. In Jesus' name, Amen.

Rejoice always, pray without ceasing, in everything give thanks;
for this is the will of God in Christ Jesus for you.
1 THESSALONIANS 5:16–18

As you develop your prayer life and mature in your faith, your attitude has to be adjusted continually. Paul taught that believers should seek to develop and maintain an attitude of rejoicing. A prayerful heart can result in a life of rejoicing. Circumstances will attempt to rob your joy, but when they seem to be pressing in on you, remember: you can pray.

You can pray anytime, anywhere, about anything. When we begin to understand God's ceaseless availability and willingness to see us through anything, then an attitude of thanksgiving will begin to arise from the depths of our souls. Rejoicing, praying, and thanksgiving—this is God's will for our lives.

The power of prayer is seen most clearly in the lives of people who have attitudes of joy and thanksgiving. Only prayer can adjust our attitude. We cannot do it on our own.

Today, pray about your attitude. Choose to rejoice when things do not go well for you. Choose to be thankful regardless of what Satan throws your way. You may ask, "How can I do that?" The answer is to be committed to praying at all times about all things. When you do this, you will see the power of prayer!

EVENING

Oh God, as I reflect on this day, I see that You have helped me adjust my attitude continually. Thank You for teaching me the power of prayer. You are amazing. You alone are awesome. I am Yours, and I pray that You will be praised through my life. Amen.

Father, I am thankful for everything in my life this morning. I am thankful for my family, my friends, my job, my church, and my pastor. I am thankful for the role in life that You have entrusted to me. I am thankful this morning for every problem I have and every problem that may come my way today, because they are opportunities for me to grow closer to You and for You to have glory. Help me remember that You are calling me to Yourself through everything in my life. I choose to live for You today. In Jesus' name, Amen.

I say to you, whatever things you ask when you pray, believe that
you receive them, and you will have them. And whenever you stand praying,
if you have anything against anyone, forgive him, that your Father in
heaven may also forgive you your trespasses.
MARK 11:24, 25

We begin to realize the power of prayer when we pray according to God's Word and God's will. As He directs our prayers and we navigate by His Word and sovereign will, we learn that the power of prayer is limitless. What we can pray about is limitless, but more importantly, what God can do is limitless.

One of the most tragic barriers to powerful prayer is the refusal to forgive others. I believe that is the greatest obstacle for personal revival and revival in the church. Jesus died for all of your baggage. You have checked it at the Cross. You must not keep trying to drag it around. Get over it! Let it go. Forgiving others makes it possible.

If you want to experience limitless power while praying, then you have to experience limitless genuine forgiveness. There is nothing anyone has ever done to you that cannot be forgiven. If God can forgive it—and He has—you can, too. When you let it go, you will be able to experience the power of prayer.

EVENING

Dear Lord, I choose to forgive everyone in my life. I choose to treat others like You treat me. Enable me to extend loving forgiveness to others. I ask You to do great things in my life. I believe only You can accomplish them. In Jesus' name, Amen.

MORNING

Dear God, keep me alert in my time with You today. I am a weak person. At times I get so distracted that I forget I am talking to You. Keep me focused. I come to You in prayer because I need You—I even need You to help me pray. Teach me to pray, Lord. I give You my all today. Speak to me now. Amen.

> *He came and found them sleeping, and said to Peter, "Simon, are you sleeping? Could you not watch one hour? Watch and pray, lest you enter into temptation. The spirit indeed is willing, but the flesh is weak."*
> MARK 14:37, 38

Have you ever gone to sleep while you were praying? When I was in college, my friends and I would have late night prayer meetings together, and one of my friends became known as one who went to sleep from time to time. I have written books on prayer, yet there have been times when I have fallen asleep while praying, too.

Can you imagine Jesus asking you while you are praying, "Are you asleep?" Can you imagine the penetration of the next question: "Could you not just pray for one hour?" When Jesus was about to go to the Cross, Peter fell asleep. Jesus told him that he had better watch and pray or he would fall into temptation. Peter's spirit was willing, but his flesh was weak. Some say this weakness resulted in Peter denying Jesus three times.

While so many things compete for your time with God, your time with Him should be your priority. Therefore, when you are fulfilling that commitment to pray, be focused and do not lose the moment in any way. When you get into your place of prayer, do not get so comfortable that you can go to sleep easily. At times, get up and walk around while you pray. Prayer is so powerful that when practiced in the right manner, it can help you overcome all temptation—even the temptation to sleep and to be distracted.

EVENING

My precious heavenly Father, may I not be one who sleeps when I pray. Help me to be so in tune with You that I am focused on the matters at hand. Forgive me for the times I have failed to do that, and equip me to become a powerful prayer warrior for You. Amen.

DR. RONNIE FLOYD, SPRINGDALE, AR

God, teach me to pray. I need to talk with You, and I feel, like so many other times, inadequate to do so. I am grateful for the blood of Jesus that makes me worthy to stand before You. I am grateful for the presence of the Holy Spirit that never leaves me. I am thankful to You, Father, for enabling me to do everything I do, including praying. Amen.

The Spirit also helps in our weaknesses. For we do not know what we should pray for as we ought, but the Spirit Himself makes intercession for us with groanings which cannot be uttered.
ROMANS 8:26

This scripture is always such a comfort to me. There have been many times I have not been able to pray—times when my heart has been so heavy about a situation that I have not known how to talk to God about it, and I have felt helpless and weak. Has anything like this ever happened to you? The Spirit of God helps you during these moments in life. He prays for you even when you do not know how to pray for yourself. He intercedes for you, carrying your greatest needs to God the Father and Jesus the Son.

Fans of the Texas A&M football team have a tradition of never sitting down during a ballgame. They call it "The Twelfth Man" because a twelfth player is one who is always nearby and ready to jump in the game if the team needs help. For years, the student body has stood to show their support. Win or lose, rain or shine, they are standing.

The Holy Spirit is so much more than this for you. He never exits, He never leaves you, and, yes, He prays for you even when you do not know what or how to pray. This means that God is for you. If God is for you, who can be against you? He is pulling you toward victory, standing with you and for you at all times—and I mean at all times! Take comfort and be encouraged by this right now: God is for you.

EVENING

Lord, thank You for Your Spirit. As this day is closing and my heart is heavy over various issues, I am thankful that Your Spirit will be interceding for me even while I rest physically. Thanks, Lord. Amen.

MORNING

Lord, thanks for the past week. I am thankful for both the good and tough moments. I am thankful for what You have taught me about the power of prayer. As I enter this weekend, continue to teach me. While I am away from the grind of life, speak to my heart. Please prepare the heart of my pastor to preach the Word, and help me hear what You want to say to me while I listen. Amen.

> *Beloved, I pray that you may prosper in all things and be in health,*
> *just as your soul prospers. For I rejoiced greatly when brethren came and*
> *testified of the truth that is in you, just as you walk in the truth.*
>
> 3 JOHN 2, 3

The apostle John was very impressed with the life of a man named Gaius. He was evidently a very spiritual and godly man who walked in the truth of God. When we follow John's example and ask God to give fellow believers health and prosperity according to their spiritual lives, that is powerful praying.

This weekend, get your life in order. Draw near to the Savior. Appeal to Him to clean you up and prepare you for service. Ask Him to make you the kind of Christ-follower that walks in His truth. Is your soul prospering, such that you'd want someone to pray for you like John prayed for Gaius? Ask God to grant you good physical health as well as spiritual, relational, and even material blessings.

Today, declare to God, "I am counting on You alone!" Count on God to get you through the coming week. Count on Him to get you through the adversities of life you presently face as well as those you will face in the future. Prayerfully express your dependence on Him in all things every day.

EVENING

Father, I pray that You would help me to draw near to You and walk closely with You, so that others will see You through me. As you empower me to walk with You, I pray that You will find me worthy of Your blessings in my life. Dear God, I am counting on You for everything I need. Amen.

Week 43, Monday

Gracious Father, I commit this week to Your purposes. Thank You that You always hear my prayers and consider my meditations. Even in the midst of uncertainty and anxiety, I will look to You and depend on Your strength. Today, I will walk in Your power and rest in Your promises. Amen.

Give ear to my words, O LORD, consider my meditation. Give heed to the voice of my cry, my King and my God, for to You I will pray. My voice You shall hear in the morning, O LORD; in the morning I will direct it to You, and I will look up.

PSALM 5:1–3

David was known as a man after God's own heart. David was not perfect, but he passionately pursued God with a heart that longed to know Him personally and powerfully.

One of the reasons David was described as a man after God's own heart is the way he started his day—his first thought of the day was prayer. He said to God, "My voice You shall hear in the morning."

It is likely that this psalm was written during Absalom's rebellion against his father, David. The word *meditation* literally means "brooding sorrow or incessant groaning," so this psalm describes a time when David encountered great sorrow. While being pursued like a wild animal, he directed his gaze toward God and depended on Him.

Where do you turn in times of distress? It is easy to believe the world's lies that the answers we look for in troubling times come from experts, best-selling authors, psychiatrists, talk-show hosts, spiritual gurus, or casual acquaintances. The Enemy would like nothing more than to point you away from the only true Source of help.

Develop a habit of turning to the Lord. Live in a way that says, "My help comes from the Lord, who made heaven and earth" (Psalm 121:2).

EVENING

Lord, I thank You that in both good and bad times, I can depend on You. In times of distress, I can rest in Your promises and provisions. I cast my cares upon You and take shelter in the shadow of Your wings. Thank You that nothing can harm me unless it is filtered through Your loving and wise hands. I take comfort in knowing that the God of the universe takes care of me. Amen.

Jesus, thank You for another day to serve You. I begin my day by spending time with You. I commit myself to Your will. Give me an unquenchable passion to see the gospel expand to the nations and the lost come to know You. In Jesus' matchless name, Amen.

Masters, give your bondservants what is just and fair, knowing that you also have a Master in heaven. Continue earnestly in prayer, being vigilant in it with thanksgiving; meanwhile praying also for us, that God would open to us a door for the word, to speak the mystery of Christ, for which I am also in chains.
COLOSSIANS 4:1–3

As Paul was in chains, he requested the church to pray on his behalf—not that he would be released from prison, but that he could continue to spread the gospel where he was. Paul's prayer for an "open door" is not referring to the door of his prison cell, but to the door for the gospel to reach those who need salvation.

Paul instructed the church to pray earnestly for the expansion of the gospel. As followers of Christ, this must be our steadfast and sincere desire. Our hearts should long for what the prophet Habakkuk proclaimed: "The earth will be filled with the knowledge of the glory of the Lord, as the waters cover the sea" (Habakkuk 2:14).

Have you prayed for God to open the door for the expansion of the gospel in your life? Have you prayed for the gospel to reach your family, friends, neighbors, community, nation, and unreached people groups around the world? Many of us spend our prayer time concerned about our comfort or complaining about our problems. Too often we pray for our prosperity instead of praying for the furtherance of the gospel. Paul's example teaches us that the spread of the gospel trumps personal comfort. Our passion should be the same as Paul's—"to speak the mystery of Christ." Ask God to make this your earnest, constant desire.

EVENING
Lord, give me a heart for prayer that reaches well beyond my wants and wishes. Preoccupy my heart with the world's greatest need—the gospel of Jesus Christ. May my mind be set on seeing all nations bow before Your throne in worship. I die to a life of ease and comfort for the sake of Your precious, saving grace. Amen.

Father, may I follow the example of Jesus and surrender completely to Your will. I abandon all thoughts of selfish gain or worldly success and submit my life to Your desires. I commit this day to You. May You be honored in everything I think, say, and do. Amen.

> *When He came to the place, He said to them, "Pray that you may not enter into temptation." And He was withdrawn from them about a stone's throw, and He knelt down and prayed, saying, "Father, if it is Your will, take this cup away from Me; nevertheless not My will, but Yours, be done."*
>
> LUKE 22:40–42

Throughout the Gospels, Jesus often withdrew to quiet, secluded places to pray because His strength came from personal communion with God. Jesus is the ultimate example for Christians. His selfless obedience and faithful determination provide the perfect model for us. As Jesus agonized over His approaching death and the devastating effects of God's wrath, He prayed, "Not My will, but Yours, be done."

In these verses, Jesus revealed two major prayers that every Christian should pray. First, He said, "Pray that you may not enter into temptation." This is a prayer for holiness. Believers should seek close fellowship with God that leads to holy living. Second, He prayed, "Not My will, but Yours, be done." This is a prayer for obedience. Christ was concerned with the plan of redemption and perfectly followed His Father's plan. Personal holiness will always lead to a life of obedience.

Prayer is surrender—surrender to God's will and cooperation with that will. If I throw out a boathook from a boat and catch hold of the shore and pull, do I pull the shore to myself, or do I pull myself to the shore? Prayer is not pulling God to my will, but aligning my will to God's will.

Our personal agendas and aspirations must take a backseat to God's will for our lives and this world. That's what prayer is about—not what we want, but what God wants. When you pray, do you give instructions, or do you report for duty?

EVENING

Jesus, You are the perfect example of total surrender and devotion. May I live a life of personal holiness that leads me to unhindered obedience. Teach me to follow Your example of prayer and faithfulness in my life each day. Amen.

Loving Savior, thank You for Your measureless grace and boundless love. Today, may I experience and display Your love. Amen.

> *God is my witness, how greatly I long for you all with the affection of*
> *Jesus Christ. And this I pray, that your love may abound still*
> *more and more in knowledge and all discernment.*
> PHILIPPIANS 1:8, 9

The world will know you are God's child by your love. You cannot build a life for God's glory if the foundation is not love. So many have tried to build upon doctrine or good works, but doctrine and good works without love is legalism. The God of Scripture *is* love, and He instructs us to love as He loves.

Paul prayed not that believers' love would begin, but that their love would abound. He hoped that it would keep on overflowing in a perpetual stream. This love is not some indiscriminate feeling; it is based on "knowledge and all discernment." It is a love with necessary limitations. "Knowledge" is more than just factual information about God's Word, or even the acknowledgement of its truth and infallibility. Real knowledge produces holiness through sincere devotion to His Word. "All discernment" appears only here in the New Testament and refers to a high level of biblical, theological, moral, and spiritual perception. It points to the Holy Spirit's leading in a believer's life.

The picture in this passage is that our love should flow like a mighty river, but be kept within the banks of knowledge and discernment. Biblical love is far from blind. It seeks to know Christ's mind and heart in order to follow His leading.

As we seek to live for God's glory, the only place to start is with love. Godly love is only produced by the Spirit of God. How can we pursue growth in this area? Through prayer. Andrew Murray, the South African minister and author, said, "God's child can conquer everything by prayer. Is it any wonder that Satan does his utmost to snatch that weapon from the Christian or to hinder him in the use of it?" Prayer is the place to start as you seek to love others in Christ's name today.

EVENING

Dear Jesus, I pray that You would give me a heart to love others as You have loved me. May my life be marked by the indelible imprint of Your perfect love. Amen.

DR. JIM PERDUE, MILLINGTON, TN

Father, teach me to pray for others more than I pray for myself. Today, bring someone to my attention who needs the ministry of prayer. Amen.

> *I pray to God that you do no evil, not that we should appear approved,*
> *but that you should do what is honorable, though we may seem disqualified.*
> *For we can do nothing against the truth, but for the truth. For we are glad when we*
> *are weak and you are strong. And this also we pray, that you may be made complete.*
> 2 CORINTHIANS 13:7–9

Paul constantly prayed for others' needs. Even in his weakness, he was glad for others' strength. He prayed that the church would be restored and be made complete. The Greek word for *complete* describes the setting of bones and the reconciling of alienated friends. Paul prayed for reconciliation of divisions and restoration within the church.

We are called to lift up others' needs to God's throne. Prayer is more than just mentioning our needs to God; it is connecting with God intimately and interceding for others faithfully. S. D. Gordon said,

> The greatest thing any one can do for God and for man is to pray. It is not the only thing. But it is the chief thing . . . The great people of the earth to-day [sic] are the people who pray. I do not mean those who talk about prayer; nor those who say they believe in prayer; nor yet those who can explain about prayer; but I mean those people who *take* time and *pray*.[16]

When was the last time you prayed for someone else more than you prayed for yourself? Paul's prayer was kingdom-minded. He understood that church divisions hinder the expansion of the gospel. He desired reconciliation not so he would "appear approved," but so Christians would do "what is honorable."

Prayer will align us with God's will and unite us with other believers. Only then can we be "made complete."

EVENING
Jesus, teach me to be an intercessor. Direct my heart to be more concerned about Your kingdom and others' needs instead of my desires. Amen.

Father, I commit this day and my life into Your hands. Lead and instruct me according to Your perfect will. You are the God of my life, and I thank You for Your indwelling presence. Fill me with Your Spirit and lead me in Your truth. Amen.

The Lord will command His lovingkindness in the daytime,
and in the night His song shall be with me—a prayer to the God of my life.
PSALM 42:8

———— ∽ ————

S ir Isaac Newton said that he could take his telescope and look millions and millions of miles into space. Then he added, "But when I lay it aside, go into my room, shut the door, and get down on my knees in earnest prayer, I see more of heaven and feel closer to the Lord than if I were assisted by all the telescopes on earth." Prayer connects you to the very heart of God.

As you prepare for corporate worship this weekend, remember that God is always present with you. Corporate worship is the overflow of what God has done in your life throughout the week. The psalmist describes an ongoing, personal relationship with God. The Lord is everything to him—his steadfast love during the day and his song at night.

He directs his prayer to the God of his life, not the God of his Sundays or the God of his parents. God was his all-consuming purpose in life. His relationship with God was everything. Can this be said of you? Have you surrendered every aspect of your life to the lordship of Jesus Christ? This is true worship—allowing Christ to live in you through the power of the Spirit.

The church needs men and women who will surrender all to Jesus and allow the Holy Spirit to direct them according to His will. E. M. Bounds, a nineteenth-century American pastor, wrote, "What the Church needs today is . . . men whom the Holy Spirit can use—men of prayer, men mighty in prayer. The Holy Spirit does not flow through methods, but through men. He does not come on machinery, but on men. He does not anoint plans, but men—men of prayer."[17] Will you be a person of prayer?

———— ∽ ————

EVENING
Lord, thank You for being forever present with me. May I live each day in complete submission to Your will and in the power of Your Spirit. Amen.

DR. JIM PERDUE, MILLINTON, TN

Week 44, Monday

Lord, I am nothing. When You found me, I was in a pit of sin. Thank You for quarrying me out of that pit and, by grace, cementing me into Your spiritual church. Today, help me extend to others the grace You have extended to me. In Jesus' name, Amen.

> *By grace you have been saved through faith,*
> *and that not of yourselves; it is the gift of God.*
> EPHESIANS 2:8

Salvation is a gift of God. He offers it in His grace, and we receive it in faith. Salvation cannot be bought or earned; it is not the result of church membership, baptism, keeping the Ten Commandments, or taking communion. We only receive salvation by placing our faith in what Jesus did for us on the Cross.

When Jesus was a twelve-year-old lad, He told His parents, "I must be about My Father's business" (Luke 2:49). When Jesus was a thirty-three-year-old man, He said on the Cross, "It is finished!" (John 19:30). The Father's business was finished. Jesus came to this earth to provide salvation for us. This work of salvation is His work, not ours.

If God would allow us to enter heaven on the merit of our good works, it would then be right for us to say, "I'm here because of my good works," or "I'm here because I did this or didn't do that." If we could boast of our works that earned our salvation, heaven would be filled with that which God hates—pride. Furthermore, if we were prideful in heaven, then God would have to kick us out, like He did Lucifer.

Salvation is God's gift, and you can't work for or earn a gift—that is a contradiction of terms. The only two things you can do with a gift are to receive it or to reject it. Salvation is free to sinners, but was very costly to Jesus. His nail-pierced hands will remind us throughout eternity of the high price of our salvation.

EVENING

Lord, I thank You for Your grace that has pardoned me and cleansed me. In Jesus' name, Amen.

Oh Lord, I desire to use what Your grace has given me to benefit You, Your kingdom, and others today. May my life bring glory to You. Amen.

To each one of us grace was given according to the measure of Christ's gift.
EPHESIANS 4:7

———————————— ✸ ————————————

God's grace is unifying. We have one body, one Spirit, one hope, one Lord, one faith, one baptism, and one God (Ephesians 4:4–6). The grace that saves us also unifies us in the body of Christ. We have much in common, and we are not to live in isolation—we are all part of the same body.

However, unity is not uniformity. God created each of us uniquely and gives His church a variety of spiritual gifts. Every follower of Christ receives at least one gift useful for building up the body of Christ—we receive them so we can serve Him and other believers in a way that glorifies Christ and edifies the church. Grace is all about giving. God gave us His Son, Jesus gave us His life, and the Holy Spirit gives us spiritual gifts. With these gifts we are to give ourselves to each other and to the cause of Christ in the world.

Spiritual gifts are not toys to play with or weapons to fight with, but rather tools to build with. That is why our gifts must be complemented with grace. This grace was missing in the Corinthian church, and its absence led to division, not diversity. Using spiritual gifts without grace produces pride, friction, egotism, and carnality. The more gifts we have, the more grace we need. There are two extremes in evaluating our spiritual gifts. We can over-appreciate our gifts and our importance, or we may under-appreciate our gifts to the point of false humility. It is wrong to boast about God-given gifts, and it is wrong to belittle the gifts we do have. Once we understand that God's free and undeserved grace has given us gifts, we will be more diligent in developing them and using them with humility, just as God intends.

———————————— ✸ ————————————

EVENING
Oh Lord, I pray that my life has showcased Your grace this day. In Jesus' name, Amen.

Week 44, Wednesday

MORNING

Lord, I am chief among sinners. My sin has shamed me and crucified Your Son. For Your grace that has rescued me, I am grateful. For Your unmerited favor, I cry out and praise Your holy name. In light of my rebellious ways, Your grace is astounding. May Your grace permeate my life and set me apart as Yours this day. In Jesus' name, Amen.

I thank my God always concerning you for the grace of
God which was given to you by Christ Jesus.
1 CORINTHIANS 1:4

In Paul's opening remarks to the Corinthian Christians, he expressed his thankfulness for the grace they had received from God. Paul went on to address many issues in the Corinthian church, but he was sure to find something for which to be thankful. This attitude is one of the keys to a victorious life. In the Old Testament, Jacob's fourth son was named Judah, which means "praise." Judah was a praising man, and that was the secret to him being a prevailing man.

Grace is unmerited favor—receiving something you don't deserve. Creation itself is a gracious act of God, but because of our sin, God's grace also takes on the character of undeserved forgiveness toward His people. Paul stands in the forefront of a great host of saints through the ages who experienced the unmerited favor of God. Paul sank low as a sinner, but soared high as a saint.

Many of Paul's converts had been saved from a life of depravity in the city of Corinth, the home of wickedness and immorality. We, likewise, have been saved from the filth and faithlessness of our culture and drawn into the glorious hope of Christ. Many of Paul's converts were Jews who looked down their noses at the sinful nature of these worldly Corinthians, yet some of these Jewish converts still relied on a works-oriented religion and didn't fully understand God's grace. Yet, whether rebels or religionists, all need the grace offered only by our Lord. God's grace is found in Jesus. "The law was given through Moses, but grace and truth came through Jesus Christ" (John 1:17). In Christ, God's grace has been shown to us and shared with us. Hallelujah, what a Savior!

EVENING
Father, I shudder to think where I would be without Your grace. Thank You for Your unrepayable favor to me. Amen.

ONE YEAR DEVOTIONAL PRAYER BOOK II

Week 44, Thursday

Lord, as I wander through the wilderness of this world, I do so with the Promised Land of heaven in mind. May Your grace guide my feet to walk with You, for You, and toward You this day. In Jesus' name, Amen.

The Lord God is a sun and shield; the Lord will give grace and glory;
no good thing will He withhold from those who walk uprightly.
PSALM 84:11

It is the Lord who gives "grace and glory." Grace begins our journey with the Lord, and that journey ends in the Lord's glory.

We need God's grace to enjoy the journey. Even though the writer of this psalm could not attend the feast in Jerusalem, he desired to be there in the presence of the Lord. Forty years of wilderness wandering taught the Jews that they were pilgrims in this world, and once they were in the Land of Promise, they celebrated annual feasts that reminded them of that reality. A pilgrim is one who is not home, but is heading home. But just because we haven't reached heaven yet doesn't mean we can't experience the joy of being in fellowship with the Lord.

We need God's grace to endure the journey. The psalmist mentions "the Valley of Baca" in Psalm 84:6, and the word *Baca* actually means "weeping." It is the grace of God that sees us through the valleys of despair and hopelessness. His grace enables us to take one step at a time. As we journey through the Valley of Baca, He is our shield and defender. As we trust Him, He leads us out of the valleys so that we will love and trust Him more.

We need God's grace to end the journey. The Lord is not only a shield, but He is also a sun. Without the sun we have no physical life, and without the Lord we have no spiritual life. Safely home in heaven at the end of our journey, there will be no need of the sun because the Son is its light (Revelation 22:5).

If we will walk by faith through this journey with the Lord, that which began with grace will end in glory!

EVENING
Thank You, oh Lord, for Your saving grace, Your sufficient grace, and Your sustaining grace. In Jesus' name, Amen.

ARDEN TAYLOR, JONESBOROUGH, TN

Jesus, pour out Your Spirit of grace on me so that I might understand and appreciate more fully what You did for me on the Cross. In Jesus' name, Amen.

> *I will pour on the house of David and on the inhabitants of Jerusalem the*
> *Spirit of grace and supplication; then they will look on Me whom*
> *they pierced. Yes, they will mourn for Him as one mourns for his*
> *only son, and grieve for Him as one grieves for a firstborn.*
> ZECHARIAH 12:10

The day is coming when the Lord will pour out His Spirit of grace on those who have previously rejected Him, namely the Jews. For two thousand years and counting, Jews have rejected Jesus as their Messiah, but there will be a day when God will pour His grace on them. They will see the nail-pierced hands of Jesus and recognize Him as their Messiah. In that day, the Antichrist will come to defeat Israel, but the Lord will come to defend Israel.

Israel has rejected God; they have killed and stoned God's prophets and crucified God's Son. Yet, in that day, God will deliver Israel by His grace. When they finally recognize Jesus, they will ask Him, "What do these wounds mean? We didn't expect our Messiah, our King, to come with nail-pierced hands and feet." Jesus will answer, "I got these wounds when I came the first time, but you rejected Me and cried out 'Crucify Him.'" Israel will look back at their past, and they will be broken-hearted, just as Zechariah said: "In that day there shall be a great mourning in Jerusalem" (Zechariah 12:11).

Perhaps, like me, you look back on past sin, failures, and rejection of Christ or His Word, and it breaks your heart. It was for those things that Jesus died. As there will be in Jerusalem one day, there ought to be mourning, weeping, and repentance in our lives and in the church today.

Annually, Israel has a Day of Atonement, but this coming day will be a real Day of Atonement, and it is all because of God's grace!

EVENING
Lord, when I realize what my sin cost You, it devastates me. Only by Your grace can I have any hope or existence. Thank You, Jesus. Amen.

God, when I was drowning in an ocean of sin, Your grace rescued me. When the road to You was too long and winding for me to travel, Your grace came and delivered me. When there is a great chasm between who I am and who I want to be, Your grace bridges the gap. Your grace has made me what I otherwise could not be. I love You and thank You in Jesus' name. Amen.

> *Of His fullness we have all received, and grace for grace. For the law was given through Moses, but grace and truth came through Jesus Christ.*
> JOHN 1:16, 17

We learn two things about God's grace in these verses. First, we learn about the completeness of God's grace. The word *fullness* means "being filled; completeness; abundance; a fulfilling." This speaks of the sum total of the attributes and power of Christ. Out of God's inexhaustible supply of resources, He gives believers all they need. Moses gave the Law to highlight the reality of sin, but where sin increased, grace abounded all the more. If God dealt with us according to the Law alone, we could not survive. But on the Cross, Jesus' sacrifice and blood met all of God's demands. In the Law, every animal sacrifice was an expression of God's grace, but in Jesus, we have the grace of God in its completeness. The abundant supply of this grace will never be diminished because we receive "grace for grace."

Second, we learn about the coming of God's grace. The Law was more impersonal than grace is. The Law was carved into cold tablets of stone, but grace came to us in the incarnate Son of God. Jesus had to come to earth as He came (born of a virgin) in order to be what He was (a perfect man). He had to be what He was in order to do what He did (die to save us). He had to do what He did so that we might have what He has (eternal life that we lost in Adam). And we must have what He has in order to be what He was (a perfect man).

Praise God that grace and truth came to us through Jesus Christ!

EVENING
Thank You, Lord, that Your grace was not exhausted at the time of my salvation, for I need it every hour. Amen.

Week 45, Monday

Lord, help me live in the supernatural power of Your grace today. Help me die to myself and crucify my flesh. May I live in the power of Your resurrection. I need Your grace . . . touch me, fill me, and use me to bring others to You. I love You, Lord Jesus. Amen.

> *The multitude of those who believed were of one heart and one soul; neither did anyone say that any of the things he possessed was his own, but they had all things in common. And with great power the apostles gave witness to the resurrection of the Lord Jesus. And great grace was upon them all.*
> ACTS 4:32, 33

How do you live unselfishly? How do you become a giver and not a taker? How do you take the ordinary, mundane aspects of life and turn them into the supernatural? How do you put others ahead of yourself? How can you experience unity with so many different thoughts, ideas, and opinions all around you? The first believers had experienced the wonderful grace of God in salvation. They had all things in common: they had common faith, love, and grace in their hearts. Nothing was done out of compulsion or manipulation; it was spontaneous. They voluntarily gave of themselves and their possessions. The grace of God had a marvelous effect on their lives and their relationships. They had great power and great grace. What a combination!

Are you lacking power in your life? Make sure you are full of grace. Do you struggle giving away grace that has been given so freely to you? You have the power of the Holy Spirit at your disposal. God's power and grace are abundantly available to each believer. The question is, are you? Appropriate the grace that God has poured out on you. Grace in you and on you will spill out to everyone around you.

EVENING

Lord, I am excited to live in the power of Your love and grace. Help me give myself to You and devote my life to sharing Your grace with others. I desire Your power in my life, and I long to be used to make a difference for You. Lead me and direct me in loving people and being a dispenser of Your grace. Amen.

Lord Jesus, I worship You and bless Your name. Thank You for shedding Your blood and paying the penalty for my sins so that I might have new life in You. Give me boldness today to share Jesus with everyone I meet. In Jesus' name, Amen.

If by the one man's offense death reigned through the one, much more those
who receive abundance of grace and of the gift of righteousness will reign
in life through the One, Jesus Christ . . . so that as sin reigned in death, even so
grace might reign through righteousness to eternal life through Jesus Christ our Lord.
ROMANS 5:17, 21

The Book of Romans is a documentary of the sinfulness of humanity. When Adam sinned in the Garden, sin entered the world, separating us from holy God and sealing our fate. Humanity's sin gave God the opportunity to display His grace. Adam's sin brought sin and condemnation to our lives, but God's gift of grace through His Son's death on the Cross provides forgiveness and justification and eternal life to all who receive Him. God's amazing grace justifies us and offers a free pardon so that we are acquitted. God's justification is God's declaration that we have been absolved of all sin. Our standing before God is perfect. We do not fall in and out of grace. That may sound too good to be true—that's why it is called *amazing* grace. God gives this gift of grace that is not deserved and cannot be earned.

People all around us are in need of God's grace. Can you think of a family member, friend, or co-worker who needs a pardon from sin? Are you willing to share this gift of amazing grace with others and offer them the opportunity to be forgiven and experience freedom?

EVENING
Father, I stand forgiven because of what Jesus did for me on the Cross. Thank You for establishing my right standing with You and for the hope of eternal life in heaven. Use me to share Your grace with everyone I know. I pray all this in my Savior's name. Amen.

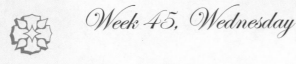

I ask You, Lord, to give me a generous spirit. Help me not to be stingy with the grace that You have so generously poured out on me. May I in turn pour it out on others. Keep me grateful, not only for salvation, but also for all Your blessings in my life. May I be a person of grace who loves my brothers and sisters, treats them with kindness, and gives them what they do not deserve. Send people into my life today who need Your salvation and grace, and use me in sharing with them. Amen.

You know the grace of our Lord Jesus Christ, that though He was rich, yet for your sakes He became poor, that you through His poverty might become rich.
2 CORINTHIANS 8:9

The context of this verse is Paul's challenge to the church at Corinth to give like the church at Macedonia. God's grace in the hearts of the Macedonians gave them a desire to give to others. God's grace in their lives sensitized them to the needs of others. That's what grace does. It makes you sensitive to the needs of people around you. When you have experienced grace, you are moved to give it away.

Although the believers in Macedonia were poor financially, they were rich in grace. Jesus Himself became poor by giving up all of His rights as God and becoming flesh. He left the glory of heaven to come and live on earth as a common man. Because we were spiritually bankrupt, Christ abandoned His riches so that through His power, we might become rich in His grace!

His gift of salvation and eternal life is the ultimate example of grace. We must not only enjoy that gift of salvation but also actively share it with other people. His grace is too good to keep to ourselves; we must give it away. Whether that means sharing the gospel through our witness or giving our money to further His kingdom, grace will open our hearts and our hands.

EVENING

Father, it's only because of Your grace that I have lived another day. Thank You for Your power and Your gift of grace that I do not deserve. Help me always be mindful of the needs of others—both their physical and spiritual needs—and guide me in sharing Your grace. In Jesus' mighty name, Amen.

MORNING

I worship You, Father, for Your amazing grace. You know the pain and frustration in my life. You know all that happens in my heart. Cover me with Your grace. Help me trust that Your grace is sufficient in all things. I am desperate for You, Lord Jesus. I need You. Amen.

Concerning this thing I pleaded with the Lord three times that it might depart from me. And He said to me, "My grace is sufficient for you, for My strength is made perfect in weakness." Therefore most gladly I will rather boast in my infirmities, that the power of Christ may rest upon me.
2 CORINTHIANS 12:8, 9

A t times we face situations that overwhelm us, perhaps in the form of a tragedy or unexpected event. In this text, the apostle Paul addressed his "thorn in the flesh" (2 Corinthians 12:7). We are not told what Paul's thorn was, but I am guessing that you know what yours is! You may have also asked God to remove your "thorn," but that may not be His intention. The thorn is there to direct you to Jesus and remind you that His grace is sufficient. His grace, His power, His plan, and His un-merited favor are all sufficient for you. When we try to tell God what He should do about our situation, we fail to hear Him assuring us that His grace is sufficient! The word *sufficient* means "to be enough." It is in the present tense, indicating a continuing action. God's grace goes on being enough! For all of the overwhelming situations and pressures in your life, there is sufficient grace.

Paul also said that the thorn was a reminder of the power of the Cross. In our human weakness, God's strength is manifested. Human weakness opens the way for more of Christ's power and grace to be applied. Christianity is not a guarantee for exemption from pain and problems; instead, it provides the promise that God's grace is sufficient through every circumstance. Today, give God glory for showcasing His strength in your weaknesses.

EVENING

God, please forgive me for allowing life's problems to overwhelm me and for not relying on Your grace. Increase my faith and my dependence on You. Help me remember that You are in control and Your grace is sufficient, no matter how big or small the situation. In Jesus' name, Amen.

STEVE FLOCKHART, HIRAM, GA

Lord, sometimes I feel so unworthy. My sin, my failures, and my poor attitude all feed my need for Your grace. So many times I base my value on how I perform, how successful I am, what possessions I have, what job I hold, or what relationships I have. Let me see life through Your eyes of grace. Let me see myself like You see me—forgiven, cleansed, and valuable. Thank You, Lord Jesus, for Your blood, for Your forgiveness, and for the richness of Your grace. I love You, Lord Jesus. Amen.

In Him we have redemption through His blood, the forgiveness of sins, according to the riches of His grace which He made to abound toward us in all wisdom and prudence.
EPHESIANS 1:7, 8

The word *redemption* means "to release by paying a price." It literally has six different meanings tied to salvation. It is the legal term used for purchasing. God purchased our salvation on the Cross. We had a need to be purchased, and only God could pay the price. We are each dead in our trespasses and sin. We are all separated from God. God in His marvelous grace paid the ultimate price for you. Jesus shed His blood and gave His own life to purchase you. You are so valuable to God that He sent His only Son to shed His blood and make this purchase possible. Your value is not dependent on your own estimation of yourself or the fickle opinions of other people. Your value is based on the love of God! That's grace! Grace is always based on who God is and what He has done, not on who we are and what we have done. What difference would it make in your life if you walked around knowing this and feeling valuable all of the time?

God has given His grace to forgive you, cleanse you, and reveal to you how much He loves you. Walk in grace today!

EVENING
Father, thank You for Your precious Son. Thank You for Your unmerited favor in my life. Thank You, Jesus, for Your endless grace. I praise You that I am a daily recipient of the grace that cost You so dearly. I praise You for removing my transgressions as far as the east is from the west. I am grateful that I stand forgiven and cleansed. Amen.

MORNING

Father, today, I am going to need Your grace. I know many things will come my way that will discourage me and defeat me. I am still grateful. I walk by faith and live in grace. Keep my eyes and my heart fixed on You. May Your grace sustain me. In Jesus' matchless name, Amen.

Now may our Lord Jesus Christ Himself, and our God and Father, who has loved us and given us everlasting consolation and good hope by grace, comfort your hearts and establish you in every good word and work.
2 THESSALONIANS 2:16, 17

The word *grace* is mentioned 200 times in the New Testament—130 times by the apostle Paul. Paul's epistles begin with grace, end with grace, and include grace everywhere in between. Paul was a man who exemplified the grace of His Father, "the God of all grace" (1 Peter 5:10). Grace is God's kindness toward us—His unmerited and unlimited favor lavished on us. Grace is God's love wrapped up in Jesus Christ.

God the Father has infinite compassion and unconditional love toward you. The Father's heart burns with immense desire for you to know Him. He sent His Son so you could know His love toward you. Grace was declared as Jesus lovingly and compassionately poured out His love for you on Calvary. God's love for you is eternal. His love has no beginning and no end. He has always loved you, and He will always love you. His love for you does not change when you do bad things or increase when you do good things. His grace is greater than your sin.

Paul's words in today's passage comfort and encourage us with thoughts of God's grace. Grace is a blanket of God's love that covers us in both good and bad times. The reality of Christ's life and love is what spurs us on in the midst of the trials and setbacks of life. May God's grace give you hope and comfort today!

EVENING

God, help me comprehend Your "forever grace." I know that I can never truly fathom all that You went through to have a relationship with me. Thank You for Your great love for me that led You to experience such agony. Thank You for pursuing me and giving me grace because You love me. Consume me with love for You! Amen.

STEVE FLOCKHART, HIRAM, GA

Father, You know my weaknesses, my breaking points, my struggles, and my hurts. I pray that You would cover me in Your grace today. Lead me through the challenges I might face. I need Your strength. Your grace is sufficient, but my faith is sometimes weak. Help me to depend completely on You. Let my weakness be overshadowed by Your strength within me. May Your love shine through me. I pray this in Jesus' name. Amen.

> *You therefore, my son, be strong in the grace that is in Christ Jesus.*
> 2 TIMOTHY 2:1

Have you ever had a day where everything seemed to go wrong? Of course you have; we all have, and we will continue to experience those kinds of days. In the midst of those days, we sometimes feel as if we are all alone or that no one cares. Today, realize that God cares and He will be with you during life's greatest trials. He will also be with you in the mundane repetition of everyday life.

The Bible tells us repeatedly to depend on God, to trust Him, and to believe in His promises. Yet there are many days in our lives when we still question His care for us. First Peter 5:7 tells us to cast all our care upon Him, for He cares for us. The Greek word for casting is *epiripto*, which means "to throw upon." This passage tells us to throw our problems upon our Father God. Release them without a second thought. When we do this, we will always find that His grace is indeed sufficient.

In the moment of weakness and insecurity, be strong. Not because of your ability, but because of the grace of our Lord and Savior.

EVENING

Father, today You've been faithful. I've trusted You completely, and I've sensed Your presence in my life. Thank You for caring for me and for caring about my problems. Thank You for Your amazing grace that gets me through days just like this one. Lord, I pray that You will continue to strengthen my faith and increase my dependence on You. Help me to realize my need for You more tomorrow than I did today. I love You, Lord. In Jesus' name, Amen.

MORNING

Lord, I thank You today for saving me. I don't deserve Your favor, Your love, or Your gift of salvation, yet You gave them anyway. Lord, I'm humbled that You've made me Your child. Help me live in a way that honors You so that others might see You through me. I thank You for giving me the opportunity to be Your ambassador to a hurting world. Help me share Your love unashamedly with others so they might trust in You as well. Guide my steps today, and for that I will give You praise and glory. In Jesus' name, Amen.

Having been justified by His grace we should become heirs according to the hope of eternal life. This is a faithful saying, and these things I want you to affirm constantly, that those who have believed in God should be careful to maintain good works. These things are good and profitable to men.

TITUS 3:7, 8

———

Salvation is a difficult concept to grasp. Our human minds struggle to understand how a holy God could leave the splendors of heaven, put on flesh as a man, and walk toward the Cross to atone for our sins. Yet that's exactly what Christ did for each of us because He loves us.

Romans 5:8 tells us, "God demonstrates His own love toward us, in that while we were still sinners, Christ died for us." I love the word *still* in that verse. It assures us that God loves us regardless of what we've done. Christ died for us, in spite of all the sins we've committed, so that we could become His children. Christ wanted us for His own—what a wonderful thought! The God of the universe wanted you and me for Himself. We are heirs to the throne. Today, live like it! Walk in His light. Honor Him in everything you do. You're a child of the King!

———

EVENING

Jesus, tonight I thank You for loving me so much that You died on the Cross for me. I thank You for making me Your child. Lord, I ask You to keep me close to You. Give me the strength to follow You, to seek You, to trust You, and to honor You in all that I do. Keep my heart fixed on You and the grace You've shown to me. I love You, Lord. Amen.

JONATHAN FALWELL, LYNCHBURG, VA

Lord, I ask You to lead me in paths of righteousness. Help me sense Your holiness as I walk through this day. I trust You to give me the wisdom I need to navigate the challenges today might bring. Help me serve You with a passion like never before. I pray that You will draw me ever closer to You and that nothing will pull me away from You. I need You to strengthen me today. May Your grace cover me. I ask this in Your precious name. Amen.

> *Since we are receiving a kingdom which cannot be shaken,*
> *let us have grace, by which we may serve God acceptably with*
> *reverence and godly fear. For our God is a consuming fire.*
> HEBREWS 12:28, 29

Holiness. Righteousness. These are attributes that God wants to be evident in our lives. The gracious, unmerited favor God has lavished upon us should lead us to a life of holiness. In the Old Testament, God manifested Himself as the "pillar of fire" and led the Israelites in the midst of uncertainty (Exodus 13:21). God presented Himself in this way as an awesome display of His power. In today's passage, the writer of Hebrews draws our attention back to the "pillar of fire" as a picture of God's power to encourage us to pursue holiness.

God's love for us is absolute, but that love also requires a reverence toward Him that should not be compromised. Today, let your fear of almighty God draw you ever closer to the flame. Let God be the light you need to expose the sin that could easily move you away from His perfect plan for your life. God will not turn His back on you. He will never leave you or forsake you. But He does want you to serve Him with a passion. And this kind of passion demands the pursuit of holiness.

EVENING

Lord, I am nothing without You. Your love and grace have made me what I am today. Forgive me for the times I have strayed from Your will. Give me an all-consuming passion to seek after Your ways, to desire Your best, to bask in Your light, and to experience Your presence. Thank You for that unmerited favor that has drawn me to You. May I continue following after You all the days of my life. I love You, Lord. Amen.

MORNING

Lord, I need Your protection today. I know that Satan desires to lead me away from serving You. I know that he wants to destroy me. But I know that Your grace will guard my heart from Satan's attacks on me. Draw me near to You today. Keep my heart focused on who You are and what You've done for me on the Cross. I submit to Your desires and Your will. I pray for Your strength today. Amen.

He gives more grace. Therefore He says: "God resists the proud, but gives grace to the humble." Therefore submit to God. Resist the devil and he will flee from you.
JAMES 4:6, 7

Having humility is the first step in avoiding Satan's attacks. It is vital for Christians to understand that Satan is a very real threat and only God can deliver them from him. Human beings are sometimes predisposed to believe they can tackle anything, but God presents a different picture in John 10:10: "The thief does not come except to steal, and to kill, and to destroy. I have come that they may have life, and that they may have it more abundantly." Christ came to deliver us from Satan's destructive grip and to give us abundant life. But we do play a pivotal role in Christ's master plan: we must seek Him every moment of the day. Psalm 34:4–7 encourages us to seek the Lord and says that He will hear us and deliver us. He will protect us from the life-draining effects of trying to do life on our own.

Pride will always lead to Satan gaining a stronghold in our lives, but God will always deliver us when we humbly submit to Him. First Peter 5:8 tells us that Satan wants to "devour" us, but God's grace is more than enough to make Satan run for the hills!

EVENING

Father, You've been faithful today. You've protected and delivered me. Your grace has been sufficient for me, just as You promised, and I give You thanks. Lord, I know that all things are possible for those who believe. Tonight, I affirm my belief in You. I trust You to be everything I need for life. Continue to be the protector I need. Thank You for saving me and loving me. In the precious name of Jesus I pray. Amen.

JONATHAN FALWELL, LYNCHBURG, VA

Week 46, Friday

My Father, I am humbled by the grace You show me each day. As this day begins, I pray that You will shower me with Your love and guidance. I desperately need You to guide my steps and light my way. I know that Your desire is for us to serve and love the special people You have brought into our lives. I pray that You will help me be the person that others need today. In Jesus' name I pray. Amen.

Husbands, likewise, dwell with them with understanding, giving honor
to the wife, as to the weaker vessel, and as being heirs together of the
grace of life, that your prayers may not be hindered.
1 PETER 3:7

God desires for us to travel the paths of life with others. He does not wish for us to be alone. He wants us to enjoy the benefits of His amazing grace together. Today's passage says that believers are "heirs together" of God's grace. This is a wonderful truth and encouragement for life. But as wonderful as it is to enjoy the gift of grace together, we must also strive together to live our lives according to His purposes. Nothing can stunt our spiritual growth more than surrounding ourselves with people who are not walking in His grace. Psalm 37:4 says, "Delight yourself also in the LORD, and He shall give you the desires of your heart." As you delight in Him, He will also give you the desire to be with others who delight in Him.

I once heard a man say that he knew his wife was "the one" because she helped him become more holy. That's God's grace in action. Today, look for ways to help your fellow heirs of the grace of life grow spiritually.

EVENING

Lord, tonight, I thank You for bringing people into my life who draw me nearer to Your love and grace. Thank You for using them to encourage me in my passionate pursuit of holiness. Lord, if there is anyone in my life who leads me in the opposite direction, I ask You to give me wisdom and strength to distance myself from that person's path. God, I rejoice tonight in the relationships You've blessed me with. I ask that You continue to grow them daily and that they would help make me more like You. In Jesus' name, Amen.

MORNING

Father, I am so humbled that You bestowed Your loving grace on me and made me Your child. Thank You for saving me. Today, draw me near to You and let nothing draw me away from You. I pray for Your wisdom and guidance in everything I say and do. Let it all be for Your glory, for You are the only One worthy of my praise. Thank You for Your love. Amen.

> *You therefore, beloved, since you know this beforehand, beware lest you also fall from your own steadfastness, being led away with the error of the wicked; but grow in the grace and knowledge of our Lord and Savior Jesus Christ. To Him be the glory both now and forever. Amen.*
> 2 PETER 3:17, 18

What an awesome God we serve! Christ came with one purpose in mind: to reconcile us to God, which includes the forgiveness of sins. We certainly don't deserve His work of grace. While His gift still amazes me, it also amazes me that we continue to struggle in our relationship with Him. We know what He's given for that relationship to exist. That struggle is a direct result of our not growing in His grace and knowledge.

Every day, Satan tries to lead people away from the Father, and often they succumb to his attacks. But God continues to call out, "Draw near to Me and I will draw near to you!" (see James 4:8). When we draw near to Him, we will grow in His grace and knowledge. How are you responding to that call? Are you walking closer to Him each day? Are you striving to grow into what He wants for you? If not, why?

Isaiah 53:5 tells us what Christ's sacrifice has done for all of us: "By His stripes we are healed." Christ gave His all so we could have it all. Never let the temptations of this world lead you astray. Seek Him every day. As you surrender to Him daily, you will grow in your faith.

EVENING

Lord, Your grace amazes me. I don't deserve it, but You gave it anyway. Help me never forget the price You paid for me. I am so grateful for Your love. I give You everything, because You gave everything for me. I love You. To You be the glory! Amen.

JONATHAN FALWELL, LYNCHBURG, VA

Father, as I begin this day and this week, help me to dwell on the reality that my life is hidden in Christ and that by trusting in Him, I have crossed over from death to life. Help me live with faith, knowing that You have promised to walk with me in the midst of whatever this day will bring, and resting in the assurance that You have made provision for my eternal future. I believe in the One You sent, and I believe every word You say. Amen.

> *Most assuredly, I say to you, he who hears My word and*
> *believes in Him who sent Me has everlasting life, and shall not*
> *come into judgment, but has passed from death into life.*
> JOHN 5:24

It is no small thing to avoid condemnation. We do not often use the word condemnation in our everyday conversations, but the weight and meaning of that word does not escape us. The Lord Jesus contrasts the word condemnation with another phrase: *eternal life*. Condemnation is the pathway of death. It is the payment for a life of active or passive independence from God. It is the just punishment for sin and the ultimate wreckage of humanity.

Eternal life, however, describes both a quality of life and an unending quantity of life. It is the beautiful reality of a full life now and a forever life in the future. It is the place at which we arrive when we cross over the abyss of death and separation from God and enter the realm of real existence. We cannot get there on our own. It requires the heroic action of a Savior, our Lord Jesus, to rescue us, the justly condemned, from the eternal death we deserve. When we hear and embrace the words of the gospel—the great news that God has made a way of reconciling humanity to Himself through Jesus' death and resurrection—and also embrace the Person of the gospel—the Lord Jesus—then we can live in the light of life, never to face condemnation again.

EVENING

Father, I will rest tonight, knowing that my life has been rescued and protected by Jesus' work. I believe with all my heart that the Lord Jesus is trustworthy for this task. Thank You for the precious gift of knowing You now and for the promise of living with You forever. Amen.

Father, I worship You for who You are. You know me intimately, better than I know myself, and yet You still love me unconditionally. I want to know You more. I want to hear Your voice, trust in You, and obey You, just as sheep respond to the shepherd. Amen.

> *My sheep hear My voice, and I know them, and they follow Me. And I give them eternal life, and they shall never perish; neither shall anyone snatch them out of My hand. My Father, who has given them to Me, is greater than all; and no one is able to snatch them out of My Father's hand.*
>
> JOHN 10:27–29

Not many of us have "Shepherd" on our résumés. As an industrialized, modernized nation, we have little familiarity with shepherds and sheep. But Jesus compared Himself to a shepherd and likened us to sheep, so it is important to understand a few things about them. One of the more obvious characteristics of sheep is that they follow; they don't lead. Sheep need a leader, and Jesus tells us in this passage that we, as sheep, are to listen to His voice and follow Him.

A good shepherd will lead his sheep well. He will take them to green pastures to eat and to flowing streams so they can drink. He will also protect his sheep from predators. Our Good Shepherd, Jesus, does so much more. He leads us to eternal life—a place where we can taste and see that the Lord is good in our earthly existence, and a promise that following Him in this life will allow us to follow Him in the never-ending life to come. The security our Good Shepherd gives us is grounded in the full resources of God. His sheep can never be snatched from the Father's hand, and we have the awesome power of the Trinitarian God—Father, Son, and Holy Spirit—to take us safely through our journey in this life and the life to come.

EVENING

Shepherd of my soul, thank You that the security of my life is wrapped up in Your hand. The awesomeness of who You are gives me assurance that I cannot be snatched from You, no matter what predators may assault me. Strengthen me to follow You and to grow in my dependence upon Your leadership in my life. Amen.

JERRY GILLIS, BUFFALO, NY

Week 47, Wednesday

Father, thank You for the salvation You have provided in Jesus. I confess that this incredible gift of salvation and life is a gift of Your grace, not a product of my deserving deeds. I am humbled by Your graciousness, and I pray that You will empower me to live in light of this grace today. Amen.

No one has ascended to heaven but He who came down from heaven, that is,
the Son of Man who is in heaven . . . that whoever believes in Him should not perish
but have eternal life. For God so loved the world that He gave His only begotten
Son, that whoever believes in Him should not perish but have everlasting life.
JOHN 3:13, 15, 16

Most people, whether they are people of faith or not, have some familiarity with John 3:16. It is a verse that has been disseminated widely. Familiarity, however, can be dangerous. It occasionally causes us to sip casually, instead of drinking deeply, the richness of meaning, especially when it comes to the things of God. This passage is far too rich just to sip casually on its meaning. We need to submerge ourselves continually in the awe-inspiring reality of what God has done for us in Jesus.

God did not delegate the responsibility to save a world in bondage to sin. He didn't outsource the rescue operation. No, God so loved this precious creation called humanity that He gave of Himself because we were helpless to rescue ourselves. His only begotten Son—the One and only unique Son of God, Jesus—stood in the place of sinful humans like you and me, took our sin upon Himself, and as the perfect, sinless sacrifice He satisfied the justice of a holy God. Because of what God has done through Jesus, we do not have to experience condemnation or eternal separation from our loving God. Through belief in the Person and work of Jesus, we will live with God forever!

EVENING

Father, may I never fail to be stunned by the wonder of how You have rescued me from sin, death, and condemnation through Jesus. Make my familiarity with You increase my awe of You, and help me live each day looking through the lens of this reality. Let my gratitude for Your grace be seen in a life authentically yielded to You. Amen.

Father, I want to experience Your love today. I know that my ability to love is based on the fact that You loved me first. Help me receive and experience Your love so that it can flow through me to other people. Help me not to love just a little; I want to learn to love You big—to love You with all that I am and have. Amen.

> *Behold, a certain lawyer stood up and tested Him, saying, "Teacher, what shall I do to inherit eternal life?" He said to him, "What is written in the law? What is your reading of it?" So he answered and said, "'You shall love the LORD your God with all your heart, with all your soul, with all your strength, and with all your mind,' and 'your neighbor as yourself.'"*
>
> LUKE 10:25–27

Jesus had a habit of answering questions with questions. This was not particularly unique; it was part of the Jewish culture and a common thing for a rabbi to do. Although the lawyer answered Jesus' question correctly, the real issue was whether he was living out the reality of the answer. Knowing the right answers and living the right life are not necessarily synonymous.

That can be true of us as well. We so often know the right answers but have trouble living out the reality of the truth. It seems that here in our passage Jesus wanted to remind us of a priority that we must remember. If we learn to love God first, we will then be able to love others well. Simply put, loving God with every ounce of our being (heart, soul, strength, and mind) is what enables us to love our neighbors as ourselves. When we love God well, we begin to see people the way He sees them—as objects of His love. And since they are objects of His love, they should be objects of our love. This, Jesus said, is what it really means to live: to demonstrate authentically an eternal kind of life in the present. Ask Him to help you do just that as you go about today's activities.

EVENING

Dear Lord, teach me to love like You love. Help me to be so overwhelmed by Your love that it spills into every relationship I have in my life. Amen.

Father, it is so liberating to know I have been set free from the ultimate consequences of sin and that I am free—free to live a life of holiness that shows the world Your glory. What a gift eternal life is! Help me to remember the preciousness of this gift and the price You paid to offer it, and may I live with a deeply grateful heart. Amen.

Now having been set free from sin, and having become slaves of God,
you have your fruit to holiness, and the end, everlasting life. For the wages
of sin is death, but the gift of God is eternal life in Christ Jesus our Lord.
ROMANS 6:22, 23

One of the most precious truths of God's gift of salvation is that we are freed from slavery to sin. We are also rescued from the ultimate consequence of sin— death. Death is the payment for our sin, but Jesus Christ conquered death through His own death and resurrection.

This truth rings loudly when we look death square in the eye. I was recently at a funeral for a thirty-eight-year-old wife and mother. I couldn't help but feel anger at death and realize what an enemy it is to the original intent of God's design in creation. But my anger that day was drowned by the reality that the gift of eternal life in Jesus Christ is bigger, stronger, and greater than death. Death's most cruel blow is the ending of earthly life, but Jesus Christ makes death only a shadow through His own death and resurrection and through His promise of eternal life for those who believe on His name. In Jesus, death gives way to life, darkness gives way to light, hopelessness gives way to hope, pain gives way to joy, and sin gives way to holiness. Praise the One who died to free you from death's grip!

EVENING

Jesus, thank You for conquering death, hell, sin, and everything else that opposes life. Your life and strength are greater than death. Help me live out the fruit of everlasting life—a life of holiness. Because You have conquered death, and because I will be raised up with You in the resurrection, empower me to live in light of eternity and to face this life with grace and confidence in Your strength. Amen.

Week 47, Weekend

MORNING

Father, I ask You to direct my thoughts toward desiring You above all. May the lesser things of life that sidetrack my focus—pride, ambition, greed, lust—fade into oblivion as I bask in Your presence. May I fight the good fight of faith and continue to confess before You the same confession I made when I surrendered my life to You: You are Lord. Amen.

> *You, O man of God, flee these things and pursue righteousness,*
> *godliness, faith, love, patience, gentleness. Fight the good fight of faith,*
> *lay hold on eternal life, to which you were also called and have confessed*
> *the good confession in the presence of many witnesses.*
> 1 TIMOTHY 6:11, 12

Today's passage reminds us that Christ-followers are to be distinctive people. We are not like everyone else. Because Christ lives in us, we will run away from things that bring our destruction, and we will pursue things like righteousness, godliness, faith, love, patience, and gentleness. But it will not be easy. We will have to fight.

This is not a fight we win with our abilities or willpower. This is a fight that must be undertaken with faith, because without faith it is impossible to please God (Hebrews 11:6). As we live lives of faith, we begin to understand what it means to "lay hold on eternal life." Eternal life is not something we can earn; it is the gift of God made possible through the death and resurrection of our Lord Jesus Christ. But we have to learn both to appreciate and to appropriate eternal life. Because eternal life is a promise for the future, we can live our lives in appreciation for what Jesus has done for us, and we do not have to fear what tomorrow holds! But because eternal life is also about the quality of the new life we have in Jesus right now, we must learn to flee things that cloud the quality of our new lives and sprint toward God so that His life can shine through us. Today, pursue the things of God with everything you've got!

EVENING

Lord, the precious gift of eternal life gives me hope for my future and encouragement for my present life. Give me wisdom to run from empty and destructive things, and grace to run to You and find satisfaction. You alone are my sufficiency. Amen.

JERRY GILLIS, BUFFALO, NY

Lord, I pray that I will live my life in light of Your sacrifice on my behalf. Allow me to rest in Your finished work and trust that Your Spirit lives inside of me, giving me the ability to live the Spirit-filled life! Amen.

> *If we receive the witness of men, the witness of God is greater; for this is the witness of God which He has testified of His Son. He who believes in the Son of God has the witness in himself; he who does not believe God has made Him a liar, because he has not believed the testimony that God has given of His Son. And this is the testimony: that God has given us eternal life, and this life is in His Son.*
> 1 JOHN 5:9–11

Whether it's a starting position on the team or a promotion at work, it's generally assumed that you have to earn what you receive. After all, "you have to earn your keep." Being a hard worker is an honorable characteristic to cultivate, but if we're not careful, that characteristic can become debilitating in our relationship with God.

Hard-working people have trouble receiving something for nothing. It is difficult to grasp the concept that salvation has nothing to do with human effort or the ability to "earn our keep." God doesn't love you any more today than He did yesterday. He wouldn't love you more if you read every word in this book in one sitting.

We must come to grips with the truth that God has done all the work through His Son, Jesus Christ. It's His life, death, and resurrection that provide our atonement—not ours. Hard work is honorable, but we have to remember that when it comes to salvation, "God has given us eternal life, and this life is in His Son."

Our hope is in Him. That is very good news!

EVENING

Lord, I come to You this evening grateful for Jesus. Thank You that our relationship does not depend on my effort, but rather on Jesus' finished work on the Cross. I am grateful that as often as I fell short today, You were there to pick me up. Thank You for being my friend that sticks closer to me than a brother. In Jesus' name I pray. Amen.

MORNING

Dear Lord, I ask for Your strength this morning. Empower me to carry out Your will for my life. Allow me to grow in my understanding of Your love and grace. Thank You for the gospel and its effects on my life. I live this day for You. Amen.

This is the will of the Father who sent Me, that of all He has given Me I should lose nothing, but should raise it up at the last day. And this is the will of Him who sent Me, that everyone who sees the Son and believes in Him may have everlasting life; and I will raise him up at the last day.
JOHN 6:39, 40

Very few things in life are as frustrating as being lost. Driving aimlessly with no clue how to get to your desired destination can cause even the most even-tempered person to suffer from a case of temporary insanity. We can find ourselves feeling lost in many other situations—it could be a marriage, a college class, a career, or relationships with family and friends.

The chaos of life will undoubtedly thrust you into seasons of doubt and overwhelming feelings of not knowing which way is up. During those seasons, don't lose hope! The Father has given everyone He has chosen to the Son for salvation. If you have placed your faith and trust in Him, you can advance in confidence, knowing that Jesus never loses hold of you—no matter how lost you might feel. What a faith-enhancing, empowering statement! When the battle is raging and it looks like you are down for the count, stand firm. Some of God's greatest miracles have occurred when His people were facing insurmountable obstacles. It will be no different with you.

You don't fight your battles alone. He has your back!

EVENING

Dear Lord, thank You for having everything under control in my life and for refusing to let go of me. I hand You every worry, fear, and anxiety, understanding that You alone are capable of raising me up for the glory of God and for the good of others. I love You, Lord. I end this day grateful for Your grace, which is consistently on display in my life! In Jesus' name I pray. Amen.

J.R. LEE, ACWORTH, GA

Dear Lord, I come to You today grateful for the freedom that comes from following Jesus. Living my life within the parameters of Your Word has set me free to live the life You have called me to live. Help me walk in that freedom today and represent You well to those around me. I pray that those who are far from You would experience life in Christ as a result of Your life living through me. Thank You for Jesus! In Your name I pray. Amen.

> *Most assuredly, I say to you, he who believes in Me*
> *has everlasting life. I am the bread of life.*
> JOHN 6:47, 48

The religious leaders during Jesus' day had a perception problem. And that led to more problems, because the way you perceive people dictates the way you will receive them. In other words, what you see is what you get. Because the religious leaders didn't perceive Jesus to be the Son of God, they couldn't receive Him as such. Their inaccurate perception and works-oriented religiosity turned them away from a potential relationship with the Son of God.

The wrong kind of religion can be a bait-and-switch tactic. It promises acceptance, but it delivers isolation. That's the nature of mere religion without a true relationship with God—it promises more than it can deliver. This type of religion may be the greatest weapon in Satan's arsenal. I think that's why Jesus used His harshest words in combating the religious elite's inaccurate perceptions. We can never solve our sin problem through religious effort. Even our best attempts fall embarrassingly short of God's standard.

What is your perception of Jesus Christ? If you see Him as anything less than the Son of God and Savior of the world, it could be that you have a perception problem. Salvation comes through Christ alone. Quit relying on religion—Jesus is the answer.

EVENING

Dear Lord, I ask You to open my eyes to the Person and work of Jesus. When I'm tempted to lean on my own effort, help me realize that my sin has already been paid for and that You are enough. Thank You, Jesus! In Your name I pray. Amen.

MORNING

Lord, this morning, I beg You to live Your life through me. Replace my doubt with faith that pleases You. Help me trust You with the things that come my way today. You are a trustworthy God, and for that I am extremely grateful. Empower me to run to You consistently as my unending supply of hope and fulfillment! In Jesus' name I pray. Amen.

> *Jesus answered and said to her, "Whoever drinks of this water*
> *will thirst again, but whoever drinks of the water that I shall*
> *give him will never thirst. But the water that I shall give him will*
> *become in him a fountain of water springing up into everlasting life."*
> JOHN 4:13, 14

Sin is fun—for a season. This is a lesson most have learned the hard way. We've sustained emotional battle wounds in an attempt to fill our lives with that which we should have left alone. The truth is that there are desires that only God can satisfy.

The woman at the well could testify to the veracity of that statement. A large amount of short-term pleasure had not added up to long-term fulfillment. The sin that had promised so much had fallen short of its promise. In an encounter with Jesus, she discovered that He alone could provide what she had been looking to find. He alone could deliver on the promise that "whoever drinks of the water that I shall give him will never thirst." She could continue toying with sin in an attempt to fill the void in her heart, or she could place her trust in Jesus, forsaking sin and trusting His work on her behalf. Reading the rest of the story will show that she made the right decision. We have the opportunity to do the same!

EVENING

Lord, thank You for the opportunity to experience eternal life through the sacrifice of Your Son. Give me wisdom to trust and to act on Your Word, rather than trying to forge my own path. You alone are worthy of my allegiance, and I am honored to place my faith and trust in You! Amen.

J.R. LEE, ACWORTH, GA

Week 48, Friday

Dear Lord, I come to You this morning reminded of the power of the gospel. Thank You for Jesus and His activity on my behalf. Thank You that I don't have to attempt to live this day on my own. May Your power work in me and through me today as I seek to honor You in every way. In Jesus' name I pray. Amen.

Do not be deceived, God is not mocked; for whatever a man sows,
that he will also reap. For he who sows to his flesh will of the flesh reap
corruption, but he who sows to the Spirit will of the Spirit reap everlasting life.
GALATIANS 6:7, 8

My four-year-old daughter would gladly give up all other food if we would allow her diet to consist of juice, coffee, and cereal bars. As a matter of fact, she has been known to grab one of the aforementioned bars on her way to bed and hide it in her pocket for a midnight snack. She can be rather sneaky. Sneakiness seems to be a common characteristic of the average person. We would rather keep our sin and faults hidden in hopes of protecting our own image. Hiding seems more appealing than confession and repentance. We have become quite adept at putting our best foot forward and keeping our sin under the radar.

We can fool the majority of people most of the time, but at no point do we fool God. He knows everything about us. He is not taken in by our public persona or extreme religiosity. We can fill our pockets with sin and walk around as if all is well, but we can't pull one over on the Creator of the universe.

Today, choose to rely on the Spirit of God to enable you to "sow to the Spirit." Harvest time is coming, and we always reap what we sow.

EVENING

Dear Lord, I come to You again tonight grateful for the eternal home You have secured for me in heaven as a result of the sacrifice of Your Son. You have blessed me beyond measure, and I end this day expressing my gratitude to You. Thank You, Lord, for my salvation! Thank You for Your forgiveness! Thank You for Jesus! In His name I pray. Amen.

MORNING

Dear heavenly Father, I praise You for Your mercy and Your power. Thank You for sending Your Son into the world to save a person like me. I am forever grateful to You, and I will spend my life telling others about the gospel message that has changed my life forever! In Jesus' mighty name I pray. Amen.

> *This is a faithful saying and worthy of all acceptance, that Christ Jesus came*
> *into the world to save sinners, of whom I am chief. However, for this reason*
> *I obtained mercy, that in me first Jesus Christ might show all longsuffering,*
> *as a pattern to those who are going to believe on Him for everlasting life.*
> 1 TIMOTHY 1:15, 16

———

The church exists so that people far from God can experience life in Christ. Every week I look into the eyes of people who used to make a living running from God. To hear the stories of how the gospel has changed their lives is nothing short of amazing. The apostle Paul had a similar story. He was notorious for dragging families out of their homes, having followers of Christ arrested, and even standing by during the murder of a well-known Christian. Through an awe-inspiring turn of events, Jesus changed his life and called him to further the very movement that he had worked so hard to defeat. The gospel changed the trajectory of his life.

The power of the gospel has not diminished! Regardless of how far from God people might be, Jesus is fully capable of rescuing them from the slavery of sin and death. The life of Paul provides a vivid example of the fact that nothing keeps a person out of the reach of God's grace. Don't be surprised when God breaks through the heart of a person set against the purposes of God. Keep praying! The gospel is more far reaching than any sin!

———

EVENING

Dear God, I pray the gospel will advance more rapidly now than at any point in history. Continue to draw people to Yourself as I live my life to lift up the name of Jesus. I beg You to break through even the hardest of hearts for Your glory and for the good of others. I love You, Lord! Amen.

J.R. LEE, ACWORTH, GA

Week 49, Monday

Father, as I begin this day, I praise You for the evidence of Your presence in my life. I have heard You by the power of Your Word, experienced You by the power of Your Spirit, and been led by You in my daily life. You are as real to me as my closest friend, and I thank You for the fellowship we share together. I pray that You will allow me to be a powerful witness of Your life through my daily walk. Amen.

That which was from the beginning, which we have heard, which we have seen with our eyes, which we have looked upon, and our hands have handled, concerning the Word of life—the life was manifested, and we have seen, and bear witness, and declare to you that eternal life which was with the Father and was manifested to us.

1 JOHN 1:1, 2

In our study today, we can see that John was dealing with an early form of a heresy known as Gnosticism. This false teaching that was infiltrating the church contended that knowledge is the greatest virtue and that Jesus was spirit only. John reminded believers that their faith walk with Christ was to be personally experienced, not just a religion to learn and know.

We have an experiential faith. My first pastorate was in a county seat in Oklahoma. I learned much about my faith from living with and listening to godly farmers. Kenneth Laufer was such a farmer. I remember that whenever someone called on him for help, he always responded and did all he could for them. Kenneth said, "I may not be able to solve their problem, but I can sit with them, love them, and pray for them so they can see Jesus in my life." May it be said of you that others can see and experience Jesus manifested in your life.

EVENING

Father, thank You for giving me life today and for providing me with opportunities to help others see You. Tomorrow, may I be Your eyes, Your ears, Your hands, and Your heart to those You bring across my path. I thank You that You are more than knowledge to me—You are my way, my truth, and my life. Amen.

Father, there is nothing more wonderful than You and Your glorious gift of eternal life. Help me live in the reality of eternal life today, remembering it is not just a life I look forward to experiencing in heaven—it is an abundant life for today. Amen.

> *Whoever denies the Son does not have the Father either; he who acknowledges the Son has the Father also. Therefore let that abide in you which you heard from the beginning. If what you heard from the beginning abides in you, you also will abide in the Son and in the Father. And this is the promise that He has promised us—eternal life.*
>
> I JOHN 2:23–25

W hat does it mean to abide in the Son and the Father? To me it means that I don't have to wait until I die to experience the glory of eternal life. I have the privilege of living in that reality today. As a small boy playing baseball in the backyard of our home, I found myself arguing a disputed call with a neighborhood friend. The disagreement heated up, and my older friend decided he would settle the situation by fighting. He started at me with fists raised and then suddenly froze in his tracks. I knew my ninety-seven-pound frame was not that intimidating, so I wondered why he stopped his attack. I turned around to see my father standing at the back door. Because of my proximity to my father, he saw the trouble I was in and stepped into the situation to ensure my personal safety.

Every time we are confronted with the problems of life, we have two options: we can try to handle the situation in our strength, or we can turn around and remember that we are abiding in Christ. An abiding child says, "Father, You are with me, and I am with You. Lead me to Your truth and give me Your power to work through this situation for Your glory." Today, abide in the Son and Father, and rejoice in the gift of eternal life!

EVENING

Lord, at the end of this day I ask myself, "Have I trusted the Lord by abiding in Him throughout this day?" I pray that You will give me the wisdom, strength, and knowledge to live in the reality of Your gift of eternal life today. Amen.

LARRY THOMPSON, FORT LAUDERDALE, FL

Week 49, Wednesday

Lord, the longer I live, the more I realize I don't have all the answers. The closer I walk with You, the better I see how far I am from Your perfect will for my life. Search me, try me, and lead me today. May I bring glory to Your name in all I do, say, and think. Amen.

Search me, O God, and know my heart; try me, and know my anxieties;
and see if there is any wicked way in me, and lead me in the way everlasting.
PSALM 139:23, 24

No other nation in the world takes security more seriously than Israel. I have made the trip to and from the Holy Land several times, and by now I know what to expect in the Tel Aviv airport. During my first visits, I was disturbed by the intense security. I was frustrated by the long lines and many questions about where I had been and what I had done. But that completely changed on September 11, 2001. I can now appreciate that the security procedures at the airport are for my own safety and protection.

Many people feel scrutinized when they are inspected for security reasons in a public setting because it seems invasive, but we should never have that attitude with God. As Christians, we desire to please our righteous Master, emulate our holy God, and love our heavenly Father. We should continually go to Him with our hearts laid open and welcome His examination. How else will we know how to grow? We need His help.

Are you trying to grow spiritually without God's help? Don't shy away from His "inspection"—it's for your good and His glory. Inviting Him to search your heart isn't about allowing Him to see something new—He already knows you intimately. It's about expressing your willingness to submit to Him. If you want to please the Lord with your life, humbly request His loving correction on a daily basis.

EVENING

Father, help me welcome Your examination of my life and make me quick to respond to Your loving correction. May I never be a stumbling block to others. Forgive me where I have failed You and prepare my heart for a new day and new opportunity to represent Your love to this world. Amen.

Lord, allow me to season the world in which I live by demonstrating Your power, love, and truth to all who cross my path today. Amen.

You are the salt of the earth; but if the salt loses its flavor, how shall it be seasoned?
It is then good for nothing but to be thrown out and trampled underfoot by men.
You are the light of the world. A city that is set on a hill cannot be hidden.
MATTHEW 5:13, 14

My wife's grandparents were great examples of faithful Christians. Grandfather Carl loved his farm, but he loved his Lord even more. I will never forget my first visit to his farm. I walked outside with Carl, and he told me to look at the brilliant stars in the cloudless Oklahoma night. "You'uns won't see a sight like that in the city," he said. It was true; the activity of the city crowded out the magnificent brilliance of starry nights. Carl did more than show me the light I had missed growing up in the city. As a loving servant, he lived his life in a way that shined Christ's light to me and to all who knew him.

As Christians, we are called to reflect the radiance of Jesus Christ to this sin-darkened world. I once read in a book, "You don't need to say a word to let others know you are a Christian . . . just live your lives in a way that there is never a doubt." I disagree with that statement. If we never open our mouths to let others know that Jesus has changed our lives, then we are only demonstrating our own good works and not His glorious power to change our lives. We must be sure to give Him all the credit He deserves! Make your life fit the description Jesus has given you—"the light of the world." Faithfully point others to Him and His gospel every way you can.

EVENING

As this day ends, I ask You, Father, if I have been the light You requested me to be in this sin-darkened world. Forgive me for the times during this day that my words or actions have hidden Your life from a world desperate to see the truth. Help me shine faithfully for You tomorrow. Amen.

LARRY THOMPSON, FORT LAUDERDALE, FL

Father, help me not to be deceived by my spiritual Enemy today. Encourage me to live in Your truth and to be thankful for Your perfect gift of eternal life. Amen.

Do not be deceived, my beloved brethren. Every good gift and every perfect gift is from above, and comes down from the Father of lights, with whom there is no variation or shadow of turning. Of His own will He brought us forth by the word of truth, that we might be a kind of firstfruits of His creatures.
JAMES 1:16–18

———————————— ✽ ————————————

Every Christmas we are encouraged to give the perfect gifts to the people we love. As a husband, I enjoy the challenge of trying to find the perfect gift for my wife. But I must admit that there have been times I have failed miserably! One Christmas I bought my wife a handheld mayonnaise maker. I just knew she would love it . . . but sadly it was not the perfect gift, and it made its way to the garage sale in record time.

God, however, always gives His children the right things. The phrase "every perfect gift" indicates that anything God provides is everything it is intended to be—complete and lacking nothing. The Greek word translated "comes down" is a present participle, implying a continual action; it is a gift that continually comes down from heaven. The expression, "Jesus is the gift that keeps on giving," is more than a mere cliché.

Today's passage reminds us that we are to reflect our Creator. We are called *firstfruits*, a word that has two important connotations in Scripture. First, firstfruits were considered sacred, or set apart, and belonged to God. Second, they were a continual reminder that there was more to come—an even greater harvest.

We are the firstfruits of God's creation, and we are commanded to give back to Him and to others. By His will, God gave us the perfect gift of eternal life so that we could continually give from the abundance Christ has provided for each of us. Reflect your Creator—be both a receiver and a giver of God's good gifts.

———————————— ✽ ————————————

EVENING
Lord, thank You for giving me so many perfect gifts. I praise You for Your goodness and grace. Lead me to give You everything for Your glory. Amen.

Father, I ask You to bring young believers into my path and make me an encourager in their lives. May I be both an example to them in their walk and a student to learn from them as they follow You. Amen.

Let no one despise your youth, but be an example to the believers in word, in conduct, in love, in spirit, in faith, in purity . . . Do not neglect the gift that is in you, which was given to you by prophecy with the laying on of the hands of the eldership. Meditate on these things; give yourself entirely to them, that your progress may be evident to all.

1 TIMOTHY 4:12, 14, 15

I remember my call to ministry as if it were yesterday. After I told my pastor about what I sensed God was doing in my life, he said, "Well, keep praying, and if God is really calling you, someday He will open the door and you will know it." I often say that my pastor knew me so well that he could never believe that God would actually call me to full-time ministry. However, God did call me, and I had the privilege of working for this godly man for many years before becoming a senior pastor myself.

Paul was wise to remind believers not to discredit what God was doing in and through the lives of young people. When you trace the history of the world's greatest revivals, you will find that the majority of them were born when students gathered to pray. God used their enthusiasm, purity, and faith to ignite the fires of real renewal. Paul reminded young Timothy to be an example of a man of God in his words and behavior and to maintain a spirit of love, faith, and purity.

I believe in today's young believers. They will not preach and minister the exact way that I have through the years, but they possess God's fire and vision, and I believe He will use them to bring revival to their generation. Every chance you get, do all you can to encourage the leaders of tomorrow's church!

EVENING

Lord, please bless the students in my church. Call them into Your service, and use them to win this generation for Christ. Help us never discredit them because of their youth, but always encourage them in the race. Amen.

LARRY THOMPSON, FORT LAUDERDALE, FL

Week 50, Monday

Lord, You are love. Your love never ends, and it never fails. Thank You for loving me first. Today, help me to know and love You more and to express my love for You by loving others. Help me to see people with Your eyes and to love them as You love them. Change my heart and mind, and give me the desire and opportunity to express my love for people in a true and authentic way today. Amen.

Beloved, let us love one another, for love is of God; and everyone who loves is born of God and knows God. He who does not love does not know God, for God is love.

1 JOHN 4:7, 8

Would you rather be known as a nice person or as a loving person? It sounds like an odd question, and you may ask, "Aren't they the same thing?" But there is a difference. Choosing to be nice and choosing to love may actually come into conflict.

Being nice means you say the things people want to hear, and you may not connect with people in an authentic way. It typically means you don't allow yourself to get into the relational messiness that comes with being involved in other people's lives.

However, if you want to love people, you must speak the truth in love, even when it is uncomfortable. You must not be afraid of the relational tension that can happen when you boldly love and engage people. Simply said, love goes beyond being nice. Loving people means being real and being willing to get into the messiness of people's lives. Loving people means seeking the best for others.

Choose today to love people, even if it means that someone will think you aren't being nice.

EVENING

Lord, thank You for showing me Your love. I admit that it is often easier to be nice to others than to love others. Help me live a life of love the way You did and still do. Help me continue to love others even when they insult me or do hurtful things. This is the path You have asked me to take as I follow You, and it is an honor to follow You. There is nothing greater I can do than love people the way You do, especially people who I think don't deserve Your love. Amen.

MORNING

Father, thank You for Your love and promises. I know there is nothing that I might face today or in the future that will separate me from the love found in Jesus. Even though I may face trials and difficult situations today, I know You are with me. I believe and accept Your promise that I am more than a conqueror. I pray that this truth would affect my thoughts and emotions as I walk with You through this day. Amen.

I am persuaded that neither death nor life, nor angels nor principalities nor powers, nor things present nor things to come, nor height nor depth, nor any other created thing, shall be able to separate us from the love of God which is in Christ Jesus our Lord.
ROMANS 8:38, 39

When you experience difficult circumstances, you may feel like God has abandoned you. You may feel alone in your trials. Aloneness is a heart-wrenching state for the human soul. Being separated from the ones we love is a very real source of grief and heartache. That is why death and divorce are two of the most difficult life situations people can experience. These verses are your promise and reminder that absolutely nothing can separate you from God's love.

No matter where you go, no matter whom you encounter, no matter what you do or don't do, no one and no circumstance will be able to separate you from His love. You may experience suffering and difficulties, but that doesn't mean He has forgotten or abandoned you. In fact, suffering actually carries you toward the goal of being conformed to the likeness of Jesus. You will overcome the world just as Jesus did. You will prevail. Don't allow the circumstances or people you face today to cause you to forget this promise. God is for you and with you.

EVENING

Lord, nothing compares with Your love. Thank You for comforting me with this promise today. May I continue to walk in the truths that I am more than a conqueror and that nothing can separate me from Your love. Though I may not always feel like You are with me when I am going through difficult circumstances, I know by faith that You will never leave me. Thank You for always being with me. Father, I love You with all my heart, soul, mind, and strength. Amen.

RODNEY HUNT, DALLAS, GA

God, help me comprehend how deep and wide Your love is for me. I know I can't understand this without Your revelation. Help me to see the small things in my world that are expressions of Your love for me and to know the fullness of You and Your love in my emotions. Thank You for rooting and grounding me in Your love. Help me see You in a new way as I experience Your love throughout the day. Amen.

That Christ may dwell in your hearts through faith; that you, being
rooted and grounded in love, may be able to comprehend with all the saints
what is the width and length and depth and height—to know the love of Christ
which passes knowledge; that you may be filled with all the fullness of God.
EPHESIANS 3:17–19

———————————— ∽∾∽ ————————————

One of the greatest revelations you can experience is God's love for you. This love was expressed completely in the Person of Jesus Christ and His sacrifice for you. He completely demonstrated His love for you by this one act. This is because love is the essence and nature of who God is.

We often run after knowledge, thinking that we grow the most as a follower of Christ by seeking knowledge. Scripture reminds us, however, that knowledge puffs up while love builds up (1 Corinthians 8:1). If your pursuit of knowledge doesn't lead you to a greater appreciation of God's love for you, then you are simply missing the point.

Relationships are far more important than any pursuit of knowledge. Your relationship with God does involve your mind, but it most importantly involves your heart. To comprehend this truth, you must soften your heart and allow God to open the eyes of your heart. Allow God's love to penetrate your emotions, heart, and the deepest part of you. This experience is foundational to everything else you do in life. Allow yourself to experience the fullness of God's love on a heart level today.

———————————— ∽∾∽ ————————————

EVENING

Thank You, God, for showing me Your love today and for displaying the complete depth of that love in Your Son when He poured out His life and sacrificed Himself for me. May my pursuit of knowledge always lead me to a greater appreciation of love. May Your love continue to set the course for my life. Amen.

Heavenly Father, I pause this morning to take my eyes off the temporary to look at the future hope I have in Christ. It is easy to forget what You have in store for me. Help me develop an eternal perspective as I face difficulties and troubles in this world. I want to gain a new appreciation of the future I have in You. I am so thankful for the promise of Paradise restored. Remind me today of Your kingdom that is coming in power and glory. Amen.

> *Hope does not disappoint, because the love of God has been poured out in our hearts by the Holy Spirit who was given to us.*
> ROMANS 5:5

We all face disappointment, discouragement, and difficulty in this life. It is easy to allow these times of discouragement and even depression to dictate how you live your life. Your momentary troubles can cause you to lose sight of your eternal future and hope. Sometimes you have to step back and remind yourself of the hope you have in Christ and ask God to give you an eternal perspective.

There is nothing disappointing about living eternally in God's presence in a restored heaven and earth, where sin, death, and sickness will be forever destroyed and will play no part in your life. There is nothing disappointing about seeing God face-to-face and not worrying about sin affecting your relationship with your heavenly Father or other people you love. You long for Paradise restored—for things to be made perfect as they once were in the Garden of Eden. God has adopted you, and by His Holy Spirit, He has put His seal on you as a deposit of these incredible things that are to come. In the midst of your temporary troubles, don't lose sight of the eternal.

EVENING

Father, thank You for reminding me of my future and the hope I have in Christ. May I never lose sight of the eternal and my future in light of the troubles and difficulties I have in this life. May this hope continue to give me strength as I face troubles in this world. Your hope doesn't disappoint. I am so thankful that You are preparing a place for me. Help me continue to run the race with my eyes on this finish line. You are my hope and my future. Amen.

RODNEY HUNT, DALLAS, GA

Week 50, Friday

Father, help me remember how You saved me. I don't want to forget what I would be without Your saving work in my life. Restore to me the joy of my salvation. Thank You for loving me before I loved You. Thank You that You cared enough to seek me, find me, and cleanse me from all sin and unrighteousness. You sought and found me, and I want to tell You today that I love You for loving me. Amen.

In this is love, not that we loved God, but that He loved us and
sent His Son to be the propitiation for our sins.
1 JOHN 4:10

———— ⁓⁓⁓ ————

God took the first step in loving you. He took the initiative not only to seek you but also to do the work of atonement for your sins. He paid a great price to rescue you. This act of love involved a great deal of suffering and sacrifice. We often say that we found God, but the truth is, we didn't find God—He found us.

You are like the one sheep that He left the ninety-nine for in the parable of the lost sheep (Luke 15:3–7). He truly cares about you and loves you that much. You matter greatly to God. Jesus left heaven's comfort for Your sake. He would do this even if you were the only one who was lost. That is the heart of God. You are wonderfully made, and thus, very valuable in His sight. This is not based on anything you have done or haven't done, but on His love, mercy, and grace for you. That is the wonder of His salvation and the reason we call Him our Savior, Rescuer, Redeemer, and Friend.

Bask in the Father's love for you today.

———— ⁓⁓⁓ ————

EVENING

Father, thank You for leaving heaven's comfort for my sake. Thank You for loving me before I knew You or loved You. I am so thankful that You took initiative and made the sacrifice for me. I know You experienced real pain and real hurt for my sake. Because of this, I can now say, "I was lost, but now I am found." Your grace truly is amazing; nothing else compares to Your love. I love You and I never want to take for granted the price You paid for my sin and my salvation. Amen.

Father, I come to You today as Your adopted child, and You have made it clear that I am greatly loved by You. I realize that the way I treat others and live out my faith expresses my understanding of Your love. Search me today and show me any area where I am falling short or missing out on the opportunity to see Your love perfected in me. I also realize that being obedient to You is directly tied to how I love others, especially my fellow believers. Help me to live in obedience to Your Word and to love others. Amen.

Whoever keeps His word, truly the love of God is perfected in him. By this we know that we are in Him.

1 JOHN 2:5

———————— ❧ ————————

While your performance doesn't affect God's love for you, your obedience does express the extent to which you understand His love for you. When you apply His Word to your daily life, His love is made perfect in you. God's love should affect your decisions and how you live your life. You cannot experience the love of God without experiencing life change. His love puts a desire in you to live obediently to His calling for your life. Faith, love, and action go hand in hand. Experiencing God's love isn't passive, but active. It involves your heart, mind, and soul. It causes a response and a change in your thoughts and actions.

As you think about your day, make the decision now to obey Him no matter what circumstances you may face. Let your answer be, "Yes, Lord." Make the decision to allow God's love to affect your behavior. Don't think of obedience as a legalistic rule to follow, but as an outward expression of your relationship with and love for your heavenly Father. Allow God's love to be perfected in you today as you keep His Word.

———————— ❧ ————————

EVENING

God, thank You that Your love is being perfected in me as I learn to obey You. Help me to be able not only to read Your Word but also to apply it to my life. I realize that the greatest area of obedience has to do with my relationships and how I love other people. Open the eyes of my heart so I can see people the way You see them and love them the way You love them. Amen.

RODNEY HUNT, DALLAS, GA

Dear Father, I come to You this morning to say thank You for a brand new day. I look forward to experiencing Your love and grace today. Help me demonstrate that same love and grace to others. In Jesus' name, Amen.

By this we know love, because He laid down His life for us. And we also ought to lay down our lives for the brethren. But whoever has this world's goods, and sees his brother in need, and shuts up his heart from him, how does the love of God abide in him? My little children, let us not love in word or in tongue, but in deed and in truth.
1 JOHN 3:16–18

From Genesis to Revelation, from earth's greatest tragedy to earth's greatest triumph, the dramatic story of humanity's lowest depths and God's highest heights can be described in twenty-five beautiful words: "For God so loved the world, that He gave His only begotten Son, that whoever believes in Him should not perish, but have everlasting life" (John 3:16).

Many people misunderstand God's attribute of love. "God is love" does not mean that everything is sweet, beautiful, and happy, and that God's love could not possibly allow punishment for sin. God's holiness demands that all sin be punished, but God's love provided a plan of redemption for sinners. God's love provided the Cross of Jesus Christ by which sinners can have forgiveness and cleansing. It was the love of God that sent Jesus Christ to that Cross.

Who can describe or measure the love of God? The Bible is a revelation of the fact that God is love. When we preach justice, it is justice tempered with love. When we preach righteousness, it is righteousness founded on love. When we preach atonement, it is atonement planned by love, provided by love, given by love, finished by love, and necessitated by love. When we preach the resurrection of Christ, we are preaching the miracle of love. When we preach the return of Christ, we are preaching the fulfillment of love.

Live in God's love—make it the foundation for all you do today.

EVENING
Dear Father, thank You for the way You have demonstrated Your love to me today. I worship You, and I am thankful to be a child of the King. Amen.

MORNING

Dear Jesus, thank You for dying on the Cross and paying for my sins. Give me the opportunity and the power of the Holy Spirit to love and tell others about You today. In Jesus' name, Amen.

> *By this we know that we love the children of God, when we love God*
> *and keep His commandments. For this is the love of God, that we*
> *keep His commandments. And His commandments are not burdensome.*
> 1 JOHN 5:2, 3

———— ‹⁓› ————

Most people have little knowledge of any language other than their own. That's why it is difficult to comprehend the abilities of a person such as the eighteenth-century Italian linguist Mezzofanti. He was fluent in 114 languages and dialects. We certainly admire men of great knowledge. But we as Christians know one language that stands above all others: the language of love. It is essential for communicating the gospel. It is our responsibility to share our knowledge of the Savior, but if we fail to demonstrate care and compassion, we are wasting our breath.

In his book *Dropping Your Guard*, Charles Swindoll told an alarming true story: "It concerned a man who had been walking along a pier when suddenly he tripped over a rope and fell into the cold, deep waters of that ocean bay. He came up sputtering, screaming for help, then sank beneath the surface. For some reason he was unable to swim or stay afloat. His friends heard his faint cries in the distance, but they were too far away to rescue him. But within only a few yards was a young man lounging on a deck chair, sunbathing. Not only could the sunbather hear the drowning man plead, 'Help, I can't swim,' but he was also an excellent swimmer. The tragedy is that he did nothing. He only turned his head to watch indifferently as the man finally sank and drowned."[18]

This is a sorrowful picture of believers casually watching the unsaved sink into a Christ-less eternity. We know that Jesus is the only way to life! May we have a love that will reach out to those around us who are dying in sin.

———— ‹⁓› ————

EVENING

Dear Jesus, thank You for another great day. What a privilege it is to serve You and to allow You to live through me. I glorify Your name. Amen.

KELLY BURRIS, VIRGINIA BEACH, VA

Father, I bless Your name for the way You have demonstrated Your love, mercy, and grace to me. Help me demonstrate that same love, mercy, and grace to others so they can see You. In Jesus' name, Amen.

You, beloved, building yourselves up on your most holy faith,
praying in the Holy Spirit, keep yourselves in the love of God, looking
for the mercy of our Lord Jesus Christ unto eternal life.
JUDE 20, 21

There is a legend about a pastor who welcomed a weary traveler into his home for a night of rest. After learning that his guest was almost a hundred years old, the pastor asked him about his religious beliefs. The man replied, "I'm an atheist." Infuriated, the pastor ordered the man out saying, "I cannot keep an atheist in my house." Without a word, the elderly man hobbled out into the darkness. The pastor was reading Scripture when he heard a voice ask, "Son, why did you throw that old man out?" "Because he is an atheist, and I cannot endure him overnight!" said the pastor. The voice replied, "I have endured him for almost a hundred years." The preacher rushed out, brought the old man back, and treated him with kindness.

When we treat unbelievers with contempt, we're not serving God. He wants us to love them as He has loved us. In today's passage, we read, "Keep yourselves in the love of God, looking for the mercy of our Lord Jesus Christ unto eternal life." Later in Jude we read, "On some have compassion . . . but others save with fear, hating even the garment defiled by the flesh" (vv. 22, 23). We can still love sinners while hating their sin. Receiving abundant mercy from God motivates us to be merciful to others.

EVENING

I praise You, Lord, for this day. Thank You for allowing me in my small way to show others Your love, mercy, and grace. I pray they will find Your peace in their hearts as I have. It is an honor to be an ambassador of the King of kings and the Lord of lords. Amen.

MORNING

Father, thank You for first loving me, in spite of my sin. Today, help me to extend the same kind of grace to my brothers and sisters in Christ. Amen.

> *As the Father loved Me, I also have loved you; abide in My love.*
> *If you keep My commandments, you will abide in My love,*
> *just as I have kept My Father's commandments and abide in His love.*
> JOHN 15:9, 10

What is the great, overwhelming evidence that we have passed from death unto life? It is love! Jesus prayed for His church that "they all may be one, as You, Father, are in Me, and I in You; that they also may be one in Us, that the world may believe that You sent Me" (John 17:21). Jesus Christ clearly spoke of visible unity, such as can be seen by the world. He prayed for believers' unity to prompt the world to believe in Him. There is a kind of unity possible in diversity—a unity compatible with variety—and Christ established a way for His church to live it out.

All through the Book of Acts, we see this phrase: "with one accord." The apostles were not given to quarreling over secondary points of doctrine. When difficulties did arise, every attempt was made to settle them in a reasonable and charitable spirit under the direction of the Holy Spirit. We as believers are to approach our problems, good works, and even our differences in the spirit of true humility, compassion, consideration, and unselfishness, reflecting the mind of the Lord Jesus.

James protested against the bareness of an orthodoxy that is divorced from love and good works (James 2:14–26). John filled his epistles with discussions about the love that Christians are to have one for another. In 1 John 3:14, he said, "We know that we have passed from death to life, because we love the brethren." It is not because we know every doctrine in the Christian faith and have studied the Bible from cover to cover. The one great test is love!

EVENING

Dear Jesus, forgive me for the times I was not a channel of Your love to others today. Help me to be a blessing that demonstrates Your love. Amen.

The psalmist said, "This is the day the Lord has made; we will rejoice and be glad in it" (Psalm 118:24). Help me, Father, to rejoice in Your love and grace, and to be ready always to say, "Yes, Lord!" I want to show You how much I love You today by the way I obey Your commands. In Jesus' name I pray. Amen.

> *He who has My commandments and keeps them, it is he who loves Me.*
> *And he who loves Me will be loved by My Father, and I will love him*
> *and manifest Myself to him . . . If anyone loves Me, he will keep My word; and*
> *My Father will love him, and We will come to him and make Our home with him.*
>
> JOHN 14:21, 23

I love to read church signs. Some are quite comical and others are very thought provoking. I appreciate that public word of witness for Christ. The other day I drove past a church's sign that contained just two words: "Yes, Lord!" While I was running errands that morning, the words stayed in my mind. Was there any situation to which they did not hold the key? I couldn't think of one. What great joy it would bring to Jesus if I began every day with those two words!

"Yes, Lord. I'll be content where I am instead of wishing I were somewhere else." "Yes, Lord. I'll trust You for the outcome of the uncertainty gnawing at my mind." "Yes, Lord. I'll open my heart and hands to others with the joyous generosity You love." The resolution of every trouble we face today begins with this trusting response to our Savior: "Yes, Lord!" You can never go wrong when you choose to obey Christ.

EVENING

Father, it is a joy to be in Your abiding love and to see how You work to reveal Your wonderful plan and purpose in my life. Help me always remember that the safest place to be is in the center of Your will. I am committed to continue saying, "Yes, Lord!" to You tomorrow! In Jesus' name, Amen.

MORNING

Father, as I begin this day please help me rely upon Your strength and courage. I want to thank You for the Holy Spirit residing in my heart and giving me the power to do Your will. Amen.

Finally, brethren, farewell. Become complete. Be of good comfort,
be of one mind, live in peace; and the God of love and peace will be with you.
2 CORINTHIANS 13:11

L oving an enemy is not natural—it's supernatural. When we feel the first impulse to strike back at our foes, we must call on the Lord to enable us to pray for them, to desire their salvation or spiritual well-being, and to have wisdom as we interact with them. Loving them for Jesus' sake will be challenging, but its reward will be great.

In August 1983, Russell Stendal was held hostage by guerrillas in a Colombian jungle for almost five months. But Stendal had an uncommon response. In a letter, he wrote, "I am in danger only of losing my life; they are in danger of losing their souls." He was so kind to his captors that he truly befriended them. One day the commander told him, "We can't kill you face-to-face; we like you. So we will have to kill you in your sleep." Naturally, Stendal couldn't sleep for the following ten days and nights. The guards came to him in the night with guns but couldn't bring themselves to kill him. Eventually, Stendal was released, and when he said good-bye, his captors actually had tears in their eyes. God enabled Stendal to forgive and love his enemies with sincerity and consistency.

Jesus taught that we are to do good to those who hate us (Matthew 5:44). When we do, it may create a change in others' hearts. Even when it doesn't, the benefits of loving others are great. We receive God's supernatural grace and strength, and we can be confident that we are faithfully representing our heavenly Father. For the Christian, that in itself is rewarding.

EVENING

Father, forgive me for the times I have not demonstrated Your love to my enemies. When I face conflicts, help me not to do what is natural, but what is supernatural by the power of Your Spirit. In Jesus' name, Amen.

KELLY BURRIS, VIRGINIA BEACH, VA

Dear God, while the world around me is unstable, I find blessed assurance in You. Your love brings me security, peace, strength, and joy; help me to be aware of that today. I pray that I will give others the kindness and care You want them to experience through me. I yield to You as I receive Your perfect love for me. Now, may I share it with others. Amen.

> *There is no fear in love; but perfect love casts out fear, because fear*
> *involves torment. But he who fears has not been made perfect*
> *in love. We love Him because He first loved us.*
> 1 JOHN 4:18, 19

Many people are afraid to love because they have been involved in hurtful relationships. Are you one of those people? Have you been rejected, taken advantage of, abused, or scarred by those you loved? Are you afraid to love again because it hurts so much? Jesus was rejected by His own family because of God's call on His life. Not until after His death and resurrection did Jesus' brother, James, finally believe in Him. God Himself is not immune to rejection. People reject Him every day, but He keeps on loving them.

You can do the same. Our passage today says that "perfect love casts out fear," and this makes it possible for you to be vulnerable again. God's eternal gift to you is love. Use His love to overcome your fear of rejection, and you will receive more love in return.

Today, be filled with the Lord's love so you can freely give it away. Be someone who loves extravagantly, as the Lord does.

EVENING

Dear God, thank You for spending today with me. Your love covered all my weaknesses and protected me. You are amazing, Lord. May I never take Your love and protection for granted. Each day is a gift. Loving others in Your name is an honor. As I reflect on the people I interacted with today, I pray for them. I ask that Your love would reach down from the heavens and touch their lives. I praise Your name because Your love is perfect and it fills my heart. I love You, Lord. Thank You for loving me so I may love others better. Amen.

MORNING

Dear God, when I look at people today, help me see them the way You see them. May I be selfless and caring so that Your love can shine through my life. I step forward today with a love to share that comes from You. In Jesus' name I pray. Amen.

A new commandment I give to you, that you love one another;
as I have loved you, that you also love one another. By this all will know
that you are My disciples, if you have love for one another.
JOHN 13:34, 35

How do we love one another? How can we express God's love to others when we can hardly stand being around them? Love is not a feeling; it is a gift. You choose to give the gift of your love to whomever you decide should have it—your spouse, a close friend, a family member. To love is to give the most precious gift you have: your heart.

Many times when love is given it is not reciprocated. But that is the miracle of true love—it doesn't require anything in return! In fact, love grows in the fertile soil of the unknown just as well as in the soil of loving relationships. Where is your love planted? Have you reserved it only for the safest places? Maybe it's time to reconsider.

There is no greater gift you can give than your love. Ask God to enable you to love as He loves. Today, focus on others' needs and concerns more than your own, and try to love them the way you want to be loved. As you rely on God to help you love others as He has loved you, His kingdom comes to earth. Your witness to His character glorifies His name!

EVENING

Dear God, thank You for the honor to share Your love with others. I have seen how my witness reflects Your love to those around me. As I shine, You are glorified. I pray that there were many who saw You through me today. Amen.

TIM DeTELLIS, ORLANDO, FL

Dear God, I thank You for Your mercy. You are faithful and I stand in awe of You. The power of Your love exceeds my imagination. The strength of Your grip on my life holds me steady in this ever-changing world. I humbly fear You because You are truly awesome. Help me walk in the truth of Your righteousness today and to be steadfast in following Your ways every day. Guide my steps. Help me yield to You, seek You, and know You more. Amen.

> *The mercy of the LORD is from everlasting to everlasting on those*
> *who fear Him, and His righteousness to children's children, to such as keep His*
> *covenant, and to those who remember His commandments to do them.*
> PSALM 103:17, 18

God's eternal gift of love is freely given to everyone He has created. But like any gift, it must be apprehended and put to use. A gift that is rejected has no value to the one who rejected it, no matter the cost to the one who gave it.

You receive the fullness of God's love when you love Him in return. This divine relationship continues to unfold and grow as long as you stay in relationship with God and seek to please Him out of love and not out of duty. God keeps things interesting by continually revealing greater dimensions of His goodness and love. He assures you that it is impossible to fall out of His love; it has no boundary.

Are you feeling God's love? Do you sense His nearness and long for His presence? Just reach out; He is very near. James 4:8 says, "Draw near to God and He will draw near to you." Receive God's great love, and then love Him back with all that you are.

EVENING

Dear God, thank You for Your guiding hand on my life, Your strength that is always sufficient, and Your love that endures all things. I look forward to a new day. I pray that my faith will be stronger and my heart will be more in love with You tomorrow. Your holy Word is truth. May I hold on to Your promises and instructions more every day. I want more of You and less of me. Amen.

MORNING

Dear God, open my eyes to see Your everlasting love. Through the beauty of Your creation or in the eyes of those closest to me, help me see Your love. Your lovingkindness reaches me. It fills my soul and strengthens my faith. Amen.

The LORD has appeared of old to me, saying: "Yes, I have loved you with
an everlasting love; therefore with lovingkindness I have drawn you. Again
I will build you, and you shall be rebuilt, O virgin of Israel! You shall again be
adorned with your tambourines, and shall go forth in the dances of those who rejoice."
JEREMIAH 31:3, 4

When you felt most alone, you weren't alone. When you wondered if anyone cared, One did care. When you felt completely unlovable, you were loved. As a Christian, you are never apart from God's love in Christ (Romans 8:38, 39). It's time to stop listening to the lies that because you are not good enough you can never receive God's love. Step away from whatever is holding you back from living every day in a loving, strengthening, and fulfilling relationship with God. You do not need to be afraid. To fear God is to honor Him—not to be scared to draw near to Him. Reach out your hand and open your heart, because God has a gift to share.

Imagine being loved before you even existed! Imagine being loved with a love that has no beginning and no end. Imagine being loved so completely that absolutely nothing could cause it to fade. This is God's love for you. Even at your lowest points, God's eternal gift of love covers you completely. His arms ache to hold you, and His heart pounds with unfailing love.

Receive God's love for you. Unwrap the present of a lifetime. God loves you and longs for you to embrace His love. It is freely given, and it will never leave you wanting.

EVENING

Dear God, thank You for a love that is endless. In a world of fragile and temporary things, I rest in You. From failure to victory, Your love surrounds me. I am truly speechless as I try to comprehend Your eternal love for me. Though my understanding is limited, I trust You and yearn for closeness with You. I give You the glory, honor, and praise You deserve for Your amazing love. Amen.

TIM DeTELLIS, ORLANDO, FL

Week 52, Friday

Dear God, I need Your peace today. I have uncertainties in my life. May I discover a deeper courage. I ask You to hold me close and to guard my heart, my mind, and my words. Make my heart's desires Your desires as I draw near to You. I declare You Lord of my life, and I rejoice in You. Amen.

The LORD reigns, He is clothed with majesty; the LORD is clothed, He has girded Himself with strength. Surely the world is established, so that it cannot be moved. Your throne is established from of old; You are from everlasting.

PSALM 93:1, 2

D o you feel overwhelmed by the circumstances that surround you? Does it feel as if the world has gone over the edge and is pulling you down with it? Do you feel as if you have no control over your life and that nobody really cares what happens to you? Well, you are not alone. Many people feel that way and live hopeless, helpless lives, suffering in quiet despair. Satan wants them to isolate themselves and keep pulling away from God and others.

Would you like to hear some good news? God reigns over the entire universe. Today's passage says He is "clothed with majesty" and "girded . . . with strength." In His divine, sovereign power, He created the world and all the people who live in it, including you! God loves you and wants you to live fully. God's eternal gift for you is hope for a bright future. Why? So you may worship Him and love Him because He first loved you.

Live in God's great gift of hope, and seek His perfect plan for your life today.

EVENING

I praise You, mighty Lord! Your throne is established—You are greater than all, and You will reign with majesty forever. You are everlasting and You are my anchor. You are worthy of honor and glory. I offer You my praise, my devotion, my love, my all! In Jesus' name, Amen.

MORNING

Dear God, I give You praise for Your endless love. You are the Creator of the universe, yet You still think of me. I am filled with awe and wonder at Your great love. I praise You for Your amazing attention to details and Your beauty and wonder. Nothing compares to Your creativity. Today, I surrender to Your plan for my life. Speak to me, and I will listen. In Jesus' name I pray. Amen.

> LORD, *You have been our dwelling place in all generations. Before the mountains were brought forth, or ever You had formed the earth and the world, even from everlasting to everlasting, You are God.*
>
> PSALM 90:1, 2

Before the earth was formed, God was mindful of you. From everlasting to everlasting, God's thoughts included you and the life He has given you to live. Before time began or any substance was created, you were part of God's intentions for His creation.

You discover God's eternal gift as you step into the awesome plan God has for you. Whether you are making a decision, creating something with your hands, raising a child, working at a career, helping another person, or learning in school, His plan unfolds as you submit to Him. Listen! Do you hear God calling? He is inviting you to come and dream with Him about your future. His plans are big . . . bigger than anything you can imagine. And they are yours to live out in His strength and for His great glory!

EVENING

Dear God, Your hand is strong, yet gentle enough to hold me. I felt Your loving care today and thank You for Your steadfast love. Even though I am only one of many, I know You know my name. Your love is a continual reminder of how real You want our relationship to be. That You could be the Almighty and still be my friend gives me a deep respect for You, and I am honored to call You Lord. I love You with all my heart. Amen.

Endnotes

[1] Matthew Parris, "As an atheist, I truly believe Africa needs God," *The Times of London*, December 27, 2008, http://www.timesonline.co.uk/tol/comment/columnists/matthew_parris/article5400568.ece.

[2] J.C. Ryle, "A Call to Prayer," http://www.fivesolas.com/callpray.htm.

[3] Shawn Craig and Connie Harrington, "Your Grace Still Amazes Me," *Let My Words Be Few*. Compact Disc. Sparrow Records, 2001.

[4] Dwight L. Moody, *The Overcoming Life* (Orlando, FL: Bridge-Logos, 2007).

[5] Steven Curtis Chapman, "His Strength Is Perfect," *Greatest Hits 2008*. Compact Disc. Sparrow Records, 2008.

[6] Joyce Martin McCoullough, Matt Huesmann, and Grant Cunningham, "May We Never Forget," *Windows*. Compact Disc. Spring Hill Music Group, 2005.

[7] Lenny Leblanc, "There Is None Like You," *Pure Heart*. Compact Disc. Hosanna! Music, 1991.

[8] http://earthquake.usgs.gov/learn/topics/100_chance.php

[9] Mark Hall, "Praise You in This Storm," *Lifesong*. Compact Disc. Reunion, 2005.

[10] Tony Evans, *Time to Get Serious: Daily Devotions to Keep You Close to God* (Wheaton, IL: Crossway Books, 1995), 35.

[11] Matt Redman, "The Heart of Worship," *The Heart of Worship*. Compact Disc. Kingsway/Worship Together, 1999.

[12] L. B. Cowman, *Streams in the Desert* (Grand Rapids, MI: Zondervan, 1997).

[13] L. B. Cowman, *Streams in the Desert* (Grand Rapids, MI: Zondervan, 1997).

[14] David Jeremiah, *The Wisdom of God* (Milford, MI: Mott Media, Inc, N.D., 1985), 73.

[15] Steve Farrar, *Standing Tall* (Portland, OR: Multnomah Press, 1994), 201.

[16] S. D. Gordon, *Quiet Talks on Prayer*, Project Gutenberg, http://www.gutenberg.org/files/13196/13196-h/13196-h.htm.

[17] Edward M. Bounds, *Power Through Prayer* (New York: Cosimo Classics, 2007), 10.

[18] Charles R. Swindoll, *Dropping Your Guard: The Value of Open Relationships*, rev. ed. (Nashville: Thomas Nelson, 2009).

Contributors

Chuck Allen	ChurchSPEAK Communications; Duluth, GA	Week 41
Tim Anderson	Clements Baptist Church; Athens, AL	Week 29
Trevor Barton	Hawk Creek Baptist Church; London, KY	Week 34
Kie Bowman	Hyde Park Baptist; Austin, TX	Week 2
Kelly Burris	Kempsville Baptist Church; Virginia Beach, VA	Week 51
Dr. Michael Cloer	Englewood Baptist Church; Rocky Mount, NC	Week 22
Jeff Crook	Blackshear Place; Flowery Branch, GA	Week 37
Tim DeTellis	New Missions; Orlando, FL	Week 52
Chris Dixon	Liberty Baptist Church; Dublin, GA	Week 25
Adam Dooley	Red Bank Baptist; Chattanooga, TN	Week 12
Tim Dowdy	Eagle's Landing First Baptist; McDonough, GA	Week 30
Grant Ethridge	Liberty Baptist Church; Hampton, VA	Week 21
Jonathan Falwell	Thomas Road Baptist Church; Lynchburg, VA	Week 46
Steve Flockhart	New Season Church; Hiram, GA	Week 45
Dr. Ronnie Floyd	First Baptist Church; Springdale, AR	Week 42
Danny Forshee	Great Hills Baptist Church; Austin, TX	Week 9
Jerry Gillis	The Chapel at CrossPoint; Buffalo, NY	Week 47
Billy Goodwin	NewSong; Ball Ground, GA	Week 33
Dr. Michael Hamlet	First Baptist N. Spartanburg; Spartanburg, SC	Week 38
Junior Hill	Evangelist; Hartselle, AL	Week 6
Pete Hixson	Vinings Lake Church; Mableton, GA	Week 39
Dr. Johnny Hunt	First Baptist Church; Woodstock, GA	Week 1
Norman Hunt	Hopewell Baptist Church; Canton, GA	Week 35
Rodney Hunt	West Ridge Church; Dallas, GA	Week 50
J.R. Lee	Freedom Church; Acworth, GA	Week 48
Dr. Richard Mark Lee	Sugar Hill Church; Sugar Hill, GA	Week 40
Russ Lee	NewSong; Murfreesboro, TN	Week 7
Dr. Michael Lewis	First Baptist Church; Plant City, FL	Week 3
Charles Lowery, Ph.D.	Psychologist; Pilot Point, TX	Week 15

FRED LOWERY	First Baptist Bossier; Bossier City, LA	Week 14
DAVID McKINLEY	Warren Baptist Church; Augusta, GA	Week 19
DUSTY McLEMORE	Lindsay Lane Baptist Church; Athens, AL	Week 20
DR. DWAYNE MERCER	First Baptist Church Oviedo; Oviedo, FL	Week 11
DR. JAMES MERRITT	Cross Pointe Church; Duluth, GA	Week 36
MIKE ORR	First Baptist Church; Chipley, FL	Week 23
DR. JIM PERDUE	Crosspointe Baptist Church; Millington, TN	Week 43
ROBERT PITMAN	Evangelist; Muscle Shoals, AL	Week 5
PAUL PURVIS	First Baptist Church Forsyth; Forsyth, MO	Week 24
RANDY RAY	North Florida Baptist Church; Tallahassee, FL	Week 13
R. PHILIP ROBERTS	Midwestern Seminary; Kansas City, MO	Week 10
JEFF SCHREVE	First Baptist Church; Texarkana, TX	Week 32
ALLAN TAYLOR	First Baptist Church; Woodstock, GA	Week 17
ARDEN TAYLOR	Along the Journey; Jonesborough, TN	Week 44
LARRY THOMPSON	First Baptist Church; Fort Lauderdale, FL	Week 49
DR. TED H. TRAYLOR	Olive Baptist Church; Pensacola, FL	Week 8
BRAD WHITE	LifePoint Church; Tampa, FL	Week 16
RICK WHITE	The People's Church; Franklin, TN	Week 27
MIKE WHITSON	First Baptist Church; Indian Trail, NC	Week 26
DON WILTON	First Baptist Church; Spartanburg, SC	Week 18
RUSTY WOMACK	Rehoboth Baptist Church; Tucker, GA	Week 31
SCOTT YIRKA	Hibernia Baptist; Fleming Island, FL	Week 28
ROB ZINN	Immanuel Baptist Church; Highland, CA	Week 4

Scripture Index

Personal Prayer Notes

Personal Prayer Notes

Personal Prayer Notes